Political Theory and Feminist Social Criticism

In *Political Theory and Feminist Social Criticism*, Brooke Ackerly demonstrates the shortcomings of contemporary deliberative democratic theory, relativism, and essentialism for guiding the practice of social criticism in the real, imperfect world. Drawing theoretical implications from the activism of Third World feminists who help bring to public audiences the voices of women silenced by coercion, she provides a practicable model of social criticism. She argues that feminist critics have managed to achieve in practice what other theorists do only incompletely in theory. Complemented by Third World feminist social criticism, deliberative democratic theory becomes critical theory – actionable, coherent, and self-reflective. While a complement to democratic theory, Third World feminist social criticism also addresses the problem in feminist theory associated with attempts to deal with identity politics. Third World feminist social criticism thus takes feminist theory beyond the critical impasse of the tension between anti-relativist and anti-essentialist feminist theory.

BROOKE ACKERLY is Visiting Assistant Professor in the Political Science Department at University of California, Los Angeles.

D1049418

Contemporary Political Theory

Series Editor
Ian Shapiro

Editorial Board
Russell Hardin   Stephen Holmes   Jeffrey Isaac
John Keane   Elizabeth Kiss   Susan Okin
Phillipe Van Parijs   Phillip Pettit

As the twenty-first century approaches, major new political challenges have arisen at the same time as some of the most enduring dilemmas of political association remain unresolved. The collapse of communism and the end of the Cold War reflect a victory for democratic and liberal values, yet in many of the western countries that nurtured those values there are severe problems of urban decay, class and racial conflict, and failing political legitimacy. Enduring global injustice and inequality seem compounded by environmental problems, disease, the oppression of women, racial, ethnic and religious minorities, and the relentless growth of the world's population. In such circumstances, the need for creative thinking about the fundamentals of human political association is manifest. This new series in contemporary political theory is intended to foster such systematic normative reflection.

The series proceeds in the belief that the time is ripe for a reassertion of the importance of problem-driven political theory. It is concerned, that is, with works that are motivated by the impulse to understand, think critically about, and address the problems in the world, rather than issues that are thrown up primarily in academic debate. Books in the series may be interdisciplinary in character, ranging over issues conventionally dealt with in philosophy, law, history and the human sciences. The range of materials and the methods of proceeding should be dictated by the problem at hand, not the conventional debates or disciplinary divisions of academia.

Other books in the series

Ian Shapiro and Casiano Hacker-Cordón (eds.)
Democracy's Value

Ian Shapiro and Casiano Hacker-Cordón (eds.)
Democracy's Edges

Political Theory and Feminist Social Criticism

Brooke A. Ackerly

CAMBRIDGE
UNIVERSITY PRESS

PUBLISHED BY THE PRESS SYNDICATE OF THE UNIVERSITY OF CAMBRIDGE
The Pitt Building, Trumpington Street, Cambridge, United Kingdom

CAMBRIDGE UNIVERSITY PRESS
The Edinburgh Building, Cambridge, CB2 2RU, UK
http://www.cup.cam.ac.uk
40 West 20th Street, New York, NY 10011–4211, USA
http://www.cup.org
10 Stamford Road, Oakleigh, Melbourne 3166, Australia

First published 2000

Printed in the United Kingdom at the University Press, Cambridge

Typeset in Plantin 10/12pt   [CE]

A catalogue record for this book is available from the British Library

Library of Congress Cataloguing in Publication data
Ackerly, Brooke A.
   Political theory and feminist social criticism / Brooke A. Ackerly.
      p.   cm. – (Contemporary political theory)
Includes bibliographical references and index.
ISBN 0 521 65019 4 – ISBN 0 521 65984 1 (pbk.)
1. Feminist theory.   2. Feminism – Developing countries.
3. Political science.   I. Title.   II. Series.
HQ1190.A29   2000
305.42′01–DC21   99–15848   CIP

ISBN 0 521 65019 4 hardback
ISBN 0 521 65984 1 paperback

For Annlyn and her world

Contents

Acknowledgements

The problems associated with inequality and the inability of some people in a society to attain a public audience have interested me academically since college. Therefore my primary intellectual debts are to Professors of Economics Henry Bruton and Roger Bolton of Williams College who oversaw my first look into problems of inequality in Malaysia and instilled in me a passion for academic inquiry.

Next I owe tremendous personal and intellectual debts to those everyday critics in Bangladesh who educated me and to those development professionals who enabled my work with so many village women and development workers in Kustia, Tangail, and Brahmanbaria. In particular, I wish to thank Tom and Lisa Krift for inviting me to base my research in Bangladesh. Elke Kraus gave me my first home in Dhaka, introduced me to my closest friends in Bangladesh, and enabled me to spend formative time in Kustia with the women's savings group members from Tangail. My intellectual debt to her and them is obvious from the first pages of this book. By sharing their home life with me during their time of family crises, Adil and Naju Shafi let me experience their needs and concerns as if they were my own. Finally, I am grateful to Dorothy "Bina" D'Costa who, with the help of Jagadindra "Bappi" Majumder, transformed me from an outside observer to a multi-sited critic. I have learned much from our continued deliberative exchange over the years.

My intellectual debts to Joshua Cohen, Martha Nussbaum, and Michael Walzer are evidenced by these theorists' central presence in this book. Though generally critical of their conclusions, I find their scholarship engaging and important. I consider my own work to complement and further, not refute, theirs.

I am grateful to the academic communities at Stanford, Yale, and UCLA that provided stimulating environments during the development and polishing of the ideas in this book. In addition, ongoing conversations with Elisabeth Friedman, Bina D'Costa, and Anne Marie Goetz throughout this project have helped me continue to see this work in its larger contexts of political theory, development practice, and Third World women's activism.

During the writing of the book, audiences at Wellesley College, the University of Arizona, and the annual meeting of the American Political Science Association offered provocative questions that pushed me to clarify parts of the argument. Particular among these were questions from Joel Krieger, Cary Nederman, Cheryl Hall, and Melissa Lane. In addition, Victor Wolfenstein and Iris Marion Young offered thoughtful commentary based on the text of those remarks that pushed me to situate my work in the context of postmodernism and relativism.

The text itself has benefited from many readers. Mark Tunick offered careful attention to early drafts and made an inspiring investment in the quality of my writing. Debra Satz and Jim March asked provocative theoretical questions in response to early drafts. Elisabeth Hansot provided thoughtful and thorough comments on the organization and argument of the book. Ian Shapiro offered suggestions about emphasis and organization that were essential to its current form. Nancy Hirschmann read the manuscript critically and constructively twice. Her advice guided its reorganization and her comments improved its overall quality. Any errors and vagaries that remain do so despite their thoughtful efforts.

For comic relief early on and attention to the readability of the final manuscript, Rebecca Todd deserves special thanks. For ushering the book through the editorial process with the right combination of discipline and cheer, I am grateful to John Haslam. Others have read parts of the manuscript. Phyllis Barnes gave an inspired read of the first chapter. Michael Goodhart offered thoughtful comments on chapter two. Elisabeth Friedman provided critical commentary on the discussion of the women's rights movement in chapter four. In addition to their thoughtful commentary, these readers have identified a flaw or endearing feature of the book: no chapter stands on its own. In my effort to explicate my ideas while acknowledging my intellectual debts I have had to make decisions about the order of discussions. The reader may not like my choices. On occasion I refer the reader to other chapters but I expect the impatient reader to make good use of the index to find the discussions that interest her.

For encouragement I thank my family who have been a personal resource throughout this project. Specifically, Katherine Stevenson, Chris Stevenson, Ann Jacobs, Carl Jacobs, and Rick Ackerly kept the road to completion paved and plowed.

A J. William Fulbright Research Fellowship funded the Bangladesh research and the American Association of University Women American Fellowship funded the early writing process.

Finally and most importantly, I owe special thanks to two people who in different and complementary ways have helped strengthen me as a scholar and a person. Susan Okin has seen my thoughts develop from seemingly unrelated reflections on Aristotle and efforts to articulate respectful feminist criticism of power dynamics in families under the economic stress of poverty into a coherent manuscript. Her confidence has been motivational from the beginning. Moreover, her careful and respectful though critical readings of others, coupled with a clear theoretical message of her own and an enduring concern about injustice in the world, make each piece of her scholarship a model.

Bill Zinke has likewise witnessed the development in my thought. He has been convinced since its earliest articulations that Third World feminist social criticism is relevant to criticism beyond the scope of feminist concerns and thus misnamed. I agree; feminist social criticism *is* political theory. While I still hold to the label I have chosen for reasons explained in the text, I thank him for considering every deliberative exchange about feminism an opportunity to envision feminism as *human*ism.

1 Silent voices and everyday critics: problems in political theory, solutions from Third World feminist social criticism

> When you live in the water, you don't argue with the crocodiles.
>
> *(Bengali proverb)*

Prologue

In Bangladesh in September of 1993, I accompanied a group of rural women from Tangail who were members of Save the Children women's groups on their visit with rural women of Kustia who were members of Soptagram women's savings groups.[1] On the afternoon of the third day, as we walked from a workshop on women's legal rights to a meeting between the women's groups, we heard shrieks of terror coming from a household compound on the other side of a rice field. "What's going on?" I asked. Sahara, a Tangail woman, turned to me with anger and a memory of terror in her eyes and hit her right fist into her cupped left hand. She had experienced domestic violence and recognized the sounds from across the field.

After a time, Sahara asked, "Do husbands beat their wives in your country?" "Some do," I answered, "even though it is illegal." We all laughed at the irony, having just learned about women's formal legal rights in Bangladesh and noting how they differed from local practice.[2]

[1] Save the Children is a US-based international nongovernment organization (NGO) operating in Bangladesh; Soptagram is a Bangladeshi NGO operating in the western portion of the country primarily in Kustia. Tangail and Kustia are two *thanas*, a regional designation with the approximate political function of a county in the United States. Tangail is in the center of the country near the capital, Dhaka; Kustia is on the western border with India. Most of the women on the trip had never been outside their *thana*.

[2] As a result of women's activism in the late '70s against all forms of violence against women, but especially dowry-related beatings and death, Bangladesh passed laws protecting women (Jahan 1995). These include the Dowry Prohibition Act of 1979, the Cruelty to Women Punishment Ordinance of 1983, the Child Marriage Restraint Act of 1984 (making marriage illegal for girls under the age of 18 and for boys under 21), the Illegal Trafficking of Women Act of 1988 and the Family Court Ordinance of 1985. These laws are regularly violated in social practices. For example, although national statistics are unavailable, it is generally confirmed in local studies that dowry is now paid in nearly all Hindu and Muslim marriages. When the law was passed, generally Hindus

1

"Why do men hit their wives?" I asked. "Because they had a bad day. Because they are poor," answered Sahara. "Because the rice is too hot, or there is not enough rice," said Apfza, a woman from Kustia. Then she added, "A good husband does not beat his wife even when they are poor."

Then Jahanara, another Tangail woman overhearing our conversation, told the story of her women's group which went as a group to the house of a member who was being abused and asked her husband to stop beating her. This reminded another Tangail woman walking ahead of us of another group's effort to get a member's husband to allow their daughter to continue in school even though he was ready to arrange her marriage. They staged a sit-in at the member's home.

Although separately they had used their groups as bases of collective action, before their walk together in Kustia, the Tangail women's groups were unaware of each other's collective actions. Together, they recognized that their collective action caused the husbands' public embarrassment and brought public attention to their views on domestic violence and girls' education. By the time we arrived at the meeting place, the women were energized by their stories. Through their dialogue, the Kustia and Tangail women recognized that the examples of group action were not isolated. They identified collective action as a tried and effective method of breaking out of coerced silence in order to voice social criticism and to influence social decision making. And they learned they possessed the means of an effective form of activism.

The main purpose of the trip was for Save the Children to train its Tangail women's groups in leadership and group management skills so that they could sustain themselves when Save the Children ceased working in Tangail. Save the Children was in the process of focusing their efforts in the more economically challenged region of Nasrinagar, to the northeast. The conventional approach to such a training would have been to bring leadership trainers from elsewhere in Bangladesh to Tangail. However, the principal program officer proposed the training be conducted by Softagram leadership trainers in Kustia for a number of reasons. The journey to Kustia would provide the Tangail women with a life experience that would make them unique in their villages. Women and most poor men do not travel beyond their villages except (for women) to marry. The experience of *bidesh* ("foreign") travel would strengthen their position in the community, benefiting the women and their groups. The women were required to get their husbands' permission for the trip. Having one's wife go was a source of status for most

practiced dowry and Muslims, particularly poor Muslims, practiced it in less than 20% of marriages (Timm & Gain 1992: 74; White 1992: 104–106).

men, so they granted their support for their wives' trips and correspondingly, for their wives' ongoing participation in the groups.

The purpose of bringing the Tangail women to Kustia (an all-day journey) for a week was to allow women from different backgrounds who had been participating in women's groups sponsored by Save the Children in Tangail and Soptagram in Kustia to learn from each others' experiences. The program officer expected that, together, uninhibited by family pressures, the women would speak freely about their lives and honestly about the potential for their families to inhibit the success of the groups. By locating the training in Kustia, Save the Children would remove the women from their families and community temporarily and thereby free them from some social constraints that might otherwise inhibit their interactions. In addition Save the Children identified Soptagram as the ideal partner for this training as they had their own women's groups and shared the goal of women's empowerment. Both Soptagram and Save the Children thought their groups would be strengthened by meeting each other. They did not know what the Tangail and Kustia women would learn from each other, but Save the Children hoped that the Tangail women would learn that they could be self-reliant and that they did not need Save the Children to keep their groups sustained.

The groups' activism before coming to Kustia and their sharing their experiences in Kustia are examples of social criticism in a context of coercive gender hierarchy. The deliberation in Kustia between Tangail and Kustia women was a form of deliberation that resulted in the shared learning among the women in an environment secure from potentially harmful gender inequality. The activism of the Tangail women of staging sit-ins to influence their husbands is an example of critics trying to make an otherwise insecure environment one in which their voices are heard. Before a background of gender inequality, these women demonstrate deliberation as important social criticism. Ignoring the Bengali proverb, these women have found a means to argue with the crocodiles.[3]

The anecdote and social criticism

Although this anecdote does not give us a complete account of Third World feminist social criticism, it provides an illustration and a starting point for my subsequent discussion. While it seems like a story about

---

[3] Sarah C. White provides the source of the proverb in *Arguing with the Crocodile* (1992). For more general discussions of women's activism in the context of gender hierarchy in Bangladesh see White (1992) for a local and anthropological description and Roushan Jahan (1995) for a more general and political description.

particular women, the story actually reveals the critical components of my philosophy of social criticism. This anecdote raises three sets of questions about social critics and social criticism in everyday life: how do social critics do social criticism? what do social critics do? and who is a social critic? A philosophy of social criticism needs to give a general account of the method, roles, and qualifications of social critics.

Through this anecdote, I offer a glimpse of the method of social criticism practiced by women activists. Having discussed the problems of domestic violence among themselves, the women on the walk identify collective action as a potential means of making their social criticism heard. Being heard is no guarantee that their social criticism, once made, will successfully influence social change. These women live under familial, social, political, and economic values, practices, and norms that enforce women's silence.[4] However, they have identified a way to break that silence with each other and to force their husbands to hear them. As critics, these women challenge the common practice of wife battery and they assert a daughter's right to an education. Their method is to inform themselves through collective dialogue, to challenge generally accepted values, practices, and norms, and to advocate for those things they believe women should have, in this case safety in their homes and an education.

The critics in my anecdote also demonstrate the multiple roles of social critics. Critics promote inquiry. The foreign researcher asked questions: "What's going on?" and "Why do men hit their wives?" Critics promote deliberation. By asking questions I facilitated inquiry among the women. Individual women shared their understandings of the causes of domestic violence. The women described using collective action to enable their participation in deliberation about the values, practices, and norms that affect their lives. Critics promote institutional change. By bringing the women together in the first place, Save the Children under the initiative of its program officer acted as a social critic by offering a unique institutional environment for the women. I call this an institutional change because it changed (temporarily) the conventional context of women's interaction with each other and created a

---

[4] By "values, practices, and norms" I mean to include the familial, social, economic and political institutions of a society including formal laws and legal organizations (like legislatures or courts), informal practices like dating, and hybrid practices such as marriage which are guided by both formal laws, organized religion, and informal norms. I mention familial values, practices, and norms separately from social ones because I want to be able to distinguish between family activities and those social activities that are not directly related to the family. Although I refer to them as *a society's* values, practices and norms, I do not mean to imply that they are recognized or practiced universally within that society.

unique opportunity for interaction since poor rural women rarely exchange experiences with strangers. The process might promote further inquiry, deliberation, and institutional changes when the women go home to their communities. All three roles of critics can overlap and all three can be directed at visible practices such as domestic violence or at more foundational social values and norms such as gendered power inequalities. By promoting inquiry, deliberation, and institutional change in an otherwise coercive and oppressive environment, critics may promote social change that is more informed, collective, and uncoerced. By informed, I mean that all views are heard and given the respect of critical attention. By collective, I mean that perspectives are shared so that together society has more information (though some information can be misleading). And by uncoerced I mean that views are expressed freely and speakers are uninhibited by norms of behavior or by specific threats from others.

Finally, the anecdote demonstrates that the qualifications of social critics are not exclusive. The critics in the story are real people, doing their jobs and living their lives. They are a foreign researcher who asked a question, a woman who experiences domestic violence in her home, another who is familiar with it in her neighborhood, two groups of women who acted in concert to voice their criticism of wife abuse and their desire to educate their daughters, the Save the Children program officer, and the two development organizations. They are individuals and collectivities; they are foreigners, locals, and people who cannot neatly be categorized as either; they have thought about these issues alone, but they work in concert for social change. Who among these are *social* critics? All are.

Everyday people walking in an everyday place, undocumented by reporters is not what people commonly think of when they picture social critics or activists. But, I argue that these women are active in their social criticism and by example offer a model of social criticism appropriate for those otherwise silenced by the values, practices, and norms of their daily lives. This is not to say that, when using the method I outline to do the roles I describe, the critics I identify will be able to effect social change. Social criticism is one way to counter, mitigate, or undermine power inequalities, but whether a particular critical effort will be effective is a matter of politics.

Social criticism and political theory

Contemporary deliberative liberal democratic theory provides the context for the theory of social criticism I propose. Deliberative theorists have outlined principles for framing discussion, designed institutions for promoting free and equal discussion, and even brought to life a model deliberative forum. Explicit and implicit in their work is criticism of a society in which political power is unevenly disbursed and an argument that more inclusive public deliberation will enhance the legitimacy of political decision making even while those decisions remain largely in the hands of representatives.

Despite its critical implications, deliberative theorists have yet to show how to use deliberation in everyday life to bring into practice the assumptions, principles, institutions, and models that are the substance of their theories. An account of social criticism is an essential complement to deliberative theory if the latter is to be a credible attack on power inequalities.

Were deliberative theorists to give greater attention to the sources of inequality and misinterpretation in the real world, they might also recognize that an account of social criticism is a valuable component of a political philosophy. Educative deliberation – that is, deliberation for the purposes of contributing to a society's collective learning process, discovery, and knowledge – is the basis of the complementary philosophy of social criticism I propose. Given the importance of educative deliberation to social decision making, the critic's role is to promote it; critics from a variety of perspectives contribute to it; good critics make use of it in their methodology.

In the exposition of their political theories democratic theorists provide an account of how citizens generally participate in democratic society and decision making as they describe it. They give accounts of the education required to participate thus, and they give examples of the institutions that will enable citizens to participate as described. And yet, when it comes to social criticism – to giving an account of how those same citizens can participate in bringing about the polity they describe – these theorists are silent. At most they give an account of the role of the political theorist as social critic. But political theorists are not the most important political actors in bringing about social change; certainly, we ought not to base our hopes for seeing greater democracy realized on the theorists' ability to make a sound argument. Really, social change toward greater or worse democracy is brought about by those same citizens who will participate in the improved polity once achieved. And so, it makes sense that a democratic political theory should have something to say about how social criticism might influence social decision making such that social change toward a more democratic society (however envisioned) is possible. The theorist or philosopher of social criticism cannot predict how effective a given practice of social criticism will be – that is a matter of actual politics – but an account of citizens' roles in bringing about political change is a missing constitutive element of contemporary democratic theory.

Some liberal democratic theorists have made speaking, listening, exchanging arguments, and thinking critically essential to their views of public decision making.[5] These deliberative theorists might be expected to give a similar account of social criticism as being a function of a critic's speaking with and listening to others, thinking critically about their and her own ideas and exchanging arguments with others. Moreover, one might expect them to argue that the critic's job is to promote such activity in the political forum. As such, one might expect that they consider how a critic goes about promoting such deliberation under the circumstance of real world inequality, exclusivity of political fora, advantage of elite political actors, and coercion of nonelite actors. However, the more common approach among political theorists is to offer social criticism as an explicit or implied extension of their political philosophy. Whether their own social criticism is explicit or implied, the deliberative theorists do not offer a general account of what social criticism should be.

John Dewey, a forefather of deliberative democratic theory, has been explicit in incorporating a philosophy of social criticism into his political theory. His philosophy of human learning is foundational to his political theory and theory of social criticism. Dewey argues that people and society learn by listening to one another's ideas and then playing out in their imagination all of the possible scenarios to which following one suggestion would lead.

[D]eliberation is a dramatic rehearsal (in imagination) of various competing possible lines of action ... Thought runs ahead and foresees outcomes, and thereby avoids having to await the instruction of actual failure or disaster. (1983 [1922]: 132–133)

Individuals and societies make decisions similarly. Both have an interest in making the best decisions as measured by their ability to reconcile competing understandings (1983 [1922]: 134 and 1989 [1944]: 273). According to Dewey's political philosophy, for individuals to participate equally and freely in democracy, they must have the intellectual capacity

---

[5] Contemporary deliberative political theorists are numerous and varied in their theorizing, as I will discuss in chapter 2. Theorists who have written foundational arguments in deliberative democratic theory include Joseph M. Bessette (1980), James Bohman (1996) Joshua Cohen (1989a), John S. Dryzek (1990), Jon Elster (1997), David Estlund (1993), James S. Fishkin (1991), Amy Gutmann and Dennis Thompson (1996), Jack Knight and James Johnson (1994), Bernard Manin (1987), Jane Mansbridge (1992, 1988), Frank I. Michelman (1986), David Miller (1992), Thomas A. Spragens, Jr. (1990), Cass R. Sunstein (1988) and Mark Warren (1996a).

to do so. They must be able to think free, undictated thoughts, to discover and learn with others (1983 [1922]: 9–11, 134 and 1989 [1946b]: 221). In addition, deliberation requires the ability to imagine – to imagine the responses that one's actions will elicit from others and to imagine the possible consequences of one's actions (1983 [1922]: 134, 144, 217). And people must value the collective life that facilitates the equal and free participation of all (1989 [1942]: 174, 178–9). Then, in Dewey's view, deliberation is at once the means of developing in people the ability to participate equally, freely and valuably in their collective life, and it is the end of collective life. Dewey's political philosophy emphasizes the developmental role of deliberation in individuals' abilities to contribute to collective life and in the society's ability to function according to the collected understandings of its citizens. The role of the social critic, according to Dewey's political philosophy, is to educate future citizens to be critical thinkers. Of equal import, the critic must inspire current citizens to reflect thoughtfully on the existing or emerging values, practices, and norms of their society such as increasing inequality in industrializing society (1980 [1916b] and 1982 [1919]) and totalitarianism (1989 [1942]) because they may otherwise undermine the freedom and equality of liberal democracy (1980 [1916a] and 1980 [1916b]). No deliberative theorist since Dewey has appreciated the role of deliberation in bringing about the conditions for deliberative democracy.

The implied social criticism of deliberative theorists tends to focus on a society's institutional and social preconditions, and procedures of deliberative democracy. For example, Amy Gutmann and Joshua Cohen articulate a political philosophy of deliberative democracy according to which, despite moral disagreements, citizens debate political issues and reach political consensus.[6] Such a view requires that citizens tolerate opposing views, listen to each other respectfully, and make their decisions based on their thoughtful evaluation of the arguments presented. According to the deliberative theorists, deliberative democracy requires and reinforces an ideal environment for deliberated social decision making that includes self-respect, mutual respect, equality, and an agreed-upon definition of what constitutes reasonable argument in the public sphere. According to their view, where societies sufficiently approximate the ideal environment, deliberative democracy will perpetuate that environment and yield legitimate political consensus (e.g., Cohen 1989a). The implied social criticism is that societies should work to promote the ideal deliberative environment and its corresponding

---

[6] See Gutmann (1995), Gutmann & Thompson (1996), and Cohen (1989a).

necessary institutions. Cohen and co-author Joel Rogers argue that associations are such necessary institutions for deliberative democracy and they offer an idealized account of those associations, but do not offer a complementary account of how to bring about such institutions (Cohen & Rogers 1992). Gutmann implies through her discussion of *Mozert* v. *Hawkins* and *Wisconsin* v. *Yoder* that social criticism should promote an educational system that teaches critical thinking such that people learn to hold their views not dogmatically, but based on their having respectfully considered alternative views and having chosen their own views as being most promising (Gutmann 1995; see also Gutmann & Thompson 1996). The social criticism she offers is implied rather than explicit. She offers examples of what constitute (in her view) convincing arguments about what education should entail, but there is no complementary account of how society might bring about such an educational system.

Both Cohen and Gutmann (and their co-authors) offer an account of deliberative democracy that is based on the strong assumptions of self-respect, mutual respect, equality, and an agreed-upon definition of what constitutes reasonable argument preexisting in the society in question. But such preconditions are lacking in most societies (and one might be suspicious of how widespread they are in a society that someone claims nearly approximates those preconditions).[7] In the real world, inequalities are too pressing, or too invisible, for the implied social criticism of ideal political theory to be relevant. Deliberation is essential to their political vision, but they have not employed it for social criticism where the preconditions of deliberative democracy are lacking. Moreover, they require that a society agree on the form of argument that will be acceptable in deliberative fora and they describe that form as narrowly consistent with legal norms of argumentation. Following this paradigm, social criticism would be very similar to what a judge does and very dissimilar to the actions and offstage voices of silent critics.

Benjamin Barber comes closer to Dewey in incorporating a theory of social criticism into his political theory. In *Strong Democracy*, Barber includes in his argument for participatory democracy an argument about what social criticism needs to be in order to bring about such participatory democracy. For Barber, strong democracy is an ongoing form of political life where people participate in public decision making as free citizens and who, through self-legislation, together resolve conflict despite lack of common ground (1984: 117–138, 151). Social

---

[7] Jack Knight and James Johnson argue that deliberative democracy requires "*equal opportunity of access to political influence,*" but argue that there is no way to measure the capacity to exercise political influence (1997: 280, 303–304, 305).

criticism complements and promotes strong democracy according to Barber. Social criticism is an ongoing incremental process leading toward strong democracy by taking advantage of existing practices and institutions that are supportive of strong democracy (1984: 262). Of the specific institutions he proposes, some, such as television-facilitated national "town meetings" and the national referendum process have been tried in some form (1984: 274–278).[8] Barber offers explicit social criticisms that are consistent with his political philosophy and are intended to bring it about. But note, these are specific criticisms offered by him. He does not tell us how he arrived at these suggestions and not others.

In my view, strong democracy implies a philosophy of social criticism according to which many social critics from a variety of critical perspectives exchange their ideas of what constitutes appropriate social criticism. Barber has articulated that social criticism should be incremental and ongoing, but then he offers a list of suggestions that, to be consistent with strong democracy, should be offered as the result of a deliberative exchange among a variety of social critics. One might argue that the research leading up to his publishing this list included deliberative exchanges with other social scientists, but he does not tell us why he recommends these, and not other, suggestions.

I am not criticizing Barber for not doing what he did not promise to do. Rather, I use him as an example of a deliberative theorist who offers a partial sketch of what social criticism generally should be in order to be consistent with his account of strong democracy. But social criticism needs to be more than incremental, practicable, and leading toward strong democracy; it also needs to specify the roles, qualifications, and method of social critics. Recognizing that we live in an imperfect world, deliberative theorists owe society a general account of the process of social criticism so that, as a society, we can bring about deliberative democracy *in a deliberative way*. In addition, as I will show in chapter 2, deliberative democratic theory as social criticism resolves a debate among deliberative theorists about whether deliberation sets or meets an epistemological standard.

All of the deliberative theorists discussed above articulate a political philosophy and either explicitly or implicitly suggest certain corresponding social criticisms. However, real world values in conflict, competing interests, and disputed priorities generate philosophical dilemmas. A question in political philosophy is interesting only if it seems relevant to contemporary political life. Ian Shapiro takes the opposite tack from those discussed above. In *Political Criticism*, Shapiro criticizes

---

[8] Barber proposes modifications to the current state referendum process and implementing it on the national level. I discuss the proposal in chapter 4.

constructed political theory and offers in its place a view of political theory as social criticism. According to Shapiro, a political theory cannot be based on any specific principles because it is human nature to explore and question those principles (1990: 262; see also 1994). Instead political theory is the kind of social criticism that a political philosopher can give. The job of a political theorist is to offer criticism of a society's previously opaque dimensions of social actions that perpetuate systematic domination (1990: 296). Unlike other political theorists, Shapiro sets his political theorizing in the broader context of his philosophy of social criticism. The critic's basic assumption is that people "have an interest in knowing and acting on the truth" (1990: 285). By offering a political theory (an account of the "truth"), the theorist acts as a critic by revealing that some existing institutions perpetuate systematic domination.

Shapiro distinguishes the general philosophy of social criticism from a particular political theory of an individual critic. As a political-theorist critic, Shapiro argues that democracy best serves legitimate governance as a method for empowering the disempowered, securing the freedom to disagree with political decisions, and institutionalizing mechanisms for loyal opposition. Consequently, it requires citizens' suspicion of established power relationships and their education to develop their capacity for critical thinking (Shapiro 1996b). According to Shapiro, there is no blueprint for a democratic polity. Rather in a democracy, the definition of social justice is determined democratically. The values, practices, and norms of a society are suspect if they are hierarchical, but they are changeable; and political change takes place democratically (1994).

In my view, Shapiro's philosophy of social criticism and his political philosophy are promising for a general philosophy of social criticism. However, Shapiro himself is not so confident. In "Three Ways to Be a Democrat" he suspects "that there is little that is general to be said about the democratic management of tensions internal to the democratic ideal" (1994: 147). One such tension might be the tension between, say, the suspicion of a hierarchical practice and a democratic decision to maintain that practice despite the harm it causes the less powerful. In order to be relevant to the pressing problems of the day, the philosophy of social criticism needs to provide a general account of how social critics should attempt to redress the harms caused by such conflicts. However, to do so democratically, social criticism cannot be the job solely of the political theorist. She is but one kind of social critic and not one known for being particularly active in the trenches of real world inequalities. In order to complement a democratic political theory, a philosophy of social criticism needs to offer an account of the practice of social criticism which, even under the nonideal conditions of inequality, coercion, exploitation, and oppression, can promote social decision making that is more informed, collective, and uncoerced. Thus the philosophy of social criticism I present both offers a "metanarrative" about what social criticism needs to be generally in order to be sufficiently critical and is critical of specific social criticisms if they are based on a presumption of a metanarrative. Without the postmodern jargon, in order to be sufficiently critical, social critics must make use of the critical method I describe *and* be critical of their own criticism.[9]

Michael Walzer offers an account of social criticism that explicitly complements his political philosophy. In *Spheres of Justice*, Walzer (1983) advocates a social democratic society in which inequalities in one sphere of life cannot be transposed into inequalities in other spheres. Most obviously, one should not be able to convert economic wealth into political power. Further, he asserts that communities have "shared understandings" about the values according to which goods within each sphere should be distributed. Walzer does offer an account of social criticism which complements his political philosophy. According to Walzer's account of social criticism, the critic, who is an insider, interprets the practices of a society to determine whether they are consistent with its shared meanings (1987 and 1988). Walzer's account of social criticism is relativist (or anti-essentialist) because social values are determined relative to a given context. The result is an account of social criticism that is unable to deal with disagreements as to what constitutes "shared" values, that is, disagreements about morality (1987: 32). Because it does not tell a society and its critics how to proceed under conditions of such disagreement, I argue that interpretation as social criticism offers too narrow an account of social criticism. Despite its shortcomings as a comprehensive philosophy of social criticism (and although Walzer himself is only obliquely aware of it), Walzer's political philosophy includes a presumed universal value – opposition to oppression – which is useful for a more general account of social criticism, specifically, the critic's method as I will describe it.

From the perspective of a modified liberal democrat, Martha Nussbaum's social criticism also explicitly complements her political philosophy. Her self-described historically sensitive essentialist approach to social criticism allows for definitive judgments about certain social values. She argues that certain values are universally recognized as being essential to being human. Those values include the ability to meet one's basic physical needs, but they also include the ability to participate in

---

[9] Compare this view to the assumption of some postmodernists that all social criticism is founded on a metanarrative (Fraser & Nicholson 1990: 34).

decision making about matters that affect one's life (1992). In a detailed list of capabilities, Nussbaum identifies those capabilities that she argues are essential to living a life worthy of being described as human. Certain liberal democratic values are embodied in Nussbaum's list of values. The role of social critics and societies is to bring about changes such that all members of a society are able to live a fulfilling human life. Nussbaum's account of social criticism is incomplete; it incorporates no methodological requirement to consult with the silent voices of a society and, consequently, as I discuss in chapter 3, it allows mistakes in interpretation on the part of the social critic to go unchallenged. Nussbaum's main contribution to the philosophy of social criticism is, however, an important aspect of the critical method. Social criticism requires, among other things, universal standards by which to assess given local practices. Nussbaum offers a draft of such criteria.

I chose to discuss Walzer and Nussbaum in detail in chapter 3 because they outline and practice a philosophy of social criticism and because, though flawed, each makes use of one aspect of the tripartite methodology which I argue is necessary for social criticism that listens to the silent voices of a society. I accept the deliberative theorists' account of the ideal political world, but argue that their political philosophy is meaningful only as an ideal. In order to be useful for social criticism it requires not merely each individual theorist's suggestions for institutional changes, but rather a more general, complementary account of social criticism that promotes social change toward achieving the ideal. Although Walzer provides a complementary philosophy of social criticism for his political philosophy, that philosophy is based on a faulty premise. I argue that social understandings are not always well-defined and "shared." In fact, they are frequently disputed, or, under circumstances of coercion, they are shared by some and forced on others. Accordingly, in my view, social critics have greater responsibilities than merely to interpret existing "shared" understandings relative to their given context but also to be skeptical of how universally they are held within a society. Walzer's account of interpretation as social criticism is an incomplete account of social criticism. Nussbaum's account of social criticism is also incomplete, but for different reasons than those of the deliberative theorists or Walzer. Nussbaum's account of social criticism is incomplete because her critical method is ill-defined. Nussbaum's essentialist model of social criticism has no methodological check to prevent or correct critics' errors in interpreting or prioritizing people's basic needs. Were Walzer and Nussbaum attentive to the views of those whose voices are silenced, they might embrace the deliberative approach to social criticism.

In sum, while attempting to offer models of social criticism, these theorists provide incomplete accounts of the roles, qualifications, and methods of social critics in the real imperfect world. According to the philosophy of social criticism I propose, social critics help society promote informed, collective, and uncoerced social decision making in the real world where inequalities are perpetuated by social values, practices, and norms. In the process of explicating this account of social criticism I argue that the women in the anecdote and other women activists and scholars around the world have managed to achieve in practice what these philosophers do incompletely in theory.

Social criticism requires the examination of seemingly shared values, practices, and norms. Political theory might guide us in determining the ends of social criticism; but in this book I focus on the process of social criticism. For this purpose I take the end of social criticism to be the ongoing process of bringing about incrementally a more informed, collective, and uncoerced process of social change. Although they may not always be successful, the everyday critics such as those on the walk in Bangladesh, and their counterparts around the world, practice social criticism that has been successful in this regard.

The social change inspired by the practice of social criticism I describe will generally promote democracy, but the specific form of that democracy need not and cannot be specified. The account of social criticism I provide is consistent with many institutional forms of deliberative democracy, including associations and variations in party politics. This view of social criticism is conducive to any institutions that promote direct, inclusive, and collective participation in governance, but it is also open to the possibility that good representatives and institutions of representation may enable a society to achieve informed, collective, and uncoerced social decision making.

Social criticism as I outline it is a process conducive to incremental, informed, collective, and uncoerced social change. Social criticism is the means for society and its critics to evaluate existing values, practices, and norms that cause or perpetuate harmful inequalities. It promotes social discussion of, but does not guarantee resolution of, conflicts. Despite existing inequalities, there is an important role for deliberation in social criticism.

A Third World feminist tripartite methodology

In contexts of coercion where disagreements are not easily articulated, my philosophy of social criticism defines roles and qualifications for critics that together potentially challenge all forms of oppression and coercion. However, because it is difficult to recognize oppression one has not experienced and because it is sometimes difficult to understand and articulate oppression one *has* experienced, social critics need a method. As feminist legal scholar Katharine Bartlett notes, "a method neither guarantees a particular result nor even the right result. It does, however, provide some discipline" (1990: 849). My feminist methodology provides such discipline. It is a method for the critic and those within the society she criticizes to learn about people and perspectives which pursuit of one's own interests, or even genuine concern for others, might not lead one to acknowledge. I do not claim to be the author of the method of social criticism I articulate. Rather, I have distilled it from the practice of many Third World women activists.

"Third World" is a term that denotes countries of various stages of economic, social and political development. By virtue of their histories, the phrase reminds us of the dynamics of race, class, nationality, and colonialism and the struggles of identity, self-determination, and cultural survival that are relevant to their present economy, society and politics.[10] The phrase is first attributed to French sociologist Alfred Sauvy in 1952 when he referred to the countries that were not aligned with the USA or the USSR as the *"tiers monde"*, thereby likening the nonaligned countries to France's *Tiers Etat* or commoners. The changes in the world that called for the participation of the *tiers monde* in world leadership would be as important to the future of the world as the changes in France that called for the participation of the *Tiers Etat* in the French government in 1789 were to the future of France. Leaders of the postcolonial states – most notably Sukarno of Indonesia and Nehru of India – sought to outline a third way of development that followed neither of the major ideologies of the West: capitalism and communism. At the Bandung Conference of 1955, leaders of Asian and African countries asserted their common desires for world peace and development.[11] In the sixties in the USA, "Third World" became a pejorative term for referring to countries whose populations live with poverty, lack of education, high unemployment, and in the seventies with inflation and high national debt. Its usage also expanded to include communities within developed states who lived under similar conditions of poverty, lack of education, and high unemployment.[12]

[10] Struggles of identity, self-determination, and cultural survival are sometimes deemed Fourth World issues with reference to indigenous people's struggles.

[11] See George McTurnan Kahin (1956), the transcripts of speeches at Bandung published by the Ministry of Foreign Affairs Republic of Indonesia (1955), and Richard Wright (1956).

[12] See also Peter Worsley's account of the history of the idea of the "Third World" in *The Three Worlds* (1984: especially 306–344).

Recently, women from certain countries and backgrounds have appropriated the term, in part because it reminds their audience of historical and contemporary relations of power between developed and less developed countries which they want to challenge, because it is flexible enough to refer to underdeveloped communities within developed countries, and because it avoids the judgments associated with "less developed" and "underdeveloped." Chandra Talpade Mohanty criticizes those who would depict Third World women as defined by their victim status. She broadly defines Third World women as women who struggle from a combination of discriminations (1991b: 74–75, fn. 1). Gita Sen and Caren Grown argue that Third World women is "a positive self-affirmation based on our struggles against the multiple oppressions of nation, gender, class, and ethnicity" (1987: 97).

Other feminists have thought to solve problems in feminist theory by drawing on Third World women's activism (Moser 1989; Chowdhry 1995; French 1992; Jayawardena 1986; Sen & Grown 1987). Julie Mostov (1992), Marion Smiley (1993) and Jodi Dean (1996) have articulated feminist theory consistent with what I call Third World feminism by focusing on women's empowerment.

In my view, Third World women activists today seek what Third World leaders sought in the 1950s: another way. Through their practice they demonstrate a way to empower women that is a function neither of notions of women as they have been understood in their traditional roles as wives, mothers, and care-givers nor of their presumed identity with men, but rather is a function of their own attempts to oppose harmful inequalities in their lives. Thus, I use the term "Third World" to refer to those seeking a third way, an empowered way, for women and for the socioeconomic development of their countries. When describing women's activism – particularly in chapter 4, the women's human rights activism – I distinguish between western (including western-educated women who affiliate themselves with western ideas) and nonwestern women because I mean to refer to their differences in resources and education. Although I don't like the connotation of otherness associated with the term nonwestern, I use it because, as opposed to the monolithic connotation of "western," nonwestern recognizes the range of perspectives that may be excluded by following a western paradigm. When I mean to refer to women's geographic differences I use the more currently accepted terms of Northern and Southern women. In my view, Third World feminists are defined by their search for another way for feminism, not by their issues, interests, education, resources, or geography. They may be western or nonwestern, Northern or Southern. In this sense, Fourth World feminists are also Third World feminists.[13]

I call these activists and scholars "feminists" because they are engaged in activism or scholarship organized by women to transform themselves and their world. As Brazilian feminists Vera Soares, Ana Alice Alcantara Costa, Cristina Maria Buarque, Denise Dourado Dora, and Wania Sant'Anna define it, feminism is "the political action of women … as agents effecting change in their own condition. Feminism supports the proposition that women should transform themselves and the world" (1995: 302). Some activists call themselves "feminist." However, because of the negative associations that the term "feminist" has to many ears, many Third World women activists reject the label. Not all women activists or self-described feminists practice social criticism as I describe it. And not all women who practice this methodology would identify themselves with the label "feminist." However, many women activists do practice Third World feminist social criticism as I describe it, and many more through their work have contributed to this critical methodology. Although women working for women's empowerment developed this methodology, it is a model of social criticism that is appropriate for challenging institutionalized hierarchy broadly. Thus, though feminism provides the source of this method, its application is not limited to feminist issues. In fact, this view of social criticism is the richer articulation of the critique of hierarchy that some democratic theorists have been seeking.[14]

The activists highlighted in this book offer more than well-argued complaint. They offer well-strategized direction for social change. They include grassroots activists like SEWA, the Self-Employed Women's Association, in Gujarat, India, which has mobilized previously un-united self-employed workers to lobby and strike for their own interests. They include self-described feminists like DAWN (Development Alternatives for Women in a New Era), a network of women scholars and

[13] According to Paula Gunn Allen (1992) and Sherna Berger Gluck (1998), indigenous women are centrally concerned with physical and cultural survival. In addition indigenous women face the problems of respecting tradition while being critical of imported patriarchal so-called traditions (Green 1982: 172), choosing between aligning with community or with national civil rights movements (Gluck 198: 43), and challenging misogyny within their communities while supporting their communities. Many Northern and Southern women are forced by their context to prioritize physical and cultural survival and many face similar challenges though they manifest themselves differently in different contexts.

[14] For example, Thomas Christiano doubts that under conditions of inequality it is possible to design political institutions to challenge those inequalities and thus relies on an understanding of democratic societies as always changing (1996: 291–295). The feminist vision of social criticism provides an account of the democratic scrutiny of existing inequalities.

activists working in development around the world who criticize existing economic development strategies and their impact on women while offering an alternative vision for economic development. These critics share a belief that in the ideal world, social decision making is collectively informed, collective, and uncoerced. Third World women activists – whether they embrace the feminist label or not – practice social criticism intended to make it more so.

The feminist method of social criticism is a critical bridge between the ideal and the reality of social change. It guides critics in their evaluation of existing values, practices, and norms and prompts them to be strategic in their inquiry. Such critics develop their strategies for social change by analyzing the answers to three questions:

1. Do the people of the society deliberate inclusively, collectively, and without use of coercion about the values, practices, and norms that affect their lives?
2. Are inequalities exploitable to the detriment of the less powerful?
3. And how does the life each person leads compare with the life a human being should be capable of living?

These three questions correspond to the three parts of the feminist methodology: deliberation as a means of inquiry; skeptical scrutiny of elitist, coercive, and exclusionary and potentially exploitative values, practices, and norms; and the development of a set of criteria for evaluating values, practices, and norms.

Each of the critics in the Bangladesh anecdote practices this method. The researcher, skeptical of the practice of wife battery and having general criteria that include basic physical security, uses deliberative inquiry with the Bangladeshi women to criticize the practice of battery. The village women, skeptical of wife battery and husbands' authority over their wives and having criteria that include physical safety and education, use deliberative inquiry first to discuss among themselves appropriate action and then to promote public awareness of the problem by staging a sit-in in the houses of their husbands. Save the Children, skeptical of husbands' authority over their wives and having general criteria that include women's autonomy in the context of interdependent and supportive family structures, creates the conditions for deliberative inquiry among the women.

By outlining the Third World feminist critical methodology, I give theoretical coherence to what is already practiced by the critics around the world and offer it not only as a method of social criticism, but also as an effective complement to those political theorists who rely in some measure on equality in society. Although all Third World feminist critics practice the preceding method, the range of critics' roles is so broad that it requires multiple critics.

Silent voices and the roles of social critics

Though there is great variety in the lives of rural Bangladeshi women, some similarities cross regional and religious boundaries. Generally, rural women in Bangladesh depend on men for their access to markets and for their very subsistence. While men depend on women for their subsistence as well, men's and women's mutual dependence should not be interpreted as reciprocal. Men can and do leave their wives and children, move to other places, and start new lives. Generally, women can leave their husbands only by returning to their fathers' homes. Without husbands, sons, or fathers, women are economically isolated because they cannot get access to markets and are socially isolated and harassed by their neighbors for being "bad" women.[15] To use a Bengali metaphor, Bangladeshi rural women live in the water with the crocodiles. Living all their lives in the water, they develop ways to avoid arguing with them.

Occasionally, a woman endures beatings in silence, for example, for not having the meal ready for her husband when he comes home from work or for serving a meal too hot. A young bride is particularly vulnerable to battery in her husband's house if her father did not pay her husband the promised dowry. Within a given marriage, the distribution of power may vary, but most of a woman's constraints are due to the socially recognized relatively greater power of her husband. Some people mistakenly associate women's inferior position with the teachings of Islam. However, comparable conditions exist for Hindu women in Bangladesh, and many similarities exist in the gender hierarchies of Bangladesh and other countries of South Asia. The values, practices, and norms constraining women's lives, while frequently attributed to Islam, are more accurately attributed to cultural constraints more broadly. The context of rural Bangladesh – the economic constraints

---

[15] I wish I could offer a clear definition of "bad" according to Bangladeshi people, particularly men. The explanation of the use of this derogatory label always seemed tautological as in, she is "bad" because she is living in a "bad" way. For example, when I was in a conservative northeastern village, the house of a single woman with three young children was vandalized. When I asked why, men told me it was because she was a "bad" woman. When I asked in what way she was bad, they answered that she lived alone. I asked some women if there was some information the men were not telling me, but they said that, no, she was not a prostitute, but rather, she lived alone because her husband died. Conventionally, widows live with their husband's brother or return to their natal home. I do not know whether she had either of those options; nor (I suspect) did the men who vandalized her home.

that prevent women from accessing the market and the social constraints that prevent women from living autonomously regardless of their financial means – limits a woman's options so that leaving her husband is rarely a choice a woman makes.[16] In sum, Sarah White writes:

There are many coercive aspects short of overt physical violence in the social conditions in which women live in rural Bangladesh, as elsewhere. Their construction as legal minors, their exclusion from property rights, the distrust and policing of their sexuality, their isolation in an unfamiliar setting after marriage, their segregation into the least valued and least remunerative kinds of work – all these are a kind of violence which helps to enforce female submission. It is not for nothing that folk culture disproportionately represents women as weeping, as in sorrow, as undergoing loss and pain. (1992: 137)

Both a woman's means of exercising her will and her resignation not to challenge the will of her husband must be appreciated in the context of the more general constraints on women that are prevalent in Bangladeshi culture.

One might ask if it is possible for women to resist without directly challenging the will of their husbands. White identifies some weapons of resistance women employ. One is complaint masked in irony. For example, when asked why she continues to borrow from a neighbor a basic household tool for husking rice – "what isn't yours mended yet?" – a woman responds, "The work gets done this way, why should they mend it?" (1992: 137). Irony is a subtle form of complaint to which women resort because they cannot complain directly.

Another form of resistance is the appropriation by women of gender stereotyping for their own ends. White gives the example of the women of one Muslim family whose water pump broke. The women were forced to fetch water from a pump in front of a wealthy Hindu household a distance away. After six months, the women asked the head of their household for a new pump claiming that their modesty was violated by having to go out for water. White considers that the women were voicing their own standards of modesty, but judges from other remarks and observations that the women were not concerned about their modesty but rather just tired of fetching water from such a distance (1992: 138). Like the peasants in James Scott's *Weapons of the Weak*, rural Bangladeshi women's subordination is such that their objections take the form of offstage defiance rather than formal resistance (Scott 1985: 25). These examples of resistance are impressive. However, the

---

[16] Developing Albert Hirschman's thesis in *Exit, Voice, and Loyalty* (1970), Susan Moller Okin makes a similar argument about the vulnerability of women in many marriages in the United States. She argues that since their exit options are socially constrained by what she describes as the asymmetric vulnerability of women and men in marriage, their voice in their relationships with their husbands is limited (1989: chapter 7).

choice of irony over direct complaint, and complaining not about the distance but about the violation of their modesty, demonstrate that for Bangladeshi women even informal resistance is severely constrained.

To describe Bangladeshi women as silent oversimplifies both the women's judicious use of voice and the range of ways in which potential social critics are silent and silenced. Some are silent, but would speak if power and resource inequalities did not create obstacles. Obstacles include formal institutional barriers to participation such as the education required to be able to speak in the legalese of government public fora, and more subtle barriers such as discrimination resulting in the majority of a public audience not hearing or ignoring the critic. Others would speak but choose silence as a result of fear of harm. Some appear not to speak publicly, but instead exercise what Scott describes as offstage defiance (1985). Others speak publicly but anonymously, in euphemisms, by veiling dissent, or through more elaborate forms of camouflage (Scott 1990: chapter 6). Although I use "silent" to describe this range of public voice and lack thereof, the differences among these silent voices are as important to social criticism as their commonalities. Moreover, understanding the range of experiences of silence and voice of those who do not present their social criticism in politically familiar ways is more useful than equating silence with political disinterest, false consciousness, or oppression.

More generally, cases which appear to be demonstrative of a "false consciousness" on the part of some group are instead cases of (1) misinterpretation on the part of the observer who identifies the "false consciousness"; (2) an inaccurate observation of uniform beliefs where, in fact beliefs are diverse; and (3) "true consciousness" based on the available information and knowledge of the group. For example, some suspect that Arab women believe that they are impure, inferior humans whose presence "pollutes" men's activities and thoughts. In contrast, Leila Ahmed in her account of the social separation of men and women on the Arabian peninsula, argues that women's inviolable spaces are a source of deliberative inquiry among women at the exclusion of men. The women, Ahmed argues, are conscious of men's authority to promote ideology and practices that reinforce the inferiority of women and yet their own identities are not victim to those efforts: "I have never seen in any other culture, including America, women whose self-perceptions were so singularly impervious to the assertions of the dominant ideology regarding their 'natural' inferiority and 'natural' subservience, and who clearly perceived that ideology as part of a system whose object is to legitimize, mystify, and further entrench those in power" (Ahmed 1982a: 530–531). According to Ahmed, those who accuse Arab women of "false consciousness" misinterpret the women's self-understandings, mistakenly observe that Arab women share Arab men's ideology about women, and fail to appreciate that the women's consciousness is in fact true to their experience and knowledge of themselves and their society. Scott offers further insight into Ahmed's argument with his account of the apparent complicity of the oppressed in the dominant ideology while being covert or anonymous in their resistance to it (1990; see also 1985).

It is not surprising that someone oppressed does not speak out against her oppressor or against practices that are oppressive with the same directness and volume as the oppressor uses to maintain the hierarchy. Oppressed and living in a culture of developed tacit communications, a Bangladeshi woman does not openly and indiscriminately express her objections to the social devaluing of women, to oppressive practices such as wife beating, or to her practical inability to exercise her formal political and legal rights that might enable her to protect herself. In her home, lacking an economic, social or political voice, a woman may only silently *wish* that she were not beaten when her husband came in from the field and his food was not ready. Metaphorically, she lives in the water and does not argue with the crocodiles. Third World feminist social criticism gives the silent a voice.

Contrast the isolation of the Bangladeshi women with the parents described by Amy Gutmann and Dennis Thompson entering into democratic deliberations (and then a lawsuit) with the Hawkins County Board of Education in Tennessee about the content of the public school curriculum (1996: 63–69). In *Democracy and Disagreement*, Gutmann & Thompson outline a theory of deliberation for equal citizens to resolve the moral disagreements common in public policy formation. They insulate their explication of deliberation in democracy from "the contexts of ordinary politics: the pressures of power, the problems of inequality, the demands of diversity, [and] the exigencies of persuasion" (1996: 3) by assuming mutual respect and tolerance on the part of citizens. That insulation may approximately describe the courtroom of the Sixth Circuit Court of Appeals in which the parents and Hawkins County argued their cases. Gutmann & Thompson are able to discuss the case because the parents were able to go to court, the arguments for both sides documented, and the decision published. However, despite existing formal laws, there is no mechanism that rural Bangladeshi women can rely on to protect them from domestic abuse, or even to listen to their complaints. The circumstances of respectful public deliberation are unfamiliar to those who live in crocodile-infested waters. How can those who are silent due to inequalities join democratic deliberations?

Contrast the silent women in Bangladesh with the political protesters in Eastern Europe at the time of the fall of the Berlin Wall. Walzer begins his book, *Thick and Thin*, with the image of people in the streets of Prague in 1989 marching for "Truth" and "Justice," the words carried on placards and shouted by the marchers (1994a: 1). Walzer understands the marchers: they "wanted to hear true statements from their political leaders; they wanted to be able to believe what they read in the newspapers; they didn't want to be lied to anymore" (1994a: 2). Walzer's understanding of the marchers' wishes was possible because he could see the words "truth" and "justice" and because he could recognize their meaning at a general level not limited by personal or social interpretation of particulars. But, how can anyone see and interpret *wishes* that are not written or spoken?

Without prior social criticism, the silent cannot participate in legal institutions or even in social movements. Moreover, they cannot know what they would say were they to participate. Marx defines the role of criticism as promoting the "self-understanding of the age concerning its struggles and wishes." He adds, "This is the task for the world and for us," the social critics (Marx 1843: 215). Third World feminist social criticism requires the critic to help the silent clarify the struggles by listening to their unspoken wishes and asking society to do so as well. Such social criticism needs to be prior to (or at least not coincident with) legal and social action. Third World feminist social critics make the silent heard. They promote inquiry, deliberative opportunities, and institutional change in an effort to make social criticism inclusive of the perspectives of those marginalized by their silence. These forms of social criticism must take place prior to getting to a courtroom or marching in the streets if legal institutions and social protest are to be informed and inclusive practices. However, Third World feminist social criticism does not guarantee that social decision making will be more inclusively informed, collective, or uncoerced, or that social criticism will be able to effect social change, but it does contribute to those ends.

Everyday critics, multi-sited critics, and multiple critics

The anecdote of the women's exchange illustrates the contributions to social criticism by people every day, the importance of critics from a variety of critical perspectives, and the value of having multiple critics for social criticism. In general there are three kinds of critics: outsiders, insiders, and those who cross boundaries. First, as an outsider, the researcher was able to ask a question about domestic violence that the women themselves were not inclined to ask because such scenes were common. On the walk in Bangladesh, even though we had just come from a meeting on women's legal protections against domestic abuse (among other things), the scene we were passing went undiscussed until I asked the question, "What's going on?"

Second, the information about the causes of wife abuse came from insiders, the village women. The village women also discussed that, though common, they thought wife battery was not acceptable. Further, they identified appropriate means for challenging husbands who beat their wives. Women staging a sit-in in a home bring embarrassing public attention to a batterer.

Third, Save the Children and its program officer offered social criticism that neither the outsider nor the insiders could offer. Most of the Save the Children program workers were Bangladeshi; the program officer was a German woman fluent in Bengali; and the funding agency for the trip was the US Agency for International Development. Collectively, these critics from multiple perspectives sought to remove the women from their watchful familial and social environments. They did so according to acceptable practices by requiring the wives to ask their husbands' permission. They promoted incremental social change, challenging the norm of women's constrained mobility while following the convention of men's authority over their wives. Although they did not have preconceived notions about what the women would experience when working together in a special context, they expected that the result would be the sustainable strength of the women's groups. The anecdote gives examples of outside critics, inside critics, and critics whose critical perspective cannot be singly defined by the critic's origin. I call this last group "multi-sited" critics to reflect the multiple perspectives of such critics, and I explain the term further in chapter 5.

Although one may be inclined to view the last perspective as definitive of social criticism, the insider and the outsider offer critical perspectives that the multi-sited critic does not share. Critics from a single perspective cannot sufficiently bring about more informed, collective, and uncoerced social decision-making fora. However, where critics from multiple perspectives contribute to social criticism, social decision-making fora may become more informed, collective, and uncoerced. Third World feminist social criticism relies on multiple everyday critics, from varied critical perspectives.

A Third World feminist philosophy of social criticism

Social criticism is more comprehensive in its analysis than complaint because it is systematic. In the real world people complain about values, practices, norms, and each other without intending to be social critics. Complaints can be directed at individual circumstances or at general circumstances, but whether individual or general, complaints are not systematic, they are particular. For an example of individual complaint, a wife could complain about her husband's abuse. Such a complaint particularizes the complainer and particularizes the accused. Change is subject to the ability of the complainer to voice her complaint and to argue well. It is doubtful that the woman living in the crocodile-infested waters could effectively voice her own criticism or even that a representative could interpret her silence. But even where well-argued complaint is effective in specific individual circumstances, because it is specific to the individual circumstances, the argument does not affect those in similar circumstances.

Another approach to social criticism, equally ad hoc but intended to have broader benefit, is generalized complaint. For example, an activist might complain about domestic violence against women – particularly new brides – in rural Bangladesh. In this case, the complaint generalizes about women's physical abuse in marriage, or even more generally about women's vulnerability in marriage. As in the case of individual complaint, however, even where well-argued complaint is effective at raising awareness of rural women's vulnerability in Bangladesh, the context-specificity of the argument inhibits related benefits from accruing to others who are also but differently vulnerable, for example widows and unmarried girls. Whether particular or generalized, such complaint is too specific to be *social* criticism.

In order to have an impact on the values, practices, and norms of a society which perpetuate the particular harms identified by the complainers and those they have not identified, social criticism needs to be systematic and make respectful and informational use of complaint. Social criticism is distinguished from complaint in that the former recognizes oppression as systematic. The social critic sees inequalities as problems with the organization of society not merely as obstacles to achieving her own interests.

One systematic approach to social criticism is offered by Raymond Geuss in his review of critical theory as it has been developed by the Frankfurt school, with Marx as its forefather and Habermas as its best-known spokesperson (1981). As Geuss describes it, a critical theory poses epistemological challenges to traditional views. Marx's social criticism, for example, provides a revolutionary account of the nature of knowledge. Without reviewing that literature, I borrow the features of critical theory Geuss identifies and add others I argue are essential for a philosophy of social criticism that is practicable in the real world.

The three features consistent with Geuss's account of a critical theory are:

1. Social criticism should guide human action.
2. It should be coherent and consistent.
   And,
3. Social criticism should be "reflective"; that is, critics should be able to criticize the values, practices, and norms of a society according to principles which are themselves open to criticism. (Geuss 1981: 1–2, 55–95)

These are important criteria of a critical theory, but there is nothing in these criteria that *requires* a theorist to be *critical* of real world values, practices, and norms (though a particular critical theory such as Marx's may be). A society might have a coherent explanation for the exploitation of certain groups within it such that it was not critical of practices that exploit or discriminate against them. In the real world where inequalities frequently exhibit coherent patterns, critical theory needs more than the criteria of actionability, consistency, and self-reflection. It needs to be *critical*. As Marx encourages, in order to be critical a political philosophy needs to wrestle with "the struggles and wishes" of real people (1967 [1843]: 215).

Though systematic, the framework of critical theory outlined by Geuss does not systematically require critics' attention to the struggles and silent wishes of the oppressed. For example, Nancy Fraser argues that Habermas fails to incorporate into his theory analysis of the struggles of women. In her criticism of Habermas, Fraser draws attention to Marx's mandate suggesting that in order for critical theory to be *critical* it must wrestle with the struggles and wishes of women. Thus, where social criticism is most necessary, Habermas's critical theory is not critical (Fraser 1991).

Feminist theorists have consistently paid attention to the practical and critical import of political theory for the struggles and wishes of women. From a liberal perspective, Susan Okin criticizes contemporary theories of justice for assuming an idealized just family. To complement the Rawlsian assumption of equality in the original position, Okin articulates a critique of vulnerability created through social practices (1989). From a poststructuralist perspective, Chris Weedon argues that by offering feminists a critique of the epistemological power of language, poststructuralism is a useful complement to feminism (1997). By contrast, Mridula Udayagiri argues that postmodern feminism is not directed at social change and embodies a language of power all its own (1995). Sharing somewhat both views, Susan Bordo argues that postmodernism provides a tool, but that it is inadequate as feminist theory

(1990). These feminists and others have critically assessed political theory and developed its models to be more appropriate guides to social criticism. Another feminist approach has been to examine women's activism for its theoretical and practical value.[17]

My approach resembles both postmodern and anti-postmodern theoretical perspectives, but draws on Third World feminist activists for its theoretical roots. However, I take the cautions of anti-essentialist feminists against obviating differences and of their critics against being exclusive in my use of language, to heart.[18] I (and other Third World feminist activists) share with anti-essentialist theorists trust in people to know best their experience, and recognition that despite apparent similarities, differences among people and their experiences are particularly informative. However, like many Gender and Development theorists and practitioners, I (and other Third World feminist activists) do not want our respect for difference to manifest itself in ways that present obstacles to women's activism. Political theory needs to be practically and experientially grounded so that its critical relevance is concrete and its critical implications realizable. The Third World feminist model of social criticism is an important complement to democratic theory and, because it is an extrapolation from the real world activism of Third World women, is realizable.

I propose that, by defining the methodology, roles, and qualifications of social critics, the following additional defining criteria of a philosophy of social criticism systematically require critics to draw society's attention to those exploitative or potentially exploitative inequalities that are perpetuated through its values, practices, and norms:

4. Social critics must follow a methodology intended to be sensitive to the reality of an imperfect world where power inequalities enable coercion and potential exploitation to silence some within a society and to impede social criticism and social change.

5. The social critic must criticize the values, practices, and norms of a society. This may require being a critical voice as a representative of silent voices, facilitating the social criticism of others (possibly by

---

[17] Many (dare I say, most) feminists have been concerned about the disjunction between political theory and women's lives and encourage informing feminist theory with women's lived experiences; see for example Caroline Moser (1989), Chris Weedon (1997), Uma Narayan (1997), Nancy Hirschmann (1998), and Nancy Naples (1998c). Also, Naples gives a review of much feminist scholarship on women's activism (1998b).

[18] By referring to "anti-essentialists" I mean to refer to those who from either a poststructuralist or postmodernist perspective criticize the essentializing of other theorists. I generally refer to "postmodernists" when I am criticizing their elitist language. On postmodernism, poststructuralism, and anti-essentialism see Chantal Mouffe (1995).

creating a safe place for those who are excluded or exploited), or contributing to social criticism directly.

And,

6. There are no constraints on the origins or qualities that qualify one to be a social critic; social criticism requires multiple critics from a variety of origins and critical perspectives.

In specifying the methodology, roles, and qualifying perspectives of social critics, these three additional criteria require that social criticism clarify the struggles and silent wishes of an age if it is to be called *social* criticism. In other words, these criteria are necessary to transform critical theory from an intellectual project to the practice of social criticism of values, practices, and norms in the real, imperfect world.

Where inequalities are pervasive, the less powerful may not express their wishes even though existing values, practices, and norms inhibit their ability to live the life they desire. Where there are people who live according to values, practices, and norms they are unable to affect, social decision making is not informed, collective, and uncoerced. Where social decision making is not informed, collective, and uncoerced, social criticism plays important roles in promoting social decision making that is. In contexts of coercion and disagreement, social criticism is in part responsible for enabling those who live in the crocodile-infested water to participate in social decision making and to influence social change.

Outline of chapters

The book is organized to give theoretical coherence to Third World women activists' practice of social criticism and to propose this feminist theory of social criticism as a necessary complement to contemporary deliberative democratic theory, a development of feminist theory, and an improvement over Walzer's and Nussbaum's theories of social criticism. Third World feminist social criticism offers a complementary model of social criticism that enables political theory to be experientially grounded and relevant in a variety of contexts.

In chapter 2, I discuss the theoretical problems that deliberative democratic theorists face when confronted with the real world obstacles to deliberative democracy. Third World feminist theory and activism offer a practicable solution. Using the example of SEWA, I demonstrate that deliberation is important to social criticism as a means of gathering knowledge (factual information, the understanding of one another's preferences, and the skills for using deliberation to continue acquiring the first two kinds of knowledge). In addition to fostering this educative process, deliberation is important to social criticism because it promotes the ongoing discussion and evaluation of existing values, practices, and norms such that no topic is immune to potential criticism. Thus those that are coercive or that exploit power inequalities come under scrutiny. Finally, deliberation enables social criticism to have critical teeth because it enables critics and society to develop criteria with which to assess whether existing or proposed values, practices, and norms are (or potentially are) coercive or exploitative. Thus deliberation under imperfect conditions enables bringing about near-ideal conditions. Deliberation is foundational to Third World feminism's method of social criticism and has implications for the roles and qualifications of social critics.

When western political theorists do attempt to offer an account of social criticism (that is, an account of how to bring about the political context they advocate), they must provide an account of how their version of social criticism would negotiate the competing pressures toward cultural relativism and essentialism. In chapter 3, I discuss two such attempts in contemporary political theory: those of Michael Walzer and Martha Nussbaum. Though promising, Walzer's methodological flaw allows the social critic to accept existing and harmful practices as shared and Nussbaum's methodological flaw allows the social critic to make incompletely informed proposals for social change.

Feminists are particularly invested in the relativist–essentialist debate because frequently the cultural practices under scrutiny are those that have different effects on women and men. The Gender and Development (GAD) literature has been particularly self-conscious. Western authors writing from outside the contexts of the practices they criticize have been accused of essentializing about all women's experiences based on western women's experiences. Other western authors have withheld criticism in the interest of identifying what women value in or gain from those practices that seem oppressive to women. Some nonwestern authors have been able to avoid over generalized or vacuous observations by basing their criticism on intimate knowledge with the practice and using their critical perspective (that of one who has insider knowledge) to remove from their criticism of the practice any exclusive foundation in either western or local cultural understandings. Some feminists, including Norma Alarcón (1990), J. Oloka-Onyango and Sylvia Tamale (1995), and Jane Flax (1995), caution that some white feminists have taken note of the work of women of color and, rather than recognized the differences among the theories proposed by these authors, used them as local perspectives that validated white western women's experiences and ignored the substance of their critical perspectives.

While respectful of their criticism, Mridula Udayagiri is concerned about the implications of the "postmodernists' assertion that philosophy can no longer claim to ground social criticism: criticism should be local, *ad hoc* and untheoretical" (1995: 167). I share the concerns of both perspectives. The theory of social criticism I propose makes critical use of local, *ad hoc*, and untheoretical social criticism in addition to outside, formal, and theoretical social criticism. The Third World feminist social criticism I describe furthers the critical project of those who worry that the voices of Third World feminists are not heard in mainstream feminism. More significantly for feminist theory and political theory, it puts at the center of an important problem in political theory Third World feminists' offering a solution. Thus, Third World women's ideas are appreciated not only for their localized information (which is critically relevant), but also for their globally relevant advance to feminist political theory. Through their activism, Third World feminist theorists have drafted a model of social criticism that is sensitive to diversity and yet has critical teeth. Their critical arguments are at once respectful of, and informed by, the broad experience of women and thus offer potent social criticism.

In chapter 4, I outline the critics' roles and illustrate that social criticism requires broad critical input in order to be *social*, using the example of the women's human rights movement and literature. Consequently, critics' roles include promoting inquiry, deliberative exchange, and institutional change such that societies can make their existing decision-making contexts more inclusive or find new contexts for decision making. Chapter 5 broadly identifies the qualifications of social critics and shows why a range of experiential backgrounds are necessary to fulfill the roles of social critics. No perspective – not that of the insider, the outsider, or even a critic able to move between the worlds of insiders and outsiders – is privileged. Though each critical perspective provides valuable information, and sometimes information unavailable to those of other perspectives, no critical perspective alone is adequately informed. Both individual scholars and collective networks of scholars and activists contribute to broadly informed social criticism.

Finally, in chapter 6, I argue that Third World feminist social criticism advances feminist democratic, critical, and postmodern theories. Feminists, drawing on liberal democratic, critical, and postmodern theoretical perspectives, have been critical of these traditions because they presume equality where substantive equality is lacking, they fail to provide a satisfactory account of how individual and group rights can be respected in a democratic model, and they fail to consider as political those issues and interests that have been historically considered private.

However, these feminists have failed to offer a theoretical solution to the problems they reveal. Third World feminist social criticism conforms to the general view of critical theory defined by Geuss – that it should be actionable, coherent, and self-reflective – and provides a solution, not in the form of democratic institutions but rather in the form of a democratizing practice. Third World feminist social criticism promotes the democratic values of inclusion and equality through the ongoing evaluation of existing values, practices, and norms.

Conclusion: a feminist political philosophy of social criticism

In striking contrast to global statistics, there are many parts of the world where men outnumber, and live longer than, women.[19] Practices based on the social, economic, and political inferiority of women to men contribute to this troubling anomaly. Particularly in places where economic resources are scarce, practices such as female infanticide, wife battery, and giving boys and men better health care, food, and education threaten the lives of women and their children. Women's chances for life – let alone their desired quality of life – are severely limited by these and other practices. In this book, I develop a theory of social criticism that provides a foundation for the criticism of values, practices, and norms that perpetuate inequalities such as those that threaten women's lives.

In the real world, coercion impedes argument, social criticism, social decision making, and social change. People with more power are able to prevent social change or to influence the process to their advantage and to the detriment of others. Third World feminist social criticism shows how, despite power inequalities, the views of the less powerful can be heard and can influence social decision making. How can society hear the arguments of those who do not argue because they are coerced in their environment – living metaphorically in crocodile-infested water? My answer, a Third World feminist theory of social criticism, is stimulated in part by my observations of a training program for rural women in Bangladesh sponsored by Save the Children and furthered by my study of Third World women's activism.

My proposal is inspired by concern for the effects of inequality on the political and social process of a society's evaluation of its formal and informal values, practices, and norms; on deliberation about them; and

---

[19] For biological reasons, women tend to live longer than men. In the industrialized countries and in many developing countries, women have a longer life expectancy than men and women make up the same or a greater proportion of the population as men (United Nations Development Program 1994). See also Sen (1990a).

on decisions to change or to reinforce them. While deliberative democratic theory, relativism, and essentialism contribute generally to the
scholarship on social change, each is an inadequate critical perspective
from which to derive strategies for mitigating inequalities in social
decision making and social change. In the real world, many people
suffer as a function of their subordinate position in social hierarchies.
Deliberative, relativist, and essentialist political theorists have sketched
philosophies of social criticism that alone are inadequate for criticizing
some harmful social values, practices, and norms. They do not specify
satisfactorily the method, roles, and qualifying perspectives of social
critics. In this book, I specify all three. Drawing from the practical
experience of a wide variety of women activists, I give a theoretically
coherent account of a method of social criticism that women activists
have been developing. In addition, I generalize about the roles and
qualifications of the social critic. Collectively, feminists – led by Third
World women activists – have pioneered a model of social criticism that
allows them to criticize existing values, practices, and norms that
perpetuate inequalities. Activists from a range of critical perspectives
guide their specific criticisms with a method: deliberation as a means of
inquiry; skeptical scrutiny of coercive or potentially exploitative values,
practices, and norms; and a working list of guiding evaluative criteria
consisting of capabilities essential to living a good human life. The
model of social criticism I propose provides no right answers but rather
a discipline for ongoing questioning and evaluation of social practices by
a society with the help of social critics.

2 A Third World feminist theory of social criticism

Introduction: quality of and equality in participation

Although deliberative theorists do not always apply their work to the political questions of contemporary world or US politics, deliberative democratic theory is relevant to contemporary politics. In places like El Salvador and South Africa political societies have revised their basic institutions to be more inclusive and democratic. In the process they have realized that, given their histories of violence, coercion, and exploitative inequalities, they also need to revise their institutions of everyday politics such that a population unaccustomed to inclusive democracy can participate in it. Likewise, though without the need for a new constitution, pluralist societies like the USA are wrestling with histories of inequality and exclusion based on sex, sexuality, ethnicity, class, caste, religion, country of origin, national identity, aboriginal status, immigration status, regional geography, language, cultural practices, forms of dress, beliefs, ability, health status, family history, age, and education such that they too need to consider how democratically their basic political institutions and institutions of everyday politics function. Deliberative democratic theorists are likewise broadening their attention from theorizing about the basic political institutions of society (Bessette1980, 1994; Sunstein 1988) to thinking about the institutions of everyday politics as well: school boards, legislative bodies, government administration, unions, trade groups, and interest groups – what Amy Gutmann and Dennis Thompson call "middle democracy" (1996). As they describe it, in middle democracy people respect each other and come to consensus on political decisions through free and reasoned deliberation among equal parties. Gutmann & Thompson's work is a valuable component of democratic theory because it offers an account of deliberative principles for everyday democratic life that are consistent with political liberalism in a pluralist society (Gutmann 1995). Still other deliberative democratic theorists are moving beyond existing deliberative institutions to describe new deliberative institutions

(Barber 1984; Dahl 1997) and even to put into practice actual deliberative fora (Fishkin 1991, 1996; Mathews 1994). Generally, deliberative theorists seek a participatory democracy of equal voices that also protects individual rights.[1] In this chapter I focus on those versions of deliberative democratic theory that inadvertently or openly promote reasoned deliberation at the expense of broadly informed deliberation. I give less attention to those versions of deliberative democratic theory whose authors, not all of whom are recognized as deliberative theorists, ask us to implement deliberative democratic institutions.

Some theorists like Gutmann & Thompson focus on principles of deliberation to be used in democratic fora. Joshua Cohen (1989a) shares this approach. Others focus on the constitutional or institutional framework necessary to sustain deliberative democracy. These include Benjamin Barber (1984), Jane Mansbridge (1988, 1992) and Julie Mostov (1992). A few, such as Cass Sunstein (1988) and Carlos Santiago Nino (1996), have even articulated both principles of deliberation and a constitutional framework for their implementation. Likewise, in their co-authored work Cohen and Joel Rogers in their account of associative democracy offer both principles and institutions of deliberative democracy (1992). Both principled and institutional approaches seem to be committed to resolving the tensions in democracy between participatory decision making and rights-threatening political participation.[2] The concern is not only the familiar Madisonian fear of a factious tyrannical majority usurping the individual rights of the minority but also a more general fear that increasing participation in democratic decision making will make that very participation less equal. (Or that making participation more equal will institutionally require making participation less substantive.) The democratic decision making among a small group of individuals who deliberatively determine their concerns, decision-making agenda, and decision rule is qualitatively more democratic than a large population's decision making according to one-person-one-vote. The former allows and requires the people to be aware of their collective self-rule. Whether viewed as the tension between democracy and rights (Nino 1996) or between participation and equality (Phillips 1991), the problem is one of creating principles and institutions for greater quality and equality of participation.

Rather than embracing the problem as one of balancing the quality

---

[1] For a quick history of contemporary deliberative democratic theory see Bohman & Rehg (1997). For a broader look at the history of deliberative democratic theory and practice see Elster (1998a and 1998b).

[2] James Fishkin defines the tension as one of tradeoffs among four democratic values – deliberation, nontyranny, political equality, and participation (1995: 62–63, 173). See also Phillips 1991.

and equality of participation, the deliberative theorists have held equality constant in their assumptions.[3] In general, they resolve the tension between democracy and rights by articulating procedural rules for participating in deliberations such that "unreasonable" views are excluded thereby preventing the majority in a democracy from following an unreasonable idea that would undermine someone's or some group's rights. Although seemingly a basis for active participation, this solution could limit participation to only those with the skills to participate appropriately. Therefore the deliberative theorists necessarily include in the procedural rules the people's equal ability to participate. Substantively, then, the deliberative theorists rely on and strengthen background educational institutions so citizens can learn to deliberate according to the norms of deliberation set out by the theorists. While this combination of procedural and substantive norms of deliberation seemingly solves the tension between participatory decision making and tyranny of the majority, it presents a second tension – one between "reasonable" deliberation and inclusive deliberation – and introduces two other forms of tyranny: tyranny of the method and tyranny of the meeting. Deliberative democratic theory excludes "unreasonable" views at the cost of inclusive deliberation. By expecting all to deliberate according to their substantive and procedural norms, deliberative democratic theorists exclude those who don't. Those who can deliberate according to the method can exercise a form of tyranny. Deliberative theorists recast the democratic tension as a question of quality of participation holding equality constant. Through their assumptions of equal participation they are able to ignore that the procedural and institutional mechanisms for ensuring quality of participation can undermine equality of participation. In addition such models of deliberation require that people are able to participate in meetings for deliberative decision making while fulfilling the nonpolitical responsibilities and desires of their lives. Those who cannot balance their participation in deliberative fora with their other life obligations and needs experience tyranny of the meeting.

Most deliberative theorists focus their (and our) attention on the tension between democracy (as participation, representation, or republicanism) and rights (protection from tyranny of the majority). While theirs is an important theoretical and practical problem for democratic theorists to wrestle with, the tension between informed and inclusive participation (as they have set it up) subsumes the second tension between quality and equality of participation and allows them to ignore it. How we identify the problem of democracy has implications not only

---

[3] Bohman (1996) is an exception.

for theory but also for *theorists*. Can we in the academy who consider ourselves citizens of a democracy as well as theorists of democracy be comfortable with the anti-democratic and elitist implications of theories premised on "reasonable" deliberation at the expense of inclusive deliberation? Can we justify advocating, either through principles of deliberation or deliberative democratic institutions, a vision of democracy premised on agreed-upon terms of discussion or judicial review of democratic decision making? I think not because they sacrifice equality of participation. To be true practitioners as well as theorists of deliberative democracy, we must offer our insights explicitly in the context of ongoing social discussions. It is not enough to offer *reasons* for our proposed principles or *arguments* in support of our proposed institutions. If we are truly to participate in deliberative democracy and be contributors to it, our theoretical proposals must in their substance be up for collective deliberation. Moreover, not everyone is equally able to participate in such deliberations so we must be inventive in our efforts to seek their contributions to our discussions. Not only is deliberative democratic theory relevant to contemporary politics, but also it has implications for how we do deliberative democratic theory.

Even deliberative theorists are not comfortable with deliberative theory. In the conclusion of *The Constitution of Deliberative Democracy*, Carlos Santiago Nino displays apparent discomfort with his own conclusions (1996). Although he has outlined the principles, institutions, and practices of constitutional deliberative democracy, he seems uncomfortable with the degree of judicial (or external) oversight that even his constitutional practice requires in order to secure both democracy (participation) and rights (protection from tyranny of the majority). His discomfort is such that he suggests in conclusion that as a body politic and its political constitution and practices approach the ideal constitution and practices of deliberative democracy, the tension between democracy and rights no longer needs to be assessed by a judicial or external reviewer. Rather the body politic itself will function to keep these in balance.[4] Nino's appeal to a utopian state of constitutional evolution reveals both the continued importance of the reviewer in his theory (and its implied practice) and his discomfort with that importance (1996: ch. 7, esp. 222).

---

[4] In "The Ideal of Public Reason Revisited," Rawls asserts that the citizens will be able to review the deliberative decisions of their representatives following the same principles that those representatives should use in their decision making (1997: 769). Bohman outlines a model of deliberative democracy that relies on continual critical attention to its practice (1996). Chantal Mouffe, to whom I return in chapter 6, envisions a democratic people defining itself in ever-increasingly reactionary terms (1992).

Feminist theorists have given more theoretical attention to the problem that Nino finds disquieting. Feminists who engage in the discussion of and furthering of deliberative democratic theory do so cautiously. Feminists are skeptical of principles and institutions because in practice they have been used to justify the exclusion of women from participating in public dialogue or engaging in political life or used to include them in principle and exclude them in practice. Their skepticism is warranted and my criticism will reiterate some of their concerns. However, feminism's greater contribution to deliberative democratic theory comes not from critiques of democratic theorists' arguments, but rather from proposals for more appropriate methods of theorizing inclusively about inclusive political processes.[5] Some feminists who I have termed Third World feminists have individually and collectively been offering social criticism that has theoretical import for deliberative democratic theorists. They invite us to consider that the obstacles to participation in democratic decision making are not only those of the visible history of violence, coercion, and exploitative inequalities a people may have endured, but also in the invisible history of violence, coercion, and exploitative inequalities that many (including women, minorities, aboriginal peoples, the disabled, and otherwise marginalized) within nations continue to experience. Third World feminism prompts us to expand the project of deliberative democratic theory beyond identifying the principles and institutions of engagement to include discussion of those principles and institutions in the context of a broad effort to achieve informed and inclusive deliberation. For feminists, informed argument cannot be based solely or even principally on accepted forms of reasoning and argumentation. Informed argument is based more importantly on broad and ever-expanding sources of information and understanding. Thus, informed argument is inclusive.

Without promising that social criticism is more effective at bringing about social change than principles of deliberative engagement or institutional reform, I argue that social change need not wait for idealized constitutional reforms to be implemented or for representatives to model ideal decision making through their application of deliberative principles. People have been bringing about social change (including institutional change) without universally recognized principles or prior institutional reforms, without equality and without

---

[5] For example, see Mostov's account of popular sovereignty which asks us to "consider the ways in which gender relations in the family, in reproductive and other areas of sexual life, and at the workplace impede or inhibit the exercise of equal citizenship" (Mostov 1992: 13). See also Anne Phillips's reconciliation of feminism and democracy in *Engendering Democracy* (1991).

universal recognition of what constitutes a reasonable argument; and yet, they have been doing so inclusively. Deliberative democratic theory is elitist if it wrestles with the tension between popular participation and tyranny of the majority without resolving the tension between "reasonable" deliberation and inclusive deliberation. The challenge is to improve the quality and the equality of participation in public decision making.

Third World feminist social criticism complements deliberative democratic theory by providing a means for improving both the quality and equality of public participation. Moreover, it furthers the deliberative theorists' project by abandoning its strongest assumptions. I have mentioned above the assumption of equality of participation; others are the mutual and self-respect of the participants and agreement on what constitutes a reasonable argument. Third World feminist social critics have used deliberation to bring about social change despite the disrespect of their audience and the need to challenge the terms of what constitutes a reasonable argument.

As an institution of public life, deliberation is relevant not only as an alternative to bargaining and contracting as the means of reaching political agreement despite moral disagreements and diverse preferences, but also as a tool for promoting excluded interests through better information where collective decision making is a function of bargaining, contracting, or win–lose power struggles. Certain deliberative democratic theorists propose deliberative theory as an alternative to bargaining and contracting (Cohen 1989a: 17). However, according to other deliberative theorists, deliberation can play a role in making bargaining, contracting, and even win–lose decision-making contexts more inclusive through being better informed (Dahl 1997). Through the example of their activism under conditions of extreme inequality, Third World feminist social critics offer the necessary complement to both versions of deliberative theory by showing us how to change the values, practices, and norms of a given context (sometimes even by insulating the excluded from an oppressive context) such that deliberation can be more informed, collective, and uncoerced.

Deliberative democratic theory

With a diversity of approaches, assumptions, and specifications, but with consensus on the value of public deliberation for political decision making, deliberative democratic theorists have drawn on various traditions in political theory to propose a liberal democratic model of democratic institutions for political decision making that eschews bargaining, contracting and win–lose models of political decision making. This model expects engaged participation of its citizenry through the citizens' offering thoughtful proposals and exercising thoughtful consideration of others' proposals.[6] Supporters attribute a range of political and social benefits to liberal deliberative democratic theory. These include collective recognition of the common good, improved sense of political community, improved quality of public decision making, enhanced legitimacy of public decisions and public institutions, development or transformation of individual preferences to be consistent with the common good, and the citizens' development and exercise of civic virtue.[7] Within the field there are also disagreements about the goals of deliberation[8] and about standards of assessment within deliberative

[6] For Joseph Bessette (1980: 107, 115) and John Rawls (1997: 769) deliberative fora are the representative (and for Rawls also the judicial) bodies in the government such that citizens' direct participation in politics is through their holding their representatives accountable and only to a lesser extent through their own deliberations.

[7] Sunstein believes that a common good is possible but not always achievable (1988: 1555). Deliberation about the common good is an alternative to competition among interest groups (Rawls 1997: 767; Mansbridge 1993) that "focuses debate on the common good" (Cohen 1989a: 25) and strengthens the sense of community among a society's members (Sunstein 1988: 1573) while recognizing difference (Mansbridge 1992: 36–37); by contrast, Knight & Johnson reject defining the purpose of deliberation as identifying the collective will (1994: 283). Deliberation can improve the quality of public decision making by encouraging citizens to make "considered" not quick judgments (Nino 1996; Rawls 1971: 47), promoting critical thinking among citizens (Mill 1974 [1859]; Gutmann 1993b, 1995), valuing the exchange of multiple and divergent opinions (Mill 1970 [1869]; Dewey 1916a; Tully 1995; Manin 1987), by breaking down prejudices based on ignorance (Gutmann 1995), or by enabling citizens to arrive at mutually acceptable decisions despite moral disagreement (Gutmann & Thompson 1996: 3). Decisions will be more legitimate because they are the result of expression by free and equal citizens (Rawls 1997), because the process is legitimate (Manin 1987; Cohen 1989a), because power is exercised collectively (Rawls 1997: 770), because people are empowered (Mostov 1992), or because they have settled on their decision peacefully (Tully 1995). Deliberation gives citizens an opportunity to change their interests to consider the public interest (Rawls 1997; Cohen 1989a: 24), to modify or determine their preferences where they are incomplete (Manin 1987), and to develop "preferences about preferences" (Sunstein 1988: 1545). Finally, like Aristotle, some deliberative theorists believe that exercising citizenship through participation in public deliberations enhances civic virtue (Mill 1974 [1859]; 1969; Sunstein 1988: 1573).

[8] Elster rejects the view that the purpose of deliberation is civic virtue, asserting rather that its purpose is political decision making (Elster 1997: 19). Rawls (1993, 1997) and Gutmann & Thompson (1996) strive for consensus, although as Cohen notes there is no assurance of unanimity (Cohen 1989a: 23). While striving for political agreement despite moral disagreement, consensus-oriented deliberative theorists recognize that legitimate decisions can be made without unanimity if there is unanimity on the procedures and rules of deliberative decision making. Cohen defends an ideal deliberative forum and process and argues that the deliberative ideal – not a notion of fairness – underlies the political values of commitment, autonomy, and legitimacy of political outcomes (1989a). Dewey (1980 [1916b]), Nino (1996), Christiano (1997), and Estlund (1997) argue that deliberation contributes to learning and leads to the epistemologically best outcome.

fora.[9] Moreover, some theorists offer deliberation as a tool for designing the basic institutions of society (Rawls 1971, 1993, 1997), while others propose it as a process appropriate for those institutions in which citizens can participate directly (Barber 1984; Gutmann & Thompson 1996). Some outline ideal conditions for familiar institutions (Cohen 1989a, 1989b; Cohen & Rogers 1992; Gutmann & Thompson 1996), while some create or discuss actual institutions modeled on the ideal of deliberation (Fishkin 1991, 1995; Mathews 1994). Additionally, there is variety among the theorists in the attention they pay to processes of public discussion and decision making, to the preconditions of deliberative fora, and to the applicability of deliberative ideals in current situations in the United States and other democracies.

With some variation, deliberative theorists set out principles and procedures to guide the content of argumentation in deliberative fora. Although some theorists make a distinction between substantive and procedural models of deliberative democracy, both nominally "substantive" and "procedural" models embody substantive norms – of individual self-respect and mutual respect among persons – and procedural norms – that deliberation should be careful, thoughtful, and informed among multiple participants who agree that reasonable argument respects appropriate constraints and who have equal opportunity to influence deliberations by giving and listening to reasons for each others' proposals.

Bohman & Rehg make the distinction between substantive and procedural models in their introduction to *Deliberative Democracy* (1997: xxvii). For a discussion of the significance of the distinction between substantive agreement on doctrines and procedural agreement on adjudicating doctrinal disagreements see Seyla Benhabib's note in which she asserts that by virtue of living in a modern state, residents accept certain "constitutional minimums" (1996b: 89–90, fn. 14). Benhabib seems to think that substantive norms are given (universally accepted and assumed in a constitutional democracy) and thus deliberative democracy is the subject of procedural norms. Like Donald Moon, to whom Benhabib directs her response, I am skeptical of the value in distinguishing between procedural and substantive deliberative democratic theory. It seems to me that the substantive and procedural accounts require the preconditions not only of constitutional minimums but also of the participants' self-respect, mutual respect, equal ability to influ-

---

[9] Some deliberative theorists identify procedural standards by which to assess deliberation (Manin 1987; Estlund 1997). Others attempt to identify objective standards of rationality to guide the content of deliberations (Rawls 1993, 1997; Cohen 1989a, 1993; Nino 1996; Habermas 1996; Gutmann & Thompson 1996).

ence outcomes, and agreement on what constitutes acceptable deliberative content.

Other deliberative theorists also reject this distinction. For example, rather than juxtaposing substantive and procedural justice, David Estlund argues that certain procedures actually yield more substantively correct judgments (1993, 1997). Nino makes a similar point in defense of deliberative democratic constitutional arrangements:

The ideal constitution of power – to the extent that it is materialized in the historical one – leads to what should be the ideal constitution of rights. Therefore, at first sight, there seems to be no conflict between the substantive and the procedural ideal constitutions, since the ideal constitution of power is, when realized, the most reliable way of gaining access to the ideal constitution of rights. The most important goal is, thus to achieve the ideal constitution of power: deliberative democracy. (1996: 219)

Whether they view them as substantive or procedural standards for deliberative democracy, the theorists who describe and advocate the principles and procedures of deliberative democracy expect self-respect, mutual respect, functional political equality, and agreement on what constitutes a reasonable argument among participants in deliberative fora.

While deliberative theorists generally require these norms, their requirement is not always obvious in their accounts of deliberative democracy. Therefore for illustrative purposes I discuss Cohen, Gutmann & Thompson, and Estlund, in some detail. According to Cohen deliberation should be free, reasoned, among equal parties, aimed at a rationally motivated consensus (1989a: 22–23). Equality of the participants requires that each person have self-respect and that each have equal respect for the others, not necessarily their ideas. An idea should not be weighted less or more based on *who* says it. "The members recognize one another as having deliberative capacities, i.e. the capacities required for entering into a public exchange of reasons and for acting on the result of such public reasoning" (1989a: 21). Additionally, in Cohen's account the definition of what is reasonable is essential. Participants must restrict each "political argument to the subset of moral considerations that others who have reasonable views accept as well" (1993: 283). Thus, participants are constrained in *how* they contribute to public debate. Not all substantively acceptable contributions meet the procedural standards of deliberation.

Proposals may be rejected because they are not defended with acceptable reasons, even if they could be so defended. The deliberative conception emphasizes that collective choices should be *made in a deliberative way*, and not only that those choices should have a desirable fit with the preferences of citizens. (1989a: 22)

It will be particularly difficult for those who lack self-respect or are not treated with equal respect to meet Cohen's procedural standard of deliberation. In the real world, some participants lack the imperative self-respect or give other participants too much or too little respect; some participants cannot support their arguments with reasons that others will find acceptable (though such reasons may exist). Where participants are respected by others and have equal ability to influence deliberations, Cohen's procedure of deliberation would probably enhance self-respect as he suggests (1989a), but where self-respect and mutual respect are lacking, the procedure offers nothing to bring them about.

Gutmann & Thompson offer principles that rely similarly on self-respect, mutual respect, and agreed-upon norms of deliberation. "The conception of deliberative democracy that we defend: consists of three principles – reciprocity, publicity, and accountability – that regulate the process of politics, and three others – basic liberty, basic opportunity, and fair opportunity – that govern the content of policies" (1996: 12). "Reciprocity" depends on mutual respect (1996: 56); "publicity" means that the reasons and information necessary for all political decisions should be made public (1996: 95); "accountability" means that the people (officials and citizens) must justify their decisions to those bound or affected by them (1996: 128); basic liberty is constrained by the claims of basic and fair opportunity (determined significantly by welfare and employment needs and practices) (1996: 208, 211, 273, 311). As in Cohen's, in Gutmann & Thompson's account of deliberative democracy self-respect and mutual respect are the bases of reciprocity (1996: 237, 79). Beyond these basic requirements, their version of deliberative democracy expects citizens to follow procedural norms of presenting coherent arguments. Substantive equality in the deliberative sphere is achieved through reciprocity which relies on people extending equal respect to all persons, not necessarily to their ideas; however, ideas should not be weighted less or more based on *who* presents them. Thus, where self-respect and mutual respect are lacking, citizens do not have equal abilities to influence deliberations.

With a different emphasis from the preceding theorists, David Estlund argues that deliberative democracy leads to better quality decisions (1993: 1477); these decisions approximate the truth and the people understand them as approximating truth (1993: 1463–1467).[10]

---

[10] John Stuart Mill (1974 [1859], 1970 [1869]), John Dewey (1980 [1916b]), Bernard Manin (1987), and Seyla Benhabib (1996b) share Estlund's understanding of the epistemic value of deliberation.

According to Estlund, deliberative democracy requires only competent voters (1997: 185) and certain "social and structural circumstances" (1997: 190) which include allowing participation by all, a focus on common not individual or group interests, a "shared conception of justice," fair evaluation of arguments, knowledge of one another's views, pluralism in life experience and culture, and the welfare of all participants sufficient to enable people to participate in public deliberations (1997: 190–191). Because of this list of circumstances of deliberation, Estlund's epistemic claim about the quality of decisions made in such deliberative fora relies on the same substantive and procedural norms as Cohen's and Gutmann & Thompson's. Choosing to participate requires self-respect. Fair evaluation of arguments and listening to one another enough to have knowledge of one another's views requires mutual and equal respect. Procedurally, Estlund expects deliberants to offer arguments that are consistent with the common interest[11] and that conform to the society's shared conception of justice.[12] His requirements of deliberation appear to be less demanding because he sets the standards by which participants evaluate deliberative outcomes internally. Yet, competency of voters and the circumstances in fact require self-respect, mutual respect, an equal ability to influence deliberations, and agreed-upon procedures of argumentation as in Cohen's and Gutmann & Thompson's accounts of deliberative democratic theory.

These preconditions and procedures will yield outcomes of deliberative decision making that meet or aim at meeting an epistemological standard – the standard of "rational" decision making as defined by those preconditions and procedures (cf. Estlund 1993: 1476). Versions of these preconditions and procedures of deliberation are recognized by many deliberative theorists.[13] Yet some critics share my concern that, due to norms of social status, people are not equally able to participate

---

[11] Sanders argues that having to make arguments in terms of the common interest constrains the range of acceptable arguments such that group claims (she offers the example of the Japanese Americans interned during World War II) are illegitimate (1997: 361).

[12] Other deliberative theorists expect significant common ground. See for example Rawls's assertion that the society have the "public political culture of a constitutional regime" (1997: 776) or that the best reasons will be shared (1997: 771). See also Michelman's claim that the deliberative democratic approach is not circular if the people are confident that the laws are in force and that the laws are "reasonably defensible as justice-seeking" though they may be imperfect (1997: 166). Consider further Elster's caution that "one cannot assume that one will in fact approach the good society by acting as if one had already arrived there" (1997: 18).

[13] See for example Sunstein (1988), Nino (1996), Mansbridge (1988, 1992), Manin (1987).

or to influence deliberative content or outcomes.[14] Deliberative theorists expect participants to be political equals, but norms of respect in society make people differently able to influence political discussions and thus outcomes. In addition, the proposed procedures of argumentation are not universal or universally practicable. Lynn Sanders and Iris Marion Young have argued that they embody white, western, educated male norms of reasoning (Sanders 1997; Young 1996).[15] These critics are concerned that the deliberative approach discredits particular interests (Sanders 1997: 361).[16] As a means of developing mutual respect and allowing those who are not generally heard to participate in the mean time, Sanders proposes allowing the practice of giving testimonials into deliberative fora. Young more thoroughly proposes that acceptable deliberative practices include allowing 1) flattery and body language in discourse, 2) emotion and figurative language (deliberative theorists' attempts to distinguish rational and rhetorical speech are specious; persuasion is part seduction; the speaker must get and keep the audience's attention, 1996: 130), and 3) "storytelling," for revealing experiences and sources of values for individuals and revealing the social position they share with others.

Tully offers a theoretical complement to Sanders's and Young's critiques and proposals.[17] He argues that "the primary good of self-respect requires that popular sovereignty is conceived as an intercultural dialogue" (1995: 190). As such the norms of discussion for determining the rules by which a society is going to govern itself must be themselves decided using a broad range of means for presenting views. Critiquing the liberal constitutionalist model for identifying common ground through reasoning, Tully complains,

---

[14] See Knight & Johnson for a discussion of equality of opportunity to influence and equality of influence in political decision making (1997: 305). See Susan Stokes for examples of the ways in which deliberation can yield "normatively unpleasant results" (1998: 136–137). Likewise, Rousseau argued that people should form their views individually so that one could not be influenced by the rhetorical skill of another (1968 [1762]). See also Adam Przeworski (1998).

[15] In the context of her critique of Habermas, Fraser makes the same critique of what she identifies as the liberal male bourgeois public sphere (1992: 119–121).

[16] Sunstein specifically rejects this interpretation of the deliberative democratic function of liberal republicanism (1988: 1573–1576). See Knight & Johnson on the challenges of measuring effective participation in deliberative fora (1997).

[17] Tully is unique among deliberative theorists, and in certain respects should not be counted among them. He is unique because he offers his account of contemporary constitutionalism as one to be considered in juxtaposition with others, not as decisive. However, we might not want to call him a deliberative theorist at all because much of deliberative theory is built on conventions of modern constitutionalism that Tully explicitly refutes (1995).

descriptions in the abstract language of modern constitutionalism occlude the ways of reasoning that actually bring peace ... [Abstract language] shackles the ability to understand and causes us to dismiss as irrelevant the concrete cases which alone can help to understand how the conciliation is actually achieved. The perspicuous representation of the reasoning that mediates the conflicts over cultural recognition consists of dialogical descriptions of the very language used in handling actual cases. (1995: 173)

Tully asks, why can't particular and descriptive language be admissible in deliberations?

Deliberative theorists need to ask this question. One answer they may offer is that diversity in expression would undermine the thoughtful, careful, reasoning process. According to Tully's description of the treaty negotiations between Aboriginal peoples and the Crown in the colonial states and Canada over three hundred years, most recently in 1992, while thoughtful, careful, and reasoned, these meetings do not appear to conform qualitatively to the procedural norms of the deliberative theorists.

Each negotiator participates in his or her language, mode of speaking and listening, form of reaching agreement, and way of representing the people, or peoples for whom they speak ... [In these negotiations] elaborate genres of presentation, speaking in French, English and Aboriginal languages, exchanging narratives, stories and arguments, translating back and forth, breaking off and starting again, striking new treaties and redressing violations of old ones have been developed to ensure that each speaker speaks in her or his cultural voice and listens to others in theirs. (1995: 129)

Shouldn't a political theory that promotes and relies on the political participation of all be based on practices in which all adults can participate? Tully argues yes and proposes that narratives, stories, and arguments presented in the variety of styles people choose are appropriate for constitutional negotiations. To extend his argument, where norms of influencing decisions are not homogeneous, the practices appropriate to deliberative fora should be broadly defined in a best attempt to make deliberative processes inclusive.[18] Although most deliberative theorists agree that self-respect, mutual respect, participants' equal ability to influence outcomes, and agreement on what

---

[18] Young makes a complementary point that the deliberative theorists' presumption of unity on norms of argument in deliberative fora is problematic practically because in a pluralist society it is surreal to suggest that such unity is possible and theoretically because then the self-transcendence that deliberation makes possible would not be necessary (1996: 122–126). While at times sensitive to the exclusionary potential of the deliberative model of the public sphere, Seyla Benhabib rejects diversity of ways of speaking in the legislative pulbic sphere but argues that non-legislative social publics offer opportunities for deliberation using a broader set of participation norms (1991, 1996b); see chapter 6.

constitutes acceptable deliberative content are the preconditions of deliberative democracy,[19] deliberative theorists have given little attention as to how to bring about these preconditions.

Accounts of deliberative theory are subject to two theoretical and two practical criticisms that the theory of social criticism can help address. The first theoretical objection is that deliberative theory assumes significant homogeneity in constitutional background (Rawls 1993, 1997) and political norms (Sunstein 1988; Benhabib 1996b) or overstates the possibility for consensus (or the likelihood of an agreement to accept a political decision). As feminists have warned, transcending difference usually means silencing subordinate groups (Fraser 1995: 289).

There are three ways in which the possibility of consensus via reasoning is overstated. The first is that, contrary to Cohen's assertion that deliberation "advances the common good" (1989b: 34), deliberation is necessary when there is no identifiable common good. As Mark Warren puts it, social interaction becomes political *precisely* when common ground is not recognizable. "Political contests emerge when individuals judge that discomforts and hardships are important enough to risk (and the risks can be substantial) moving into an arena of social groundlessness" (1996b: 245).[20] Likewise Holloway Sparks (1997) and Iris Young (1990a) see political participation as including the dissent by those excluded and their effort to be included. Courtney Jung and Ian Shapiro argue that oppositional groups serve a democratic function and should be institutionalized outside of party politics (1996). Of course, deliberation about "political contests" may lead to identifying a common good, or common underlying values as Cohen asserts.[21] But it may also lead to recognition of underlying fundamentally competing values. Take David Miller's example of competing values about appropriate energy sources: deliberation may reveal that people's point of disagreement is their willingness to trade damage to the environment for energy cost efficiency. Even after deliberative exchange of reasonable arguments, people may continue to disagree fundamentally about the appropriate tradeoff (1992). Diego Gambetta adds a concern that

---

[19] Tully points out that even if a theorist lays out for society the right way to deliberate, theorists and members of that society are bound to disagree in their interpretation of that theorist (1995: 103–106). Similarly, my account of the common assumptions of deliberative theorists differs with others' accounts of deliberative theorists' common ground (cf. Bohman & Rehg 1997, Elster 1998a).

[20] By "social groundlessness" Warren means "spaces within which the rules, norms, institutions, identities that regulate most social interactions become contestable" (1996b: 244).

[21] Jane Mansbridge concurs that deliberation may "reveal previously unrealized areas of agreement" (1996: 47) especially if conditions such as "lack of haste and face-to-face interaction," which are conducive to agreement, exist (1988: 73).

deliberation can have a paralyzing effect, leaving deliberants unable to rank their preferences (1998: 22). The practice of politics in the USA and around the world gives us countless examples of people unable to reach political agreement. Regardless of evidence to the contrary, certain deliberative theorists are confident in the possibility of political agreement on public policy despite persistent moral disagreement (Gutmann & Thompson 1996: 63–69).[22]

The second way in which the political theorists of deliberation over-state the capacity of deliberation to result in a unified agreement is by idealizing (through simplification) the deliberative process as if it were a rational debate within a single individual. For example, in *Human Nature and Conduct*, Dewey articulates deliberation as the thought process of an individual. According to Dewey, imagination tries out the various proposals suggested by habit and impulse: "deliberation is a dramatic rehearsal (in imagination) of various competing possible lines of action … Thought runs ahead and foresees outcomes, and thereby avoids having to await the instruction of actual failure or disaster" (1983 [1922]: 132–133). In *The Public and its Problems*, Dewey anthropomor-phizes the public, giving it the capacity to reason as an individual (1954 [1927]).[23] For Benhabib, this like-reasoning leads a political community to have common understandings and thus to political agreement. According to her, respect for rights and plurality would lead us to agree that Christian Scientists cannot deprive their children of healthcare, Orthodox Muslims must send their children to school, Sikh soldiers in the Canadian Royal Police can wear their turbans in uniform, and Muslim French school girls can wear head scarves (1996b: 89–90, n. 14). These may be the agreements she recommends but she provides no evidence that all who consider themselves reasonable, concerned about rights (though probably not the same rights with which Benhabib is concerned), and aware of plurality would agree with her conclusions. All do not reason as she does.

Similarly, when Gutmann & Thompson defend (for example) the court's decision in *Mozert v. Hawkins* as properly reasoned because it respects the principles and conditions of deliberative democracy (par-ticularly the principle of reciprocity) as they define them (1996: 68–69), they are asserting that participants should all reason as one even though their fundamental values differ. Moreover, a court decision is not a deliberated agreement among disagreeing parties. Without evidence that the parents, having heard the arguments and the court's reasoning,

---

[22] See footnotes 7 and 8 for a detailed qualification of this generalization.
[23] Debra Morris and Ian Shapiro make the same observation in their introduction to *John Dewey: the Political Writings* (1993: xiii).

agreed with the court's decision, the decision represents only *hypothetical* political agreement in the face of moral disagreement. The parents may "accept" the court's decision only because the law provides them no other option of appeal. Benhabib and Gutmann & Thompson provide examples of the reasoning Dewey describes. They attempt to associate deliberative practice with a unity of thought that is not evident even on the issues they choose as their examples. The suggestion seems to be, if everyone reasoned in the way they suggest, that societies would be able to reach reasonable consensus through deliberative procedures. Gutmann & Thompson do a particularly good job at demonstrating the conclusions to which their principles lead, but rather than a theory of deliberative democracy, they have given us an account of the limits of deliberative democratic theory. Where the norms of reasoning are not universally held, their model of deliberative democracy does not apply, though some may use it to guide their own reasoning processes.

The third way in which the deliberative political theorists understate conflict is by overstating the reasoning capacity of individuals. For Cohen, the legitimacy of decisions arrived at in the deliberative arena depends on people offering acceptable reasons for their arguments (1989a: 22; see also 1989b: 32–33; 1996: 99).[24] Cohen's requirements of legitimate deliberations are two steps removed from reality. Cohen presumes first that a person is willing and able to give arguments and second that the reasons that she is willing and able to offer meet his standards of acceptable reasons. However, I think Cohen overstates people's willingness and ability to provide acceptable reasons for their proposals in both senses. According to Cohen, reasons are considerations in favor of something and are

(1) *compelling* to others, (2) acknowledging those others as *equals*, [and] (3) aware that they have alternative *reasonable commitments* ... If a consideration does not meet these tests, that will suffice for rejecting it as a reason. If it does, then it counts as an acceptable political reason. (1996: 100, *numbers and emphasis added*)

Cohen defines acceptable reasons as those that would be given in an idealized circumstance. In the nonideal world what counts as a reason when dogmatic people whose interests are at stake cannot be compelled? What counts as a reason when people do not believe each other to be equals? Which of the commitments and beliefs that people in the nonideal world have – to material interests, cultural norms, or personal obligations – are reasonable?

---

[24] Gutmann & Thompson similarly assert that people with a "sense of reciprocity" would offer arguments that would lead to the resolution of political disputes even where there are fundamental moral disagreements (1996).

Cohen tries to answer these questions by giving us examples of unacceptable reasons. Considerations based on a belief such as faith or a revealed truth, considerations which depend on a particular context and view of the public order, considerations based on personal interest, and considerations based on false assumptions of agreement through abstraction in political justification are all unacceptable (1998: 195–198). However, in the real world people disagree, for example, as to which considerations are contextual and which are universal. Rather than recognizing that people may disagree on the classification of their reasons, he points out that the sorts of disagreements likely to be argued with the wrong kinds of reasons are precisely those around society's values and morality (1996).

Around issues of values and morality, some people may not be able or willing to separate the considerations they offer from their world view. Even if they are willing to offer acceptable reasons, the personal habits of thinking that have resulted from a lifetime of believing their world view may make it difficult for them to provide other, more acceptable, reasons – though they might exist. Cohen is explicit that the only worthy proposals are those that are accompanied by such reasons. Even if acceptable reasons exist, if they are not offered, the proposal is not worthy of consideration in the deliberative arena (1989a: 22). In this way, Cohen's account of acceptable reasons in deliberation advantages those able to reason in his idealized way.

In rural Bangladesh, as a result of distribution practices within households, many women – particularly women of childbearing years – are nutritionally deficient. Many women living with such nutritional deficiency are unaware of it. If she were made aware of the possibility of improved health, what "acceptable" reasons would a rural Bangladeshi woman give to her husband or mother-in-law for wanting to increase her nutritional intake at the expense of her husband? Generally, she does not articulate her own interests, but were she to, she might articulate her reasons in terms of her own interests or those of her children, of all women, or of human rights. Cohen might argue that any of these reasons would be acceptable because they are based on considerations of equality. What if the woman does not feel claims of equality are appropriate against her husband or mother-in-law? What if she does not think she has a right to better nutrition? What if she believes she has such rights but shies away from asserting such rights? What if she does not realize the impact of her own nutritional intake on her nursing and unborn children? Should consideration of her nutritional status be then excluded from deliberation? Does she have to rely on someone else making the argument in an acceptable way in order that her request count? According to Cohen, yes (1989a: 22; see also 1989b: 32–33; 1996: 22).

> Deliberation is *reasoned* in that the parties to it are required to state their reasons for advancing proposals, supporting them or criticizing them. They give reasons with the expectation that those reasons (and not, for example, their power) will settle the fate of their proposal. In ideal deliberation, as Habermas puts it, 'no force except that of the better argument is exercised' (1975, p. 108). Reasons are offered with the aim of bringing others to accept the proposal, given their disparate ends and their commitment to settling the conditions of their association through free deliberation among equals. Proposals may be rejected because they are not defended with acceptable reasons, even if they could be so defended. The deliberative conception emphasizes that collective choices should be *made in a deliberative way*, and not only that those choices should have a desirable fit with the preferences of citizens. (1989a: 22)

A variety of reasons defined as acceptable by Cohen might be given, but what proposals will be considered in the deliberative arena if such reasons are not given? Cohen's view of acceptable reasons is too demanding for the real world and undermines the project of social criticism. Cohen's view of deliberation like that of Dewey, Benhabib, and Gutmann & Thompson relies on either unanimous or singular reasoning defined by the terms of acceptable argument.[25]

The discussion of Cohen's idealized notion of deliberative reasoning leads me to the second theoretical objection to deliberative theory. As I discussed in chapter one, because deliberative theory is idealized, it is not actually deliberative. Cohen's deliberative model does not provide for discussion about what constitutes reasonable argument. Gutmann & Thompson's deliberative model does not allow for discussions about how a society might decide to balance basic liberty and basic opportunity. Cohen & Rogers (1992) propose institutions to make public decision conform to deliberative norms, but they do not demonstrate that these proposals are a result of deliberations.[26] Fishkin proposes the deliberative poll as a construction of ideal circumstances (1995). Except to the extent that political theorists deliberate with one another through their scholarship, these proposals are not deliberatively derived. One

---

[25] Their view of the reasoning process is consistent with Rawls's account of reasoning in the original position where each would reason like the representative man (1971: 64, 138, 568). Rawls does not adequately explain how his reasoning of a representative person is different from the utilitarians' imposing the reasoning of one on the whole (1971: 29). Rawls recognizes citizens' plurality and then uses the device of the original position to homogenize their reasoning about justice. The deliberative theorists create homogeneity of reasoning through the device of requiring agreement on the principles and procedures of deliberation.

[26] One might argue that by publishing their proposals these theorists are subjecting their proposals to public deliberation. Bohman does propose a more deliberative vision of deliberative practice (1996).

wonders how the deliberative theorists would respond to popular displeasure with the deliberative model. Can a democracy choose non-deliberative democratic institutions? Might citizens of a democracy disagree about the form deliberative democratic institutions should take based on differing views of who would benefit from their functioning?[27] Sanders goes as far as to call deliberative democratic theory "antidemocratic" because it is based on disdain for democratic decisions that do not conform to deliberative norms (1997). Nino offers an exception to the general practice in deliberative theory because he explicitly presents his view of constitutional democracy deliberatively and even invites discussion around those aspects with which he is uncomfortable (1995).

By contrast Benhabib does say that the norms of deliberative democracy are among those institutions affected by the deliberation. She makes an important distinction between a Rawlsian notion of public reason and a Habermasian notion of public reasoning. According to Rawls, Benhabib argues, public reason is "a regulative *principle* imposing limits upon how individuals, institutions, and agencies *ought to reason about public matters*" (1996b: 75). By contrast, the Habermasian view is that public reasoning is a process. Although Benhabib generally interprets Cohen's and her views of deliberative democracy to be consistent with Habermas, on the meaning of public reason, I read Cohen as treating public reason as Rawls does (see Cohen 1989a: 19). Demonstrating the influence of Habermas and critical theory on her view of deliberative democracy, Benhabib argues that equality requires equal participation, an equal right to question the agenda, and an equal right to question the rules of deliberation (1996b: 70). Further, single decisions are decisive only as new starting points for ongoing discussions. "Majoritarian decisions are temporarily agreed-upon conclusions, the claim to rationality and validity of which can be publicly reexamined" (1996b: 72). In this respect Benhabib's account of deliberative democracy moves in a direction consistent with Third World feminism.[28]

Deliberative democracy's two theoretical problems of homogenizing

---

[27] Although Cohen presents deliberative democratic theory as an alternative to the contract, bargaining, and win–lose models of democratic decision making, Przeworski argues, in his critique of deliberative theory, that if all have the same information and the same ability to interpret information then deliberation will not yield changes in beliefs (1998: 144–145). If deliberation does yield changes in beliefs, then it must mean that there are differences in information resources and the ability to manipulate them and that people are doing so. If people are doing so, they must be making decisions based on their calculation of their own advantage and not on a deliberatively derived sense of common ground.

[28] For a more complete assessment of Benhabib's account of deliberative democracy see chapter 6.

and idealizing, draw our attention to problems in realizing deliberative theory in practice. In addition, there are two other practical problems with deliberative democratic theory that were not captured in the discussion of the theoretical problems. Deliberative democratic theory assumes participants can resolve all or nearly all questions regarding "constitutional essentials and matters of basic justice" (Rawls 1997: 777). This means that, if participants talk long enough, they will be able to agree on the form of institutions that should guide and promote their deliberations. Tully, describing centuries of constitutional negotiations, offers significant evidence that such agreement should not be the basis of deliberation because agreement on the legitimate form of decision-making institutions is unlikely (1995).

Even if agreement on basic principles is possible in the long run, should societies and critics delay their use of deliberation in social criticism until then? As a response, consider John Maynard Keynes's observation that the "*long run* is a misleading guide for current affairs. *In the long run* we are all dead. Economists set themselves too easy, too useless a task if in tempestuous seasons they can only tell us that when the storm is long past the ocean is flat again" (1971 [1923]: 65). Political theorists set themselves too easy and too useless a task if the theory we describe only asks that societies and critics wait until they realize the deliberative theorists near-ideal circumstances. Even while portraying the US constitutional tradition as one of liberal republican values in evolution, Sunstein does not portray constitutional scholars as being aware of their supposed near-unanimity on the underlying political values of the constitution (1988). Given the unlikely event of such unanimity, Benhabib's prescription for ongoing examination is essential.

The second practical objection to deliberative democratic theory is that in practice it is exclusionary. Just as majority factions of citizens who lack mutual respect can drown out the voices of some citizens, so too the terms of acceptable argument in deliberative fora can exclude others from speaking up. Thus, deliberative democracy can substitute tyranny of the majority with tyranny of the method. In addition deliberative democracy can impose tyranny of the meeting on those who have better things to do than to participate in meetings. According to Sanders, ordinary citizens don't want to, or don't have the time to, deliberate (1997). Furthermore, "The curse of the meeting" according to Anne Phillips is that all cannot participate equally (1991: 161–165). Moreover, in practice deliberative democracy may *prevent* open discussion because norms of social behavior (to respect certain speakers, when to speak, how to speak, and what to say) and expectations of mutual respect (despite possible actual disrespect) may inhibit inclusively informed deliberations. For example, Michael Huspek and Kathleen Kendall argue that those who are excluded from the political sphere do not use the vocabulary of the dominant culture (or use it well) not only because they do not have the experience of practicing it, but also because they morally reject those who use political vocabulary (1991). They develop a language of opposition that is consonant with their everyday life experiences. The oppositional language "supplies workers with symbolic resources of resistance but at the same time deprives them of needed symbolic resources for voicing critical interests effectively" in political deliberative fora (1991: 15). Finally, deliberative theory excludes those (introduced in chapter one) who are silent due to power hierarchies. In order to assess the Third World feminist method of social criticism as a necessary complement to deliberative democratic theory, I will need to show that it addresses these theoretical and practical problems with deliberative democratic theory.

Other critics agree that deliberative democracy can be more inclusive if it promotes listening in deliberations (Bickford 1996), allows testimony not just argument from participants (Sanders 1997), incorporates the various ways people have of persuasion (Young 1996), and admits different kinds of evidence including narrative and storytelling in addition to argument (Tully 1995). Each of these proposals contributes to a more comprehensive account of how to make democratic use of deliberation where disrespect and obstacles to equality exist and persist despite existing fora for public dialogue. These proposals assume that deliberation does not meet standards of knowledge, but rather that through deliberation participants determine what they know. According to the critics of deliberative democratic theory, deliberation sets an exclusionary epistemological standard.

In order to determine if deliberation meets an epistemological standard, as its proponents assert, or sets one, as its critics assert, theorists need first to agree on what kinds of knowledge are at issue. Deliberation's educative value is not based on liberal, democratic, or any other political values, but rather on the value of knowledge.[29] Deliberation contributes to three kinds of knowledge. Each of the deliberative theorists recognizes some educative aspect of deliberation, but recognizes its educative value only as it is instrumental to an already

---

[29] Will Kymlicka does argue that the educative value of deliberation is a value liberals hold, but even he does not claim that liberals are alone or unique in their appreciation of deliberation as a means of improving the quality of a society's important decisions, including choices about its ends. "Deliberation, then, doesn't only take the form of asking which course of action maximizes a particular value that is held unquestioned. We also question, and worry about, whether that value is really worth pursuing" (1989: 11). Kymlicka refers to Ronald Dworkin's "In Defense of Equality" (1983: 26–27).

functioning near-ideal deliberative democracy, that is, instrumental to meeting the epistemological standard of deliberative theory.

A familiar definition of knowledge is the set of available facts. Deliberation improves the set of available facts by improving the distribution of information. Individuals have private information based on what they have seen, heard, smelled, tasted, and touched. It may be subjective information such as the experience of domestic violence, or it may be more objective information such as statistics about how often incidents of domestic violence occur under a given set of circumstances. One educative value of deliberation is that it allows for the exchange of many perspectives and sources of information and therefore increases knowledge (the set of available facts) in the community.[30]

A second definition of knowledge refers to information about identity and preferences – knowledge about what I and others feel, what I and others care about, and what I and others are interested in. Through participating in deliberation I discover my own preferences, understand my own values, and develop my identity and sense of autonomy.[31] In addition, I and other participants come to know each other's preferences and to understand underlying dimensions of disagreement. Deliberation increases the knowledge of the interests and preferences of those who participate.

A third definition of knowledge is a stretch from the common understanding of knowledge as informational to knowledge as developmental. Deliberation develops in individuals and communities certain skills that are important for ongoing accumulation of the first two kinds of knowledge. People learn to learn from each other, and actually learn more through participatory learning.[32] Through deliberation, individuals develop the ability to imagine being in another's shoes in part because they gain information about one another and because through the practice of deliberation they improve their accuracy at anticipating others' perspectives on certain events, ideas, or proposals. Similarly, the practice of deliberation enables groups to get better at deliberation in

---

[30] Dewey and Cohen demonstrate this understanding of knowledge when they defend the instrumental role of deliberation in promoting the values of a liberal democracy society. This kind of knowledge has an explicit and significant function in Dewey's philosophy of social criticism. Dewey recognizes an educative value of deliberation is instrumental to deliberation's political function in the near-ideal democracy (1980 [1916a], 1986 [1916b]). For Cohen the educative value of deliberation is mentioned incidentally but plays an important role because it is essential to "any view of intelligent political decision-making: if only because of its essential role in pooling private information against a background of asymmetries in [information's] distribution" (1996: 99–100).

[31] See Cohen (1989a, 1989b, 1998), Gutmann (1993b, 1995), and Warren (1996b).

[32] For evidence of advantages of participation for childhood development see *Apprenticeship in Thinking* by Barbara Rogoff (1990).

part by learning from each other and in part by learning to cooperate with one another. Deliberation develops individuals' participation and critical thinking skills and their ability to resolve disputes through the process of deliberation.[33]

In sum, deliberation increases individual and community knowledge, self-knowledge, and ability to learn. Thus, deliberation's educative value is not only in meeting but also in setting epistemological standards, but these standards are not exclusionary. Even such a formulation belies the true ongoing nature of learning. The boundaries of what people can know individually and collectively are always expanding, and do so with increased vigor through deliberation.[34] Thus, deliberation sets an ever-changing epistemological standard.

Deliberations cannot be informed, lead to legitimate decisions, or approach consensus (or even a fair compromise) about the common good unless they are truly informed. Being informed is a function of being adequately and accurately inclusive. What one says and how one says it must be less important to a theory of deliberative democracy than that one be heard, understood, and valued. By providing rules to prevent the "unreasonable" speech of those who offend the dominant articulation of a political community's understanding of respect, deliberative theorists also disallow other "unreasonable" speech that never gets the opportunity to be heard or if heard is not respected due to cultural norms of status and persuasion.[35] Constrained by what is "reasonable," some perspectives are not included in deliberations and thus the potential for learning is diminished. However, as Mill argues in *On Liberty*, in order for people to learn and improve their arguments, they must listen to even mistaken arguments (1974 [1859]).

Moreover, by limiting the relevance of deliberation to circumstances of collective desire for political agreement despite moral disagreement, deliberative democratic theory is silent on questions of resource allocation between competing purposes where generally bargaining,

---

[33] Pateman emphasizes the function of deliberation in developing participation skills (1970). She argues that by participating in deliberation, people learn to participate better. Whether by this she means only that people learn to deliberate or also that they learn to learn from each other, Pateman offers an argument in favor of deliberation based on its value for learning and knowledge which is integral to her political argument in favor of participatory democracy. Gutmann emphasizes the function of deliberation in developing critical thinking skills (1995).

[34] The remaining empirical problem is to prove the epistemological value of deliberation. This proof is outside the scope of this chapter. Some psychological studies have demonstrated the expanding boundaries of individual and collective knowledge as a function of deliberation with others. See Rogoff (1990).

[35] Sanders gives an account of research on juries and classrooms that demonstrates that quantity of speech and social status not quality of contribution or actual education and experience determines how persuasive one's ideas are (1997).

contracting, or the exercise of power is used to make political decisions. However, the educative function of deliberation can be valuable for social change under just such circumstances. In their strategizing, deliberants challenge existing norms of political discussion and create others. Educative deliberation in social criticism is not confined by procedural norms or agreement about what constitutes a reasonable argument.

If self-respect, mutual respect, equality of influence, and agreement on what is admissible in deliberative fora are to be realized, people, not principles and not institutions, will bring them about. Deliberation can be useful to those people trying to bring about the necessary conditions of deliberative democracy.[36] Those who have sought respect for those neglected, or who have made themselves heard despite severe inequality, can show us how. I propose that deliberation is part social criticism and that as such is an ongoing process that strengthens democratic institutions where they exist and can be used to bring them about where they do not. As part of a method of social criticism, deliberation both meets and sets an epistemological standard. In order to do so deliberation must be more inclusive in order to be better informed. Borrowing from the political theory of feminist academics and the unarticulated theory of Third World women activists, I sketch an outline of social criticism that promotes inclusively informed deliberation and pushes on the boundaries of knowledge. This Third World feminist account of social criticism thus offers a necessary complement to deliberative democratic theory because it promotes democracy where democracy is imperfect. (And it does so while meeting the challenges that deliberative theorists and their critics pose.) As part of a nominally feminist and functionally broad method of social criticism, educative deliberation is a means to improving both the quality and equality of participation.

---

[36] As Sunstein recognizes, deliberation is a critical idea (1988: 1549), but as most deliberative theorists use it, it is useful only once its preconditions are met. Estlund (1993) and Tully (1995) do not tell us exactly how societies can achieve the deliberative norms they describe. They, too, desire to leave up to the deliberations themselves determinations of the norms of deliberation. Tully describes truly deliberative political institutions:

a contemporary constitution can recognise cultural diversity if it is conceived as a form of accommodation of cultural diversity. It should be seen as an activity, an intercultural dialogue in which the culturally diverse sovereign citizens of contemporary societies negotiate agreements on their ways of association over time in accord with the conventions of mutual recognition, consent and continuity. (1995: 184)

Third World feminist theory and social criticism

Without explicitly working within the framework of deliberative democracy, Third World feminists make use of deliberation to challenge existing understandings, dominant ideologies, and power structures thereby trying to make social and political understandings more informed and power structures more inclusive. The use of deliberation in Third World feminist theory makes Third World feminist theory a good starting point for a theory of social criticism with which to complement deliberative democratic theory and make deliberations more informed and inclusive despite a context of inequality.

There is a broad range of uses of the term "Third World." It can be a geographical reference to countries in the southern hemisphere, a sociohistorical reference to postcolonial countries including those with immigrant populations and populations who are descendants from slaves, an economic reference to capital-importing nations, and a cultural reference to nations that do not have Western European traditions.[37] I use "Third World" as a descriptor of a specific kind of feminism that advocates revolutionary social, political, and economic reorganization such that each woman has supreme authority over herself and that that authority is not undermined by social values, practices, and norms that dictate hierarchy based on sex, sexuality, ethnicity, class, caste, religion, country of origin, national identity, aboriginal status, immigration status, regional geography, language, cultural practices, forms of dress, beliefs, ability, health status, family history, age, or education. Third World feminists advocate scrutinizing and challenging existing values, practices, and norms based neither on the roles that societies have identified for women, nor on the roles that societies have identified for men, but rather based on an ongoing opposition to harmful inequalities in women's lives be they a function of sex or other categorization. In short, Third World feminism advances democracy for all.

Third World feminist theories are even more various than deliberative democratic theories. It is common for feminists to refer to "feminisms." For example, recognizing that her definition of feminism is one among many, Anastasia Posadskaya, a founding member of the Independent Women's Forum in Russia, says:

---

[37] Although she views Third World feminism more narrowly than I, Uma Narayan defines herself as a Third World feminist and adds to the theoretical content I describe by noting that Third World feminist scholars in the USA have the added burden of being perceived as having been westernized either by their education or by their careers in academia (1997: chapter 1).

I prefer to speak about *feminisms* ... For me, feminism implies a specific rejection of the perception that society has a gender neutral character. Feminism also brings an agenda for change on a global and not just a national level. That is not to deny the diversity of national experience. For example, the emphasis in Russia on independence from the state and from all official political structures is a result of our national experience. (Waters & Posadskaya 1995: 363)

Despite diversity, and in fact drawing on it, Third World feminists have outlined a coherent feminism based on sisterhood and solidarity, a political strategy, social reorganization, and the reorganization of feminism as a social movement.[38] Third World feminists base solidarity not on a false universalization of some women's experiences as relevant for all, but rather on a rejection of essentializing about women (Spelman 1988: 165, 174–175), learning about each other (hooks 1984: 56), examining women's experiences as taking place at various intersections of oppressions rather than considering certain oppression as being in addition to other oppressions (Crenshaw 1989; Collins 1991: 164), expecting self-evaluation including willingness to be self-critical (Collins 1991), and being explicit about group assumptions (Spelman 1988: 169). Solidarity means forming alliances with communities, with other activists, with other oppressed groups, among feminist intellectuals, and between feminist intellectuals and activists and artists.[39] Solidarity means thinking of women's interests as *collective* (as in a collection of) interests rather than as interests in common. Though commonalities may exist, focus on them can yield neglect of the actual experiences of some of those assumed to be joining in. For example, the women's human rights movement used violence against women as a common theme to unite women who were objecting to experiences as diverse as domestic violence and global socioeconomic exploitation of women in the structure of global capitalism. As such it is an example of Third World feminists' organizing around a commonality. However, the appro-

---

[38] In the following discussions I reference specific texts of feminists, primarily African American women writing in the USA because they, in their critiques of liberal, Marxist, and radical feminisms in the USA, have sketched an outline of Third World feminism. Other feminists of color from the USA critiquing the white middle-class focus of much second wave feminism (e.g., Alarcón 1990; Moraga 1993) and from around the world criticizing the societies of either their native or adopted countries (e.g., Basu 1995a; Narayan 1997), and white US feminists (e.g., Smiley 1993) have written with sensitivity in an effort to advance Third World feminism. Their work also informs my account of existing Third World feminist theory.

   In her discussion of listening in democracy Susan Bickford (1996) also draws on work by women of color, specifically Alarcón's postmodern critique of some white US women's use of *This Bridge Called My Back* (1990).

[39] For example, Collins notes the importance of black feminists' alliances with African-American men and of their seeking strength in the African-American community (Collins 1991: 33–36).

priate means of addressing the specific variations are widely divergent and the emphasis of human rights lobbyists of the United Nations has been on redressing noneconomic violations of human rights specifically those caused by national governments' actions or neglect rather than on violations by global corporations and by the regulation of the international movement of capital and labor.[40] Opposition to violence against women describes a collection of interests not an assimilation of interests. Likewise seeking a basis for solidarity, Gita Sen and Caren Grown want to provoke discussion "about the commonalities and differences in the oppression of women of different nations, classes, or ethnic groups" (1987: 24).[41] Stating the grounds for solidarity somewhat differently, Posadskaya describes the common ground of the founding members of the Independent Women's Forum, "We did not agree on everything, but we shared a hostility to the idea that women occupied a special social place, especially since it was other people who were deciding what that place ought to be" (Waters & Posadskaya 1995: 364). Deliberation enables Third World feminists to conceive of women's interests in solidarity, not as similar, and therefore, not to obscure the interests of any women.[42]

The political strategy of Third World feminism is to oppose domination in its many forms. Third World feminists critique capitalism and materialism, including the means of economic growth, commercialization, and market expansion. They challenge fundamentalism, national chauvinism, racism and sexism. They scrutinize dominant ideologies, authority, privilege, and the production of knowledge. Their political strategy intends to promote peace and equality while resisting oppression in all its unjustifiable forms. To do this Third World feminists use existing spheres of influence and, drawing on sisterhood and solidarity, create additional safe places (Fraser 1992; Mansbridge 1996). By creating alternative contexts for women to deliberate with and learn from one another, women make their activism better informed and more inclusive; women draw on their own resilience to find and speak

---

[40] In chapter 4, I discuss the women's human rights movement and give a more nuanced account of the interests collected by the movement and how well they were represented. Because the structures that cause the various kinds of violence against women vary so, women do not experience common structures of oppression or have common interests in their struggles against those structures. But they have the sisterhood of struggle. Compare to Young's account of women as a social collective (1994).

[41] See also Collins (1991: 206–207).

[42] In *Lesbian Ethics: Toward New Value*, Sarah Lucia Hoagland suggests we replace autonomy with "autokoenony" by which she means that individuals develop an understanding of self-in-community: "who we are emerges through our interactions with others." Despite people's interdependencies, she wants "to invoke a sense of ourselves as not essentially defined in terms of one another" (1988: 145).

with their own voices; in dialogue with one another women express and learn from emotion and exercise the human capacity for empathy.[43] Deliberation in enclaves is important to enhancing women's participation in mainstream deliberations. Thus, informed and inclusive deliberation is essential to Third World feminist theory and activism.

Third World feminism's goals are ambitious: the reorganization of society, international and national economics, religion, cultural practices, educational systems, international and national development strategies, investment in and use of the military, sexuality, gender hierarchy, and the ways "in which race and class inequalities have been sexualized" (Collins 1991: 165).[44] Certainly, nonfeminists have taken up many of these issues and many feminists who do not embrace the ideology and political strategies of Third World feminists have taken on aspects of these issues. The overlaps between Third World feminism and other theories and activisms are evidence that Third World feminism is broadly relevant. Third World feminism has potential practical and theoretical appeal beyond those issues that can be marginalized for being "women's" or "Third World" issues.

In their approach to addressing their concerns, Third World feminists also have advocated changes to feminism as a social movement. Their reorganization of feminism as a social movement includes mass education (hooks 1984; Collins 1991: 151), networking among women,[45] and using experience-based arguments and understandings to articulate proposals (hooks 1984: 57).[46] Most importantly, Third World feminism is activism. It takes nearly as many forms as it has advocates, but Third World feminism in each form is politically relevant activism with the purpose of changing women's lives through changing the organization of society. Though these changes may be brought about incrementally, the vision is revolutionary. Thus my account of Third World feminist theory requires accounts of the actual activism of Third World feminists.

---

[43] See for example Mohanty (1991a), Sen & Grown (1987), hooks (1984), Zein Ed-Dīn (1982 [1928]), Hassan (1991), Shaheed (1995), Spelman (1988) and Collins (1991).

[44] To list feminists who make these various points would cause more exclusion than inclusion. Most aspects of language, ideology, knowledge, values, practices, norms, or social, economic, and political power have been examined by feminists.

[45] For example, for African-American women this means recognizing bloodmothers and othermothers in the community as resources for women and their community (Collins 1990: 119–123). Among Muslim women, this has meant forming alliances across nations with other women in Muslim countries and countries with some Muslim laws (Shaheed 1994).

[46] hooks's argument is echoed in Tully's (1995), Sanders's (1997), and Young's (1996) proposals for deliberative theory.

Third World feminist activism and social criticism: the SEWA example

I began chapter one with an illustrative anecdote from an afternoon during my research in Bangladesh. In order to illustrate Third World feminist activism's realizing the solidarity, political strategy, and goals of Third World feminist theorists, let me supplement that illustrative anecdote from chapter one with a more complete account of Third World feminist activism using a different example about which there has been some social science research and documentation. The activism of SEWA (the Self-Employed Women's Association), a women's organization in Gujarat, India, develops the illustrations from the Kustia and Tangail women's groups in Bangladesh.[47] The SEWA case both demonstrates Third World feminist activists' actualization of Third World feminist theory and was a source in my identifying the model of Third World feminist social criticism. The activism of SEWA highlights the advantages of deliberation for informed and inclusive social criticism and the role deliberation can play in improving the quality and equality within deliberative processes. In SEWA women use deliberation to make social values, practices, and norms more informed, collective, and uncoerced.

SEWA was born of the Women's Wing of the Textile Labor Association, a textile labor union founded by Mahatma Gandhi in 1917. In Gujarat province of India, as in many parts of the Third World, most women are self-employed. Self-employed workers include those who are home-based producers and who therefore have no contact with other workers because the contractors bring the raw materials to their homes and pick up their final products, independent workers such as crafts people and vendors who sell in markets or house to house and who require capital to purchase their raw materials, piece-rate workers who work for contractors or traders who have monopsony buying power over their production, and service workers who work outside of their own homes in private houses and places of business as cooks and cleaners or who work for hire in construction, agriculture, or transportation (for example carrying produce from the market). Individually, self-employed women generally have no influence on the terms of their employment, including the cost of their inputs, the amount of labor they provide, and the price of their products or their labor. Because women are contracted individually, any single worker is expendable. Consequently, women are easily coerced by employers and middlemen to accept low wages and

---

[47] SEWA, pronounced "seva," means service to the community without the connotation of charity (D'Costa 1997).

wage cuts. Moreover, because they are responsible for family care giving, their income stream is in part a function of the health of their family members and their ability to devote time to income-generating work.

Because she realized that most women are employed informally, the leader of the Textile Labor Association's Women's Wing, Ela Bhatt, was inspired to set up a separate organization to work with self-employed women workers. With the support of the textile union, SEWA challenged the government interpretation of "trade union" which had required union members to be employed in the formal economy. In 1972 SEWA was registered as a trade union of self-employed workers. SEWA began during a period of awareness, and contributed to increased awareness, of self-employed women. In 1974 the Indian government published the Report of the Committee on the Status of Women in India and in 1976 began the United Nations Decade for Women. SEWA is among others in India including Working Women's Forum which have been the subject of international attention as a function of their work with self-employed women.

SEWA uses occupation-based organizing to enable women to mobilize collectively so that they are no longer expendable to their employers and so that they become socially and politically visible, especially as workers. SEWA organizers use deliberation amongst women as a means of organizing them so that, organized, they are able to bargain with their employers effectively. More generally, they are able to participate more effectively in influencing the values, practices, and norms by which they live. By participating in SEWA trade groups, otherwise marginalized women are able to have a public voice. For example women in Gujarat who subcontract to roll cigarettes acted collectively and successfully struck their employers in order to receive minimum wages. SEWA had similar success achieving a minimum wage for stitchers. Hawkers and street vendors struck to deter city planners from replacing their market of 6,000 vendors with a supermarket.

In order to form the cooperatives and trade groups, SEWA organizers conducted a large survey of the living and working conditions of women. Their activism begins with inquiry. When conducting the surveys, Nirubehn Jadav, Secretary of SEWA, says,

we kept our eyes open for one or two outspoken women with some fire ... We would get the women to go amongst their sister workers and find out what their problems were. They conveyed the problems and priorities of their trade group so that we could call these women together for a meeting. (Rose 1992: 45–46)

The fiery women and SEWA organizers fostered deliberation among the self-employed women on topics of importance to the self-employed women, and SEWA cooperatives and trade unions provided an institutional means for them to make their social criticisms heard and to change their lives. The cooperatives and unions were further strengthened by child care, legal aid, cooperative banking, milk production, artisan and home-based production, vending and trading, marketing, agriculture and forestry, land development and water harvesting, regional development, health, child care, housing, and trade-specific literacy programs.

SEWA members have improved their economic condition by increasing or stabilizing employment, gaining access to regular supply of raw materials, owning their own tools, finding adequate work space, expanding markets, and diversifying into other work activities. (Jhabavala & Bali n.d.: 7–8)

SEWA maintains its strength through the same mechanism that draws women to SEWA.

SEWA's mass membership has been built up incrementally from long-lasting social networks and cemented by collectively secured (not just received) benefits in each of the areas of SEWA's three-pronged strategy of union struggle, work cooperative and group support services. (Jhabvala & Bali n.d.: 7)

With each success SEWA strengthens the social networks that it relies on.

Not only has SEWA strengthened social networks, but also it has contributed to new social understandings through its work and lobbying. The union lobbied the government to finance the maternity benefit program that SEWA had established and to provide life insurance through the SEWA Co-operative Bank to self-employed workers. Through SEWA's work, the society and government have a greater understanding of self-employed women workers and self-employed workers generally. Changes in the society's values, practices, and norms are a function in part of this changed appreciation of self-employed workers.

SEWA is experimenting with ways to expand its reach to include men without losing the benefits to women that SEWA has achieved by being a women's organization. For example, men may join SEWA occupational or trade groups as associate members with "no voting rights and no claim to the property of SEWA" (Selliah 1989: 14, citing the SEWA constitutional revision). As of 1989, its experience had been that men's presence in meetings inhibited informed deliberation because the women were silent, but SEWA continued to experiment with ways to incorporate men into SEWA as they viewed the ability to incorporate men without compromising the benefits to women as the ultimate demonstration of achieved equality.

The SEWA story emphasizes the role that knowledge acquired

through deliberation can play in social criticism. First, the SEWA organizers and some fiery self-employed women promoted inquiry among unorganized women workers about their needs. Second, in preliminary meetings SEWA organizers promoted deliberation among women in order that they recognize their common interests.[48] Third, the combination of all of SEWA's activities contributed to institutional change in the lives of self-employed women workers. Mobilized, the SEWA members promoted dialogue with business owners and within the government about the needs of self-employed women workers, employers, and the government demonstrated their learning by changing practices and laws (including minimum wage for some home-based producers and licenses for vendors).

The example of SEWA, like that of the Bangladeshi women's groups, demonstrates that educative deliberation – deliberation that leads to improved collective factual knowledge, self-understanding, and skills of deliberation – is useful to social criticism under conditions of inequality. Deliberation among relative equals generates shared knowledge of needs, circumstances, and ways to deal with those circumstances. That knowledge can be used to try to counter existing power inequalities, enabling the oppressed and coerced to participate in deliberative fora from which they were previously excluded and to participate more effectively where they have been nominally participating. When the critics are successful, those participating in broader deliberative fora learn more about previously excluded perspectives in a way that asks them to take those views into account. (Under various political circumstances, the critics may or may not be successful politically at promoting social change, but the educative value of deliberation is no less.) Society learns the views of self-employed women; employers learn the views of their piecemeal workers; and husbands learn the views of their wives. Both kinds of educative deliberation – deliberation among the oppressed and deliberation despite inequality in the broader social deliberative arena – inform Third World feminist social criticism. Third World feminist practice suggests a method, roles, and qualifications of social critics more generally.

The SEWA experience gives us insight into Third World feminist social critics' method. Given the diversity of Third World feminist social criticism, I might refer to their methods in the plural. By referring to their similar components despite diversity in application, I by no means intend to portray Third World feminist critical methods as uniform. To

---

[48] Such secure deliberative fora are not in themselves always conflict or problem free. One of the problems facing SEWA is the challenge of the village and poor urban women having control over the organization though they frequently lack the education and experiences to think strategically on behalf of the organization (Bumiller 1990: 143).

the contrary the strength and value of Third World feminist social criticism comes from its diversity and its eagerness to learn from its diversity. Drawing on their diversity, Third World feminist social critics collectively scrutinize all existing and potentially exploitable social, economic, and political inequalities. They guide their criticism of values, practices, and norms with standards that include abstract standards such as respect and more concrete standards such as basic needs. They use deliberation to make their criticism better informed and inclusive. With this method they scrutinize familiar and comfortable values, practices, and norms and reassess their society's and their own criteria of social criticism. SEWA's founder skeptically scrutinized the practice of unionization; its members scrutinized their own work experiences. Through deliberation among self-employed workers, they determined on what basis they should criticize existing employment practices. The criteria they used emphasized income security and thus most proposed changes secured the workers' income stream.

Even where inequality exists and persists, social critics can help bring about inclusive social decision making in a deliberative way. Thus, Third World feminist social criticism requires multiple roles of social critics. Critics' roles include inquiry, hosting opportunities for deliberation both among equals and despite inequality, and fostering institutional change. SEWA organizers inquired about self-employed women's lives and problems; the women themselves inquired about their own problems and priorities. As an organization, SEWA provided opportunities for self-employed women to deliberate amongst themselves. SEWA cigarette rollers struck their employers in order to provoke deliberation with their employers despite obvious inequality. SEWA organizers promoted institutional change by representing self-employed women as workers.

As in the Bangladeshi example SEWA demonstrates that there are many ways to qualify as a social critic. Some qualifications are better suited to certain roles than others. An individual, Ela Bhatt, was a social critic who realized that self-employed women were workers unlike those in the formal economy in certain respects, but equally if not more vulnerable to exploitation as a result of being self-employed. As an educated woman, Ela Bhatt was somewhat of an outsider whose experience and perspective enabled her to perceive and act against a form of inequality. The fiery women within the trade groups are also social critics. From within the society of self-employed women they provoked the women workers to identify their interests and obstacles. Finally, providing a place for women to learn from one another and to organize themselves, SEWA as an organization is a social critic offering an institutional change in women's lives. The ability of the SEWA organizers and lobbyists, in particular Ela Bhatt, to move between the worlds of self-employed women and government bureaucracy was a definitive qualification for successful social criticism. SEWA organizers were able to use their intimate knowledge of self-employed women's lives to inform their arguments to government officials and donor agencies.

Beyond its critics' method, roles, and qualifications, Third World feminist social criticism's defining feature is its ongoing and self-critical practice. For example, the SEWA organization and its members are continually identifying new needs and opportunities and they continually examine their own practice as critics to improve upon them. The expanding programmatic content of SEWA from trade-groups, to co-operatives, to a bank, to insurance mechanisms, is evidence of their ongoing social criticism. Their attempt to allow men members and reconsideration of how best to benefit men without harming women are evidence of their self-criticism. By the standards of critical theory – the guidance of human action, coherence, and reflectiveness – and my own modifications to that model – the method, roles, and qualifications of social critics – the SEWA practice of social criticism articulates through its actions a theory of social criticism.

Third World feminist social criticism is practiced in various forms by other women activists around the world, but there is no reason that it should be practiced only by women. Third World feminist social criticism is feminist not because it is practiced by women nor because it is relevant only to and for women. Rather, Third World feminist social criticism is feminist because it contributes to a tradition and development of feminist activism and theory (though either would be sufficient to make it feminist). Like much of the tradition of feminism, its function is more broad than criticism about women's social standing. Third World feminist social criticism is social criticism.

Moreover, though practically grounded and thus realizable, it is also theoretically useful. In fact, it offers a solution to the practical and theoretical problems deliberative democratic theorists had in describing principles and procedures for deliberation that were informed and inclusive, with broad participation without the tyranny of the majority, the tyranny of the method, or the tyranny of the meeting.

Third World feminist social criticism and deliberative theory

To recall, deliberative democratic theory's problems are that it (1) requires that the participants have self-respect, mutual respect, equal ability to influence outcomes, and agreement on the acceptable content of deliberations and yet (2) has no account of how to bring about this common ground, let alone to bring it about deliberatively. In practice deliberative theorists further (1) face the challenge of reconciling their theory with the real world inability of people to reach consensus on basic let alone more particular questions of justice. Finally, in the real world, people don't want to and don't have time to participate in deliberations to the extent deliberative theorists would require.[49] Thus, the theory that relies on participation (2) needs to explain either why people will participate willingly or why their lack of participation doesn't matter for the theory.

Third World feminist social criticism does not use the procedures of deliberation to restrict the content of deliberation. Third World feminist social criticism requires critics to scrutinize existing standards of respect to expand notions of acceptable arguments such that they include those made by nonmale, noneducated, and nonwhite critics, using testimonials, stories, analogies, rhetoric, and emotion to express nonwestern and other ideas to audiences unfamiliar with nondominant ideology. Thus while promoting mutual respect, Third World feminist social criticism expands the range of familiar perspectives and understandings making deliberation more inclusive while making it better informed. Further, such inclusive deliberative inquiry promotes the self-respect of the participants if other participants listen to and respect the content of their contributions. Although in practice deliberants can ignore the contributions of some participants, the theory of social criticism tells us how to bring about their inclusion. Moreover, having multiple critics fulfilling the multiple roles using the feminist method of social criticism aggressively challenges the norms, values, and practices that allow some to be excluded. Finally, through the feminist method, critics encourage the silent to speak for themselves and represent the silent when they don't. Thus, the feminist model of deliberation works both in theory and practice to exclude those who are ignored or discriminated against. Feminist social criticism does not require equal ability of participants to influence deliberations but rather promotes the functional equality of participants.

Third World feminist social criticism faces the first practical challenge of deliberative democratic theory in that there is no better likelihood that deliberation will lead to consensus on any issue. In fact, because of their more inclusive content deliberations may be less likely to yield

---

[49] This is true for the theories both of Barber, Cohen, and Gutmann & Thompson that require citizen participation and of Rawls and Bessette that require only citizen review of representatives' decisions.

consensus on basic constitutional arrangements or particular questions. However, with respect to the second, because it functions to make existing values, practices, and norms *more* inclusive, life under Third World feminist social criticism is *in the mean time* more inclusive. Rather than waiting for consensus on political norms, Third World feminist social critics can proceed to offer social criticism and modest improvements in, or mitigating conditions for, existing harmful inequalities.

Perhaps most importantly to those social critics who worry about the exclusion of people who are so marginalized that outside critics have yet to become aware of their marginalization, Third World feminist social criticism expects its social critics to search continually for ways to create opportunities for the participation of the previously excluded. The critics' roles of promoting inquiry, deliberative opportunities, and institutional change include creating safe and convenient places for the marginalized to deliberate about their interests. Further, Third World feminist social critics make use of representatives to allow those who cannot get to deliberative fora or present their views according to existing norms of deliberation once there. Representation causes other problems, importantly among these, possible misrepresentation and the continued marginalization of the represented and in chapter 4 I offer a more complete discussion of representation as a challenging role for social critics who wish to promote inclusion of the views of the marginalized without continuing their marginalization by speaking for them. However, in the imperfect real world where mutual respect and the equal ability to influence deliberations are lacking, where the acceptable norms of deliberative participation are exclusive, and where possible participants have other obligations more immediate to meeting the needs of their families and themselves, representation promotes more fully informed and therefore functionally inclusive deliberations.

Third World feminist social criticism undermines the tyranny of the nondeliberative majority that worries deliberative democratic theorists. It promotes broad social participation in public deliberations but assesses deliberative outcomes not on substantive or procedural standards, but rather on how well they hold up to ongoing social criticism. Third World feminist social criticism challenges the deliberative democratic theorists' tyranny of the method by promoting where necessary safe enclaves of deliberation among equals to allow those marginalized in larger spheres the experience of deliberation and to make their contributions to deliberative fora more informed.[50] Third World fem-

---

[50] Drawing on Mary P. Ryan's documentation of women's public spheres of activism, Fraser argues that the liberal public sphere (of private citizens discussing issues of public concern) that Habermas idealizes is only one public sphere. However, in reifying

inist social criticism further challenges tyranny of the method by inviting all forms of expression including stories, testimonials, analogies, emotionally-charged rhetoric, flattery, and argument. And, where the existing method is exclusive, until the conventions of deliberative method themselves are subject to deliberative social criticism, Third World feminist social criticism undermines tyranny of the method by relying on feminist social critics to represent those who cannot argue in conventionally accepted ways. However, Third World feminist social criticism cannot decisively address the problem that Sanders identifies of the authority given by some to others based on their characteristics and not on the content of their proposals or information.

Further, Third World feminist social criticism cannot decisively create the time or the will to participate. However, it can undermine tyranny of the meeting by critically evaluating deliberative methods as mentioned above and thereby making deliberative fora more inviting to those with the time to participate. Further, self-conscious critics who are adequate and accurate representatives can free those without time from the tyranny of the meeting.

Finally, in thinking about how well Third World feminist social criticism deals with the practical problem of exclusion, we must consider whether Third World feminist social critics can give onstage voice and audience to those whose oppression is so profound that they are afraid to reveal their critiques of domination. In *Domination and the Arts of Resistance*, James Scott writes, "short of actual rebellion, powerless groups have ... a self-interest in conspiring to reinforce appearances" rather than in challenging their oppressors (1990: xii). Under such conditions, if social criticism isn't going to bring about substantive social change, then social criticism itself is risky. Security to deliberate may be the common assumption of deliberative democratic theorists and Third World feminist social critics. Where security is lacking, feminist social critics create safe enclaves for women to talk among themselves and with other critics. In such enclaves the powerless may cultivate their opposition through the "off-stage parody, dreams of violent revenge, millennial visions of a world turned upside down," or onstage anonymous attacks (1990: xii, 17) Scott describes, or through less violent fantasies of having the ability to speak, having the opportu-

that sphere as the public sphere, Habermas like the bourgeois liberals who institutionalized it after the French Revolution, also reify the boundary between public and private, labeling women's concerns "private" concerns, despite the public nature of their activism (Fraser 1992). Women's deliberative enclaves challenge traditional notions of appropriate boundaries between public and private spheres of life. For more on enclaves see chapter 4. For further discussion of feminist views of the public sphere see chapter 6.

nity to be heard, and being taken seriously. Although some Third World feminist critics may try to enable the voiceless to be secure in speaking publicly, Third World feminist social criticism is not a model for making social criticism more effective at bringing about social change, but rather a model for making it better informed and more inclusive, and thus a challenge to inequality.

Conclusion

The roots of the problems of deliberative democratic theory are as deep in the history of political thought as the idea that deliberation – thoughtful reflection and discussion of available knowledge – could provide political insight. In the *Eudemian Ethics* Aristotle takes up the role of deliberation in collective understanding.

> About all these matters we must try to get conviction by arguments, using the phenomena as evidence and illustration. It would be best that all men should clearly concur with what we are going to say, but if that is unattainable, then that all should in some way at least concur. And this if converted they will do, for every man has some contribution to make to the truth, and with this as a starting-point we must give some sort of proof about these matters. For by advancing from true but obscure judgements we will arrive at clear ones ... [T]here are some who, though thinking it to be the mark of a philosopher to make no arbitrary statement but always to give a reason, often unawares give reasons foreign to the subject and idle – this they do sometimes from ignorance, sometimes because they are charlatans – by which reasons even men experienced and able to act are trapped by those who neither have nor are capable of having practical and constructive intelligence. And this happens to them from want of culture; for inability in regard to each matter to distinguish reasonings appropriate to the subject from those foreign to it is want of culture ... [W]hen men are unable to see a flaw in the argument they are compelled to believe what has been said. (1216b 26–1217a14)

Like Rawls, Aristotle seeks concurrence based on existing common ground. Like Dewey, he recognizes that each makes a contribution to truth, though like Mill he does not think that every view is equally valuable. Like Dewey, Aristotle argues that our research into a question of truth should begin with collecting our knowledge. Like Cohen, Gutmann & Thompson, and Rawls, Aristotle has confidence in our ability to use reason to sort through that collected knowledge. But likewise, like Tully, Young, and Sanders, Aristotle recognizes that others can be falsely led by authoritative (if mistaken) reasoning. However, the good critic according to Aristotle does not "want of culture" but rather can take the context of the individual contributions to truth into account and consequently set aside those that are inconsistent. As I show in the next chapter, Michael Walzer also thinks that cultural knowledge of context is essential to social criticism.

Third World feminist social criticism does not rely on common political norms, self- and mutual respect, participants' equal ability to influence outcomes, and agreement on what constitutes acceptable deliberative content. It does, however, rely on some people to take up each of the roles of social critics. These roles include helping society recognize the truth in each contribution – particularly those previously unknown. As Mill argued, even those views that are wrong are valuable to finding truth because they can make individuals consider opposing views seriously and as a result strengthen their own arguments (1859). Third World feminist social critics are more like Dewey than Mill in their recognition of the valuable content of a variety of views. Like Aristotle and Dewey, Third World feminist social critics begin their social criticism with a presumption that collecting knowledge will be valuable. Like deliberative theory's critics, Third World feminist social critics are skeptical of reasons as the grounds for assessing the content of deliberation. In fact, the objects of their social criticism include the rules of deliberation. And as I show in the next chapter, more successfully than Michael Walzer or Martha Nussbaum, Third World feminists both critically assess contexts and respect variety across contexts.

Third World feminist social criticism is not only the practical application of deliberative democratic theory in the real world of inequality, disrespect, and disagreement about what constitutes a reasonable argument, but also the theoretical complement to deliberative theory's assumptions of equality, respect, and agreement and its debate over the epistemological value of deliberation. The Third World feminist theory of social criticism is derived deliberatively both in that its content results from broadly divergent contributors through their theory and practice of social criticism and in that, once outlined, it remains open to further discussion and revision. My confidence in the Third World feminist model of social criticism I present comes from the range of activists that I have witnessed using it and from common ground among various accounts of people resisting oppression.[51] However, I expect that further research and deliberation will yield an increasingly rich understanding of Third World feminist social criticism making it even more important that we recognize the plurality in Third World feminist social criticisms and critical methods. Thus, I present this model of social

---

[51] For examples see Mary Belenky, Lynne Bond, and Jacqueline Weinstock (1997), James Scott (1985, 1990), Virginia Rinaldo Seitz (1995), Farida Shaheed (1994), and Sarah C. White (1992).

criticism as a deliberative model; its form and content continue to be a subject of deliberation.

For Third World feminist social criticism, "reasonable" deliberations are those that are best informed by an inclusive range of experiences, stories, and arguments. Complemented by Third World feminist social criticism, deliberation meets, sets, and expands epistemological standards. Third World feminist social criticism enables deliberation to meet the deliberative theorists' standards of self-respect, mutual respect, participants' equal ability to influence outcomes, and agreement on what constitutes acceptable deliberative content. However, it further asks that those standards be reviewed; thus Third World feminist social criticism helps deliberative democracy be a better democratic standard. Yet, Third World feminist social criticism is ongoing such that it prods deliberative fora to expand accepted standards of knowledge, encouraging the continued assessment of standards as they change.

As a result, social criticism and deliberation are more inclusive and therefore better informed. Multiple and varied social critics promote inquiry, deliberation, and institutional change using a method of social criticism that uses guiding criteria informed by deliberative processes to scrutinize skeptically existing and potentially exclusive values, practices, and norms. Under review by Third World feminist social criticism, deliberative theory and practice becomes more informed and inclusive thus inclusive deliberation does not sacrifice public decision making to the tyranny of an unreflecting majority. Under scrutiny by Third World feminist social criticism, the norms of reasonable content of deliberation are the subject of deliberation resulting in a broader range of acceptable contributions to deliberative fora. Through the practice of Third World feminist social criticism, the form and therefore the content of deliberations become more inclusive. With Third World feminist social criticism, deliberative democratic theory becomes deliberative democratic practice.

3 Method: skeptical scrutiny, guiding criteria, and deliberative inquiry in concert

Introduction

When western political theorists do attempt to offer an account of social criticism (that is an account of how to bring about the world they advocate), they must provide an account of how their version of social criticism would negotiate the competing pressures against cultural relativism and essentialism. Social criticism should be sensitive to difference in the experiences of oppression without letting recognition of difference be an obstacle to criticism; it should have critical force without consciously or inadvertently marginalizing those whose experiences don't conform to the experiences of oppression being addressed by a specific criticism. Feminists are particularly invested in the relativist–essentialist debate because frequently the cultural practices under scrutiny have different effects on women and men, because essentializing about human beings based on men has made women invisible or their claims to justice illegitimate, and because essentializing about women based on certain women's experiences and interests risks making other women and their claims invisible. For Third World feminism the challenge is to be sensitive to anti-essentialist concerns about the inaccuracies and potential harms that can come from considering Third World women activists as a category of activist while supporting their varied projects of critical activism.

Political theory generally needs social criticism to bring its implied changes about, but not any social criticism will do. Third World feminist social criticism makes political theory and practice more informed and inclusive and thus improves both the quality of and equality in public decision making. For contrast and for their contributions to social criticism, in this chapter 1 consider two theorists who offer political theory with complementary accounts of social criticism. Third World feminist social criticism resembles certain aspects of their theories, but it is a better theory of social criticism because it leads to criticism that is respectful of social institutions but critically suspicious of all potentially harmful inequalities. Third World feminist critics are sensitive to the concerns of cultural relativists but unaccepting of cultural justifications for harmful inequalities. Third World feminist critics can learn from both relativist and essentialist criticisms, but Third World feminist social criticism does not rely on either exclusively.

Michael Walzer provides a relativist account of social criticism that relies on an insider's critical insights. Walzer's approach is based on an idealized critic whose perspective from "a little to the side, but not outside" enables him to recognize (where others can't) those practices of a society that are inconsistent with its deeply held values. In privileging the insider's perspective on the society's deeply held values, his account of social criticism allows practices that are oppressive to some within the society to go unexamined at the discretion of the critic. Nothing obliges the critic to scrutinize those practices that are familiar and accepted.

Martha Nussbaum's approach is not so limited and the resulting criticism is more decisive in its implications. Nussbaum offers essentialist social criticism that relies on the critic's use of a list of the universal criteria of a fulfilling human life. However, because she has not given theoretical or practical attention to the questions of the social critic's method, roles and qualifications, Nussbaum's approach allows for exclusionary decision making and flawed proposed solutions.

Walzer and Nussbaum make inadequate use of deliberation for influencing social criticism. Yet, they try to wrestle with the challenge of describing social criticism that is theoretically general, respects diversity, and yet substantively and meaningfully critical. Neither is unproblematically successful.

Within feminism, Gender and Development (GAD) scholars have likewise wrestled with concerns about harmful essentializing while advocating meaningful social change. Feminists from anti-relativist and anti-essentialist perspectives have worked toward promoting socio-economic development that, rather than adding women as beneficiaries to traditional development projects, asks development organizations to change their own gendered practices and to design their projects at least to take into account, and sometimes to change, a society's gendered practices. Some western authors, writing from outside the contexts of the societies they criticize, have been accused of essentializing about all women's experiences based on western women's experiences, or worse for generally portraying Third World women as victims. Other western authors have withheld criticism in the interest of identifying what women value in or gain from those practices that seem oppressive to women. Some nonwestern authors have been able to avoid overgeneralized or vacuous observations by basing their criticism on intimate knowledge of the practice and using their critical perspective (that of one who has insider knowledge) to remove from their criticism of the practice any exclusive foundation in either western or local cultural understandings. Individually, the GAD scholars have not been satisfied with one another's navigation of relativistic respect and respectful criticism.

Taken together, however, the work of anti-relativist and anti-essentialist feminists, when it is the work of insiders, locally sensitized outsiders, and multi-sited critics, is Third World feminist social criticism. In their efforts to draft social criticism that is sensitive to diversity and yet has critical teeth, Third World feminist theorists promote solidarity among women, develop political strategy, work toward the reorganization of society, and do so through a reorganization of feminism as a social movement. Moreover, GAD feminists use a method of social criticism that is similar to that illustrated by the SEWA activists. They skeptically scrutinize existing values, practices, and norms for their potentially harmful inequalities; they evaluate those values, practices, and norms based on certain criteria; and taken together, we can use their scholarship as a platform for deliberative inquiry about the inequalities to which they draw our attention and about the criteria that ought to be used to assess them.

Collectively, GAD arguments are executions of the more general account of Third World feminist social criticism I have been describing. The philosophy of social criticism implicit in their work offers an antidote to the relativists' and essentialists' critical impotence. Feminists working in the field of Third World development have struggled with the desire to challenge all forms of domination without also undermining the bases for trenchant social criticism.

A Third World feminist method of social criticism

As illustrated by the SEWA example in the preceding chapter, the Third World feminist method of social criticism involves three tools: skeptical scrutiny, guiding criteria, and deliberative inquiry. Skeptical scrutiny is an attitude toward existing and proposed values, practices, and norms that requires one to examine their existing and potentially exploitable inequalities. This aspect of the critic's methodology forces the critic to seek out all those who are silenced by coercive values, practices, and norms. Skeptical scrutiny has critical meaning only contextually. Skeptical scrutiny guides critics to question (not all at once for fear of undermining the foundations of society, but to question nonetheless) whether any and all aspects of community norms, values, and practices (no matter how "accepted" they are) presume, reinforce, cause, or exploit power inequalities to the detriment of the less powerful.

Other political philosophers have suggested a principle or guideline similar to skeptical scrutiny. I adopt the phrase from Justice Ruth Bader Ginsburg who uses it to describe the Supreme Court's standard applied in *US* v. *Virginia* to the review of state policies and institutions that might be considered discriminatory.[1] Ian Shapiro offers a similar account of a principle guiding democratic political criticism. He proposes that democracy has a "middle-ground principle" which is "suspicion" of power inequalities and hierarchies (1994: 138). According to Shapiro,

democracy is better thought of as an ethic of opposition than a system of government. At the heart of what makes it attractive is the antipathy it generates for all systems of entrenched hierarchy and its principled amateurism, its intrinsic hostility to the idea of political expertise. (1990: 277; see also 1988: 284–90; 1989b)

Shapiro portrays democracy as the realization in political institutions of the principle of opposition to oppression and to exploitation of power inequalities. In describing the political engagement of those in a democracy who dissent from its political decisions, Holloway Sparks argues that dissident democratic citizenship strengthens and enhances the democratic practice by maintaining an "oppositional stance" against those with successful political power (1997: 82). (Because it requires thorough treatment, I wish to set aside the issue of whether skeptical scrutiny of power inequalities necessarily leads to democracy and instead to discuss only skeptical scrutiny as a tool of social critics.)

Skeptical scrutiny has led feminists to question everything including the basic institutions of government, the family, and language and to critique privileged power as it is manifested in families, societies, the economy, politics, and language. Although respect for the diversity of women's perspectives has led feminists to be cautious about generalizing about women and women's claims, feminists have made progress toward developing a feminist critical method for challenging power inequalities (e.g., Soares et al. 1995 and Smiley 1993). Patricia Hill

---

[1] In the Virginian Military Institute case in which the court decided whether a state-run all-male military academy constituted state-sponsored sex discrimination, Ginsburg writes, "[t]oday's skeptical scrutiny of official action denying rights or opportunities based on sex responds to volumes of history. As a plurality of this Court acknowledged a generation ago, 'our Nation has had a long and unfortunate history of sex discrimination'" (*US* v. *Virginia* 116 S.Ct. 2264 (1996), 2274 quoting *Frontiero* v. *Richardson*, 411 US 677, 684, 93 S.Ct. 1764, 1769, 36 L.Ed.2d 583 (1973)).

Collins cautiously argues that while experiences of race, class, and gender oppression vary, critical strategies may be similar.

The search for the distinguishing features of an alternative epistemology used by African-American women reveals that values and ideas Africanist scholars identify as characteristically 'Black' often bear remarkable resemblance to similar ideas claimed by feminist scholars as characteristically 'female.' This similarity suggests that the material conditions of race, class, and gender oppression can vary dramatically and yet generate some uniformity in the epistemologies of subordinate groups. (1991: 206–207)

Skeptical scrutiny embodies an epistemological consistency across challenges to oppression.

The guiding criteria are a list of minimum standards that critics use to challenge existing values, practices, and norms. There is great variety in how feminist activists and scholars have articulated and used their lists. Some (such as women's human rights activists) have articulated universal lists, attempting to extrapolate from individual actual experience to identify the common criteria of women's lives (CEDAW 1979; Bunch 1990). Others (such as SEWA) have articulated local lists, meaning that they have identified needs specific to the lives of specific women (such as their self-employed members). Despite its specificity, a local list can have universal import. As Amrita Basu notes by drawing on the various examples in her edited volume to describe women's activism, "In fighting for what appear to be particularistic goals – finding their voices, setting their own agendas, and creating their own social spaces – women's movements are seeking the most universal objectives" (1995a: 20). Some lists, such as the Bangladeshi women's desire not to be beaten in their homes, are specific; other lists, such as the network Women Living Under Muslim Laws' (WLUML's) general guiding criteria of gender equality, are general.[2] Later in this chapter, I propose a version of the guiding criteria that is a general list of what people ought to be able to choose to do, derived from the lists of many social critics around the world. It is a universal list that requires local interpretation and prioritization by critics working in a particular context. Third World feminist social critics (whether working individually or collectively) have guiding criteria of which they make explicit or implicit use.

Deliberative inquiry is the practice of generating knowledge through collective questioning, exchange of views, and discussion among critics

---

[2] Women Living Under Muslim Laws is an international network of scholars and grassroots organizations exchanging information and ideas among women who live in Muslim countries or secular countries (such as India) which allow Muslim communities to decide certain matters (generally family matters) according to Muslim law. See chapter 5.

and members of society.[3] For feminists deliberative inquiry serves two broad purposes. First, among those who have been silenced, it promotes collective learning and understanding in a relatively safe forum. Second, having developed self-knowledge and an understanding of the obstacles they face, the previously silent then use their new knowledge to promote deliberative inquiry in the broader society where their views have previously been excluded. Critics may use deliberative inquiry to promote inquiry, analysis and interpretation, to promote deliberative opportunities in the broader society, and to promote institutional change by bringing about the conditions for deliberative inquiry.

Feminists give us many examples of critics creating fora for deliberative inquiry amongst the oppressed. SEWA's organizational meetings of self-employed working women are similar places of educative deliberation among the previously silent. The training in Kustia organized by Save the Children is an example of a deliberative forum created by a critic so that those they brought to the training could learn together. Deliberative inquiry is part of the critical method for both those who have been silent and those who want to learn from them.

Deliberative inquiry among women has been used by feminist critics as a source of strength for women, to identify and learn from women's experiences, and to develop strategies for collective action. For example, Mahnaz Afkhami criticizes the way in which elite men have controlled the discourse on Islamic beliefs.[4]

Increasingly, women are questioning the framework within which Islamic discourse has developed. The primary question is no longer what Islam has said, but who has said what on behalf of Islam and why. Thus, increasingly, the politics of achieving the right to interpret Islamic text becomes salient. (1995b: fn. 8, 13–14)

Shaheed, also writing about Muslim women's collective deliberative inquiry, concurs:

Women must start assuming the right to define for themselves the parameters of their own identity and stop accepting unconditionally and without question what is presented to them as the 'correct' religion, the 'correct' culture, or the 'correct' national identity. (1995: 95)

For feminists, deliberative inquiry means combining learning, scholarship, and activism. Collins provides an example of the interdependence of thought and action that black women have had for over a century.

---

[3] Note that according to this view and consistent with Third World feminist social criticism, all members of society are potential critics. See chapter 5.
[4] Other women asserting their right and obligation to interpret Islamic texts included Nazīrah Zein Ed-Dīn (1982 [1928]), Jane Smith and Yvonne Haddad (1982), Nawal el Saadawi (1982), Azizah al-Hibri (1982), Riffat Hassan (1982), and Fatima Mernissi (1991).

The activities of nineteenth-century Black women intellectuals such as Anna J. Cooper, Frances Ellen Watkins Harper, Ida B. Wells, and Mary Church Terrell exemplify this tradition of merging intellectual work and activism. These women both produced analyses of Black women's oppression and worked to eliminate that oppression. The Black women's club movement they created was both an activist and an intellectual endeavor. (1991: 29)

Women have been able to overcome their marginalization by drawing on their strengths. If focused on women's common experience of oppression, solidarity doesn't recognize women's strengths. As Farida Shaheed puts it,

One of the problems facing feminist groups is that definitions of the female gender shared by women across class and ethnic divides are those of limitation and oppression. This distinguishes gender identity from identities of community (ethnic or religious) that allow women to share in myths of greatness and strength, and not just oppression. (1995: 98)

Collective action enables women to regard themselves as empowered not as oppressed.[5] However, as the learning about one another's activism among the Bangladeshi women on the walk demonstrates, deliberative inquiry can yield strategic insights and be empowering. For women, deliberative inquiry has been a way for feminists to identify women's needs and interests and then to share them with the broader world. As is captured in Belenky et al.'s description of the German Mothers' Center movement, women work together deliberatively and in so doing develop their ability to bring about their vision in the larger community.

By creating public spaces that are the moral equivalent of an inclusive, egalitarian, nurturing family, full of socially responsible people, the homeplace women have created a working model of the kind of world they yearn for in their dreams. Day in and day out, the homeplace women get hands-on, practical experience in building the kind of world they long to have. As the members watch each other develop, their understanding of the importance of this kind of moral commitment deepens, their efforts intensify, and their successes multiply. The possibility of a world where all humanity is well nourished is kept alive in the face of overwhelming evidence to the contrary. (1997: 265)[6]

---

5 In their edited volume, Myra Marx Ferree and Patricia Yancey Martin collect evidence of collective action from many women's movements – movements begun by women, made up of women, or pursuing women's interests (1995). However, not all women's efforts to promote broad awareness or policy decisions have been effective. In fact most international and national development decisions continue to ignore their effects on women. For examples of feminists' critiques of development policy see Marchand & Parpart (1995).

6 The word "homeplace" comes from the term used by bell hooks (1990) for communities that sponsor the development and growth of their members and are particularly important to those marginalized or excluded from society (Belenky et al. 1997: 161–162).

Stories of their successes demonstrate women's potential greatness and strength collectively.

Learning is intrinsically valuable, but for feminist activists it is also instrumentally valuable. Collective learning, through deliberative inquiry with other women, leads women to be able to develop strategies for promoting deliberation in the broader society about the issues and concerns of women that had previously gone unheard. Concerned about social change being informed and inclusive feminists have created institutions for women to participate in local, national and international dialogues so that they can learn from each other and others can learn from them. Women participate in a women's (or a women's-interest based) organization; the organization represents their interests; and the women gain the knowledge necessary to participate effectively in social decision making. Some emphasize gathering and dispersing knowledge. Others emphasize synthesizing and summarizing information. Both are important ways for feminists to improve women's ability to participate in the deliberative fora that affect their lives and they complement each other in promoting and facilitating that participation.

Deliberative inquiry is a part of the method of social criticism that feminists use in practice and it has helped them to be strategically effective. Women have been effective at bringing about inclusive social change through, first, deliberative inquiry among themselves and, then, deliberative inquiry with others. However, alone, deliberative inquiry is not a critical method. It is merely a means of encouraging the silent voices to speak and asking the broader society to hear them. But social criticism is not just about collecting and expanding a society's knowledge, it is also about reviewing, questioning, and sometimes challenging a society's values, practices, and norms. Deliberative inquiry is one way to encourage the silent voices to speak, but it does not guarantee that some will not remain silenced by coercion or that those who speak will be heard.

Together, not singly, the three tools – skeptical scrutiny, guiding criteria, and deliberative inquiry – are the method of social criticism I attribute to Third World feminism. Deliberative inquiry promotes further examination of unfamiliar views and a search for unknown views where skeptical scrutiny has become too narrowly focused or the guiding criteria are unclear or need to be themselves the subject of criticism. For example, critiques of liberal, Marxist, and radical feminism by women of color accuse it of being too narrowly focused on concerns of white middle-class women. By drawing from a broader range of women and drawing them into feminist deliberations, Third

World feminist critics re-ignite feminism's skeptical scrutiny. Similarly, deliberative inquiry is directed at the guiding criteria that a society and feminists themselves use. For example, Kimberle Crenshaw challenges the criteria of anti-discrimination's application in legal scholarship, political theory, and feminist theory (1989). Third World feminist critics use all three aspects of their critical method – skeptical scrutiny, guiding criteria, and deliberation – in conjunction with one another; consequently, their method is effective at navigating the shoal waters of relativism and essentialism.

Gender and Development: theorizing about and by Third World women

Perhaps because questions of life and death, not just quality of life, are at issue in development, in the academic field of Gender and Development (GAD), feminist accusations of cultural relativism and essentialism have been particularly trenchant and personal. Focusing on the issues of women in developing contexts, the GAD literature has been extremely self-conscious. As an academic interest, GAD theorizing has been instrumental in the critique and analysis of development initiatives and academic discussions of development that fall under the rubric of GAD and its precursor, Women in Development (WID). In the GAD literature we see why the theoretical split between anti-essentialists and anti-relativists is practically important; women's lives are at stake. Though individual GAD theorists do not necessarily demonstrate the practice of the Third World feminist method of social criticism, each offers a criticism (or threat of a criticism) that Third World feminist theory will have to satisfy in its attempts to be respectful of difference in the context of offering incisive social criticism.

During the United Nations Decade for Women (1976–1985), WID was the development strategy that reflected an acknowledgement of women as unappreciated resources in their nation's development. The United States Agency for International Development and other governmental and nongovernmental international donor agencies created WID departments to fund various women-focused development initiatives, the most lasting of which are credit programs for income-generating activities. Caroline Moser provides a helpful descriptive analysis of various WID initiatives (1989). The GAD approach grew out of critical analysis of the WID approach as it was manifested in the Decade for Women. GAD draws attention to ways in which the social construction of male and female roles affect the impact of development strategies and programs. Therefore, development research and planning needs to be gendered in order for strategies and programs to have the desired impact on women's lives.

One approach of feminist development theorists is to interpret GAD scholars as solving a problem that they see in the earlier WID policies and scholarship. For some scholars development policy is not possible without first understanding the gendered nature of society. Gita Sen and Caren Grown writing for a consortium of development scholars and practitioners challenge the way in which familial, social, economic, and political practices are gendered and critique the impact of environmental policy and lack thereof, the debt crisis, militarization, and cultural practice including national chauvinism, racism, and sexism on women (1987).[7] Development policy aimed at improving the lives of all must be preceded by understanding the gendered obstacles to women's advancement. According to such a gendered understanding of development, a gender-aware planner cannot "'graft' gender onto existing" approaches to planning (Moser 1989: 1800). Rather, as Moser argues, a new field, "gender planning, a specific planning approach in its own right" needs to guide gendered development strategies and programs (1989: 1818 fn. 5). Moser provides an outline for gender planning as a discipline (1989). Some GAD scholars argue that GAD is a postmodern perspective on development precisely because while examining social, political, and economic obstacles to women's gains through development, it challenges existing norms of development. Eva Rathgeber, for example, argues that the GAD approach is more postmodern and appropriate as a development approach than its predecessor, the Women in Development (WID) approach, because the latter embodies "western views of 'modernization'" (1995: 204). Rathgeber criticizes WID for tending to place all women in a single category which has caused the voices of many minority women and women in developing countries not to be heard. The WID approach also tends to seek for women opportunities like those of men rather than challenging the assumptions on which the structures that determine men's and women's opportunities are based or questioning whether the opportunities available to poor men and women shouldn't be broader than those currently available to poor men. However, Rathgeber thinks the GAD approach does not repeat WID's

---

[7] For other examples of development literature that attempts to be sensitive to difference while offering trenchant criticism see Judith Bruce (1989), Amartya Sen (1990c), Irene Tinker (1990), Susan Greenhalgh (1991), Gerry Salole (1991), Eudine Barriteau (1995), Anne Marie Goetz (1995a, 1995b). See also the individual contributions to Goetz's edited volume, *Getting Institutions Right for Women in Development* (1997) which, despite the title, reflect a range of GAD approaches to development programming and program evaluation.

mistakes.[8] On this reading, the GAD approach is sensitive to the problems associated with making the generalizations that are necessary for designing public policy; but does not shy away from making policy recommendations.

Another approach is anti-essentialist and critical of attempts to talk about Third World women because the label, even before the policy addressed to them is proposed, explicitly condescends to those women or does so implicitly by critiquing Third World practices from a western perspective.[9] For example, in contrast to Geeta Chowdhry (1995) and Joan French (1992) who treat Sen & Grown's *Development, Crises, and Alternative Visions* (1987) as ground breaking in its gender analysis, Mitu Hirshman criticizes the book as an example of essentializing about gender (1995). Consistent with Mohanty's critique of development literature (1991b), Hirshman accuses Sen & Grown of treating the sexual division of labor as definitive of gender analysis. Moreover, Hirshman argues, the larger network of international scholars (DAWN) who contributed to the research for *Development, Crises, and Alternative Visions* condescend to Third World women as subjects of study and discussion rather than as agents of change in their own lives. The personal attacks on development scholars by postmodern theorists consist primarily of elitism.[10] From this perspective, the GAD approach to development policy is based on harmful generalizations about women.

Other feminists have criticized the anti-essentialist critics for *their* elitism. Postmodern theory has invented jargon and phrases that are inaccessible (in their full intended meanings) to even college undergraduates let alone uneducated Third World women (Currie & Kazi 1987). Responding to Chandra Mohanty (1991b) and Aihwa Ong (1988) and the influence of their writings on development scholarship, Mridula Udayagiri argues that postmodern textual analysis and discourse are not directed toward social change and embody a power dynamic all their own (1995). Some grouping is necessary in order to propose institutional social change. In this light, despite its flaws, the WID agenda created public space for women's knowledge to be shared (1995: 172). The WID agenda created a growing audience for scholars (frequently with some western education) whose critiques are based on intimate knowledge of the local context of their research.[11] These activist

---

[8] For critical discussions of changes in development policy and programming see Kardam (1991) and Parpart (1995).

[9] See for example critiques of feminism by Minh-ha (1987) and Lâm (1994).

[10] See for example Marchand (1995) and Parpart (1993, 1995).

[11] Most of the feminist analysis of other countries available in the West comes from people who have been educated in the USA or who interact regularly with scholars and development organizations from the West. Thus, most Third World feminists face the

scholars write about women's activism and efforts at promoting gender-aware development programming, frequently doing so while (when speaking to a local audience) avoiding words and ideas (such as "feminism" and "gender") that would allow their local critics to accuse them of being "westernized."[12] Their critiques demonstrate a range of women's interests and those interests depend on their context. However, in any given context, the critical weight of the women's social criticism depends on their employing appropriate criteria. Accordingly, social criticism relies on some categorizing and setting of criteria. This last and varied set of anti-postmodern or anti-relativist scholars criticize various values, practices, and norms within their societies, sometime overgeneralizing about women's experiences ignoring differences in ethnicity and class when they articulate the bases of their criticism.

Feminists outside of the development field are concerned about the challenge of reconciling relativism and essentialism, or perhaps more accurately given their criticisms, anti-essentialism and anti-relativism. Linda Alcoff gives an account of the problems of accommodating relativism and essentialism that face feminists (1988). More critically, in "Feminism, Postmodernism, and Gender-Skepticism," Susan Bordo argues that postmodern feminism has shifted feminist discussions from issues of practical import to issues of methodology and theory.

> Not only are we thus diverted from attending to the professional and institutional mechanisms through which the politics of exclusion operate most powerfully in intellectual communities, but we also deprive ourselves of still vital analytical tools for critique of those communities and the hierarchical, dualistic power structures that sustain them. (1990: 136)

Bordo argues that postmodernism is more valuable for its tools than for its theory (1990: 153–154, fn. 1). Hilary Charlesworth acknowledges the problem of doing international law, "which, by definition, is concerned with transnational standards" without assuming a "monolithic" women's perspective or interest (1994). Without being critical of the theoretical observations of anti-essentialists, Cressida Heyes cautions that in seeking to root out essentialism feminist theorists run the "risk of

---

challenge of being credible to an audience suspicious of their "westernization" (Narayan 1997).

[12] See for example the contributions to Amrita Basu's edited volume, *The Challenge of Local Feminisms: Women's Movements in Global Perspective* (1995) and Haleh Afshar's edited volume, *Women and Politics in the Third World* (1996). Nancy Naples's edited volume, *Community Activism and Feminist Politics: Organizing Across Race, Class, and Gender*, gives a range of accounts of US women's activism (1998). See also Lynn Stephen's *Women and Social Movements in Latin America*, particularly an interview with María Teresa Tula (1997: 52–53).

allowing critical analysis of second wave feminist theory to take prece-
dence over more constructive and pragmatic work" (1997: 143).

Third World feminist social criticism is such pragmatic work. Though
not always self-conscious of their accommodations to anti-essentialist
and anti-relativist concerns, Third World feminist social critics make use
of all feminist interpretations of GAD: GAD as social criticism, GAD as
essentializing, and GAD as rejecting relativism's elitism. The GAD
approach – its penchant for drawing on local activism and localized
research and its self-consciousness about the possible ways in which its
own criticisms can marginalize some people – is consistent with Third
World feminist social criticism. Combined, the three aspects of the
methodology improve upon both the relativist's exclusive use of skeptical scrutiny (especially when narrowly hunting for essentialism) and
the essentialist's exclusive use of guiding criteria based on generalizations (however local) about women's interests.

With relativism and essentialism juxtaposed like this, it seems obvious
that a method of social criticism which could be guided by a list of
criteria that is not a list based on only some women's experiences or
interests would enable sensitive scrutiny of gendered practices and the
variety of ways in which they have an effect on women. However, it also
seems obvious that no critic alone could articulate a complete list of
criteria appropriate for a given context. And certainly, any list of criteria
would have to vary in its particulars by context. Deliberative inquiry is
essential to estimating a complete list of criteria and to modifying it for
the particular context. Relativism reminds us to be inclusive and
essentialism tells us to get on with it. Both are important to Third World
feminist social criticism, but alone neither is adequate.

Third World feminist social criticism is not just *a* theory of social
criticism. This theory of social criticism is better than others at meeting
the challenges of both relativist inaction and essentialist marginalization
as well as the demands of respect for diversity and potent social
criticism. In their critical method relativists emphasize skeptical scrutiny
over guiding criteria and essentialists, the reverse, while both make
inadequate use of deliberation for making both their skeptical scrutiny
and guiding criteria more inclusive and therefore better informed.

In the following sections I consider two political theorists' accounts of
social criticism and argue that they too make inadequate use of all three
aspects of the feminist methodology. Michael Walzer emphasizes skeptical scrutiny and Martha Nussbaum emphasizes the guiding criteria,
but neither makes adequate use of the other or informs their skeptical
scrutiny and guiding criteria with deliberative inquiry.

Michael Walzer: contextual interpretation as social criticism

As in my account of Third World feminist social criticism, Michael Walzer goes beyond the articulation of an actionable, coherent, and reflective theory of social criticism to identify the qualifications, method, and roles of social critics. According to Walzer, the critic's qualification is his connection to the society, meaning he is an insider of sorts, his method is to use shared meanings as a critical standard, and his role is interpretation. According to his account, the social critic identifies and understands a society's shared values and interprets existing or proposed practices for their consistency with those values. Shared values vary by political community, but they always include life and liberty (Walzer 1977, 1983, 1987, and 1988). The job of the social critic, Walzer argues, is to interpret the practices and social understandings of the society around him and to criticize those that he interprets to be inconsistent with that society's values.[13] However, social criticism as he describes it allows critics and society to avoid listening to the offstage voices because (1) connection is too limiting a qualification for social critics; (2) a method needs a way of questioning a society's shared meanings; and (3) interpretation is too narrow a role for social critics. In my view, social criticism that does not give voice to the views of those who are silent as a function of inequality and coercion is not adequately critical. How can the critic hear and interpret ideas that are not voiced? How can the critic understand the values of those who do not march or shout? Should the social critic be their spokesperson? What do the needs of the oppressed and silent suggest is required of social criticism? Although the philosophy of social criticism has featured prominently in Walzer's work, the answers to the preceding questions have not. Further, critics of Walzer have accused him of being unclear,[14] of

---

[13] Interpretation as social criticism is most explicitly defined in Walzer's *Interpretation and Social Criticism* (1987). However, Walzer's social criticism as interpretation plays a significant role in other works particularly *Spheres of Justice* (1983), *The Company of Critics* (1988), "Objectivity and Social Meaning" (1993), and *Thick and Thin* (1994). Importantly, on the first page of *Interpretation and Social Criticism*, Walzer says that the interpretive account of social criticism "accords best with our everyday experience of morality" (Walzer 1987: 3). If Walzer were to mean by this only to argue that social criticism as interpretation only works to answer everyday moral dilemmas such as "should I tell the truth about such and such," then the approach would be of little value to the philosophy of social criticism. Given the order of moral and social problem he uses as examples in his works, it is clear that he means social criticism as interpretation to apply to the more significant moral dilemmas societies face every day, such as whether, and under what conditions, a society should permit capital punishment.

[14] See Joseph Raz's review of *Interpretation and Social Criticism* in which Raz is particularly

making naive assumptions about how a society forms and perpetuates its values,[15] and of being universalist, not relativist.[16]

Though criticized as a relativist with universalist principles (Galston 1989), Walzer is a good choice for demonstrating the contributions of relativism to the philosophy of social criticism because he explicitly defines for the social critic a role that is respectful of the variety of moralities in the world. Consequently, Third World feminist social criticism's definitions of the critics' qualifications, method, and roles need to do a better job of guiding respectfully social criticism than can be done using Walzer's qualification (connection), method (shared meaning as critical standard), and role (interpretation).

According to Walzer's account of social criticism, the critic's qualification is his connection to the society he criticizes. Walzer gives examples of the connected critic in *The Company of Critics* and he himself is a connected critic of US's political, social, and economic inequalities in *Spheres of Justice* and in many articles in *Dissent*. For Walzer, the most powerful critic is one whose social criticism is maximal ("thick") and universal: "rich in its detail, expansive in its scope" (1994a: 50). Criticism according to Walzer is based on the critic's extensive, intimate, and profound understanding of the values of the community he criticizes. He appreciates that some unconnected critics like Amnesty International can offer thin social criticism, based on universal values, but worries that such critics risk "claiming political authority everywhere on the basis of ideological correctness" (1994a: 49). Their work potentially prevents some within a society from asserting their political authority in the name of a particular thick morality. Walzer does not recognize how important their work is for facilitating inclusive consideration of a given maximal morality by those who have to live by it. The Walzerian critic may be unable to recognize the interests of, among others, those who live with crocodiles.[17]

To elaborate, Walzer describes the connectedness of his critic in a

critical of Walzer's undefined use of "interpretation" (1991). The word has meanings ranging from translation to artistic re-creation.

[15] See Susan Okin on Walzer's *Spheres of Justice*, specifically her critique of the relativist's use of "shared understandings" (1989: chapter 3).

[16] See William Galston on Walzer's *Just and Unjust Wars*, *Radical Principles*, "Philosophy and Democracy," *Spheres of Justice*, and *Interpretation and Social Criticism* (1989). See also Raz's reading of *Interpretation and Social Criticism* in which he argues that Walzer recognizes variety in moral codes between communities, but assumes moral coherence within communities (1991: 393).

Walzer himself writes, "I want to endorse the politics of difference and, at the same time, to describe and defend a certain sort of universalism" (1994a: x).

[17] In my view, Walzer's critic may offer valuable social criticism, but he cannot offer all necessary criticism, and no critic alone regardless of his perspective can be sufficient.

variety of ways. He is positioned within the society he criticizes: "a little to the side, but not outside" (1987: 61). By this Walzer means that the critic is from the society in question, but has had some experience that provides critical distance, "measured in inches" (1987: 61), from which to assess the values promoted and passed down in the society (1983: 198). He criticizes from within the society's framework of values, practices, and norms. The critic, like the poet, "cannot cut himself off from the community of ideas" that provide his context (1981: 382).

The Walzerian critic uses his connection not just to think critically but also to speak with the society he criticizes. "If the critic is to speak for his fellows, he must also speak with them, and when what he says sounds unpatriotic, he has to insist upon his own deeper patriotism" (1988: 234). The Walzerian critic is a masterful orator. He has a command of specialized and popular language (1988: 9) and he is "defiant, out-spoken, fearless" (1988: 12). Though not necessarily elite in the sense of being from an advantaged class of society, the Walzerian critic has unique intellectual and speaking abilities. He is uncommon.

According to Walzer the critic's method is to apply his society's values as a critical standard by which to evaluate its practices such that more of society benefits from certain of its values.[18] The critic recognizes when a society's values are hypocritically defended by the more powerful and cynically regarded by those with less power (1988: 22).

He identifies his society's common values and promotes adherence to them. The critic "believes that his criticism is a real service: it can make [his city] a better city" (1988: 18). Walzer's critic is devoted to the values of his society. By criticizing he demonstrates "a passionate commitment to cultural values hypocritically defended at the center, cynically disregarded at the margins" (1988: 22). The society's improvement cannot come from outside the society, but rather from the society's own values. Whatever the society's values, they will be consistent with its history and culture (1988: 234). The Walzerian critic is sympathetic – in Walzer's term, "loyal" – to the oppressed, "but he sees these people and their troubles and the possible solution to their troubles within the framework of national history and culture" (1988: 234). Although Walzer believes that conventions should not be "imposed by force," he generally assumes they haven't been (1994a: 29; also 1983 and 1993).

---

[18] Walzer derives his account of the connected critic in part from analyzing the work of eleven critics in *The Company of Critics*, but he does not wholeheartedly endorse their accounts of social criticism (1988). For example in his chapter on Julien Benda, he is critical of Benda's analysis of intellectual treason. Benda argues that "the national passion" of intellectual critics inhibited their criticism. Walzer asserts by contrast that Benda should have been critical of the intellectuals' use of power not of their love of country (1988: 43).

Consistent with a relativist philosophy, the society's shared values are the social critic's guiding criteria.

Thus, the effectiveness of the Walzerian critic hinges on his ability to identify the shared understandings of a society; and it hinges on there being some.[19] According to Walzer, shared understandings are more likely to exist in a political community. "[T]he political community is probably the closest we can come to a world of common meanings. Language, history, and culture come together (come more closely together here than anywhere else) to produce a collective consciousness" (1983: 28; see also 1981: 380). Although he recognizes that in "a growing number of states in the world today: sensibilities and intuitions aren't readily shared," he does not relinquish the notion that they can be shared, rather "the sharing takes place in smaller units" (1983: 29). Walzer naively asserts the congruence of political and moral communities and ignores the possibility of profound disagreements within moral/political communities. He assumes that the smaller units will have shared understandings "among the citizens about the value of cultural diversity, local autonomy, and so on" (1983: 29) despite Walzer's own examples of disagreement within a given political community.[20] For example he argues in *Spheres of Justice* that there is an underlying distributive principle – complex equality – by appealing to which he can criticize unjust inequalities (1983). His recognition of variety and disagreement within political communities makes his emphasis on the critical power of shared understandings ironic, if not hypocritical.

[19] Walzer uses the terms "shared understandings" (1983: xiv, 313), "common meanings" (1983: 28), "shared meanings" (1983: 250n, also this sense is implied in the discussion on pages 313–314), and "social meanings" (1993: 166, 1983: 313) to describe values that presumably all within a society hold freely without coercion such that the society can be described as having a "collective consciousness" (1983: 28).

[20] Some examples of disagreements within societies cited by Walzer include: in China between communist and traditional Chinese (1983: 195–196); in the USA about the content of education (1983: 197), the constitution (1983: 197), the proper length of compulsory education (1983: 208), vouchers for education (1983: 218), integration and bussing (1983: 221), marriage and kinship rules (1983: 231), difficult decisions about punishment of crimes (1983: 269); and in India about the caste system (1983: 314–315). In addition, Walzer refers to the variety of groups within the USA (Walzer 1983: 150; see also 1990b), the exclusion of groups within India (1983: 151n, 165, 175), the exclusion of African-Americans after Emancipation (1983: 165), and the different experiences of men and women on kibbutz (1983: 173–174). Similarly, in *Thick and Thin*, Walzer notes the differences among the Prague demonstrators – between Christian fundamentalists and others about the meanings of truth and justice. See also *Interpretation and Social Criticism*: after an account of a dispute between Rabbis over morality, Walzer concludes, morality "is something we have to argue about. The argument implies common possession, but common possession does not imply agreement" (1987: 32).

There are (at least) two ways to criticize Walzer's use of shared understandings. One is to argue that social values cannot be assumed to be shared. An argument that relies on shared understandings must include more than the vague allusion to a common language, history, culture, and "collective consciousness" (1983: 28). History provides plenty of examples of why this is so. For example, Southern US blacks and whites have a shared history of slavery, reconstruction, Jim Crow laws, and desegregation, but that does not mean that Southern blacks and whites experienced history similarly, that they have a collective consciousness, or that they have shared values. Given that specific practices constrain the mobility, economic resources, and ability to speak of the less powerful, before asserting that shared practices of a hierarchical system are the result of collective consciousness, one must find out whether they are collectively valued, or valued by some and forced on others. A critic's approach, Walzer argues, should be just the opposite: the critic should assume that in a society values are shared and the critic should "work out what they [in his example, women-who-are-objects-of-exchange] find valuable or satisfying in their old way of life" (1993: 176). If one is not cognizant of the potential to mistake oppressive or coerced practices and meanings for agreed upon practices and understandings, the relativist's respect for social understandings is a means of conserving existing sometimes oppressive, coercive, or exclusionary practices.

In *Interpretation and Social Criticism* Walzer tries to argue, explicitly against this point, that interpretive social criticism does not definitionally entail respecting the status quo. Although Walzer offers a convincing demonstration of how interpretive social criticism can be critical, he does not adequately defend it as being critical enough to criticize an oppressed group's seemingly collective acceptance of their oppression (1987, especially chapter 2). He does not consider the possible interpretations of silence. In *Spheres of Justice*, however, Walzer notes that in the case of slavery, masters and slaves do not have "shared meanings." Citing Orlando Patterson, Walzer argues in a footnote,

'There is absolutely no evidence from the long and dismal annals of slavery: to suggest that any group of slaves ever internalized the conception of degradation held by their masters.' Slaves and masters do not inhabit a world of shared meanings. The two groups are simply at war... (1983: 250n)

Where extreme oppression (as in slavery) is a social practice, according to Walzer understandings are not shared by oppressor and oppressed. How are we to know when social values are shared or the manifestation of a dominant ideology? In sum, the first criticism of Walzer's use of "shared understandings" is that it is too relativist, i.e., not critical enough of existing social practices and meanings.[21]

An alternative criticism of Walzer's use of shared understandings is that they are not relative at all but that they are instead a cover for his own values. According to William Galston, Walzer's philosophy of social criticism relies on three philosophical beliefs based on which Walzer defends a nontranscendent universal endorsement of democracy (Galston 1989). This second criticism is not valid because it conflates Walzer's own political philosophy with his theory of social criticism. The values important to Walzer's political philosophy are life and liberty,[22] democratic activism,[23] complex equality,[24] and "mutual respect and a shared self-respect."[25] These values are important to Walzer's political philosophy, meaning they are important to his own maximalist (thick) political theory, but they are not part of Walzer's general philosophy of social criticism. Of these beliefs, only the minimal code of life and liberty is likely part of all societies' shared understandings according to Walzer. The minimal code is a (thin) general value that is universally held and therefore important to social criticism as part of all societies' values.

The third part of Walzer's account of social critics – the critic's role, interpretation – draws on the critic's connection to and knowledge of society. The critic interprets the values, practices, and norms of his society. As Joseph Raz argues, Walzer is vague as to the meaning of "interpretation" (1991). Interpretation can be narrowly defined as translation in which case the critic is constrained from inserting his individual understandings into his interpretation (although as any translator will tell you, most translation requires some judgment on the

---

[21] According to Walzer, his account of connected critics at work in *The Company of Critics* answers this criticism because it shows connected critics doing social criticism using the principles of their own societies (1988: ix). Although not directing her argument toward Walzer, Nancy Hirschmann offers an alternative analysis of oppression (1996a). She argues that because gender norms create not only external constraints but also internal constraints, in order to counter oppressive ideology, feminist social critics need to develop countermeanings and counterdiscourses. In her critique of oppression she sees internalization that Walzer and Patterson do not see and in her solution she advocates seeking alternative norms to the dominant social meanings. Walzer's social criticism cannot easily be applied to oppressions that are internalized.

[22] Walzer refers to life and liberty as the minimal and universal moral code (1987: 24).

[23] Walzer defends democracy, socialism, and political activism in *Radical Principles* (1980: 3–19, 42, 51, 125), *Spheres of Justice* (1983: 283, 287, 303, 310, 318), *Interpretation and Social Criticism* (1987: 22), and "The Politics of Rescue" (1995: 54).

[24] Walzer defends the concept of complex equality in *Radical Principles* (1980: 242), *Spheres of Justice* (1983), "Liberalism and the Art of Separation"(1984: 321), and *Thick and Thin* (1994a: 57–58).

[25] Walzer defends mutual respect and self-respect in *Spheres of Justice* (1983: 321 and 258, 310, 320).

part of the translator in order to resolve ambiguities). Or, interpretation could be more broadly defined as artistic license to impute one's own values, judgments, and understandings into observable social values.

In either case, Walzer's critic's role is too narrowly defined. There is no scope for the social critic to help resolve disagreements within society. There is no role for the critic to inquire into the values and desires of those who are unable to voice their views in public. There is no role for the critic to promote deliberative opportunities among disagreeing parties. There is no role for the social critic in developing institutional means for reconciling disagreements within society. And there is no role for the social critic in securing a public voice for those silenced by oppression and fear. Many social problems around the world – racially experienced gender oppression in the USA and gender hierarchy in Bangladesh are just two – are a function of disagreements within society, yet the views of the oppressed are not reliably represented by the publicly articulated social values.

Particularly in *Interpretation and Social Criticism*, Walzer seems to presume that societies don't run amok; they simply lose sight of the essential underlying principles of life and liberty and the particular social values that embody them (1987: 24–25). Despite diversity among societies' values, Walzer *presumes* that social moralities always embody an opposition to oppression: "[m]orality is always potentially subversive of class and power" (1987: 22). Consequently, the role of the critic is to remind his society of its principles – life, liberty, and opposition to oppression among them. For example, he argues that in an Indian village, though adhering to the caste-based distribution system, poor villagers may repress their objection to the caste system and well-off villagers may repress their recognition of the principles that are the bases of the poor villagers' objections. He argues that the repressed principles should be revealed to the community (1983: 313–314).

Despite his faith that the universal values of life, liberty, and opposition to oppression will be revealed, in a more recent essay advocating humanitarian intervention in Bosnia he describes the challenge for the philosophy of intervention in a society where "the trouble is internal, the inhumanity locally and widely rooted, a matter of political culture, social structures, historical memories, ethnic fear, resentment, and hatred" (1995: 56). Although he is not explicit, Walzer seems to believe that the Bosnians have not lost sight of their values, but rather that their values are inhumane and a cultural characteristic or that there is "not quite a 'war against all' but a widely dispersed, disorganized, and murderous war of some against some" (1995: 56).[26] In his analysis Bosnia violates the assumptions on which interpretation as social criticism relies.

Walzer maintains two competing claims: (1) that the critic's task is to interpret the society's shared understandings and (2) that sometimes values are disputed within societies. The competing claims are reconciled if there is always a cultural value of opposition to oppression for the critic to reveal in the soul of anyone and everyone.[27] Whatever else it sees, the society under criticism must also see where and when its practices are oppressive. Throughout his work, Walzer has taken on or cited many political and social problems where a plurality of views within a given society is evident. However, Walzer has confidence in the critic from within to reveal oppression where it goes unrecognized by his own society. In sum, Walzer's philosophy of social criticism is the practice of someone from within a society positioning himself still within the society so as to be able to observe its practices and meanings and to assess their consistency with the underlying values of the society. Walzer's model of social criticism offers no basis on which to consider or criticize the underlying values themselves. Further, I doubt that, alone, the connected critic, as Walzer describes him, has an adequate perspective from which to seek out the silent voices and to criticize seemingly uncontested values, practices, and norms that are in fact oppressive. Interpretation is too narrow a role for social critics. Shared meanings are incomplete critical criteria. The connected critic, working alone, is unqualified.

Walzer's disproportionate focus on the shared meanings of a society rather than on the potential or likelihood that certain values, practices, and norms are shared by some and forced on others is rejected by feminist theorists' continual effort to examine seemingly shared values, practices, and norms. Social critics should *at least* draw critical attention to power inequalities. Moreover, taking life, liberty, and opposition to oppression seriously, Walzer's social critic must do more than interpret social values. She should inquire about potentially oppressive practices whether they are valued or not. She should provoke deliberation within society about those values. In some cases she may even bring about institutional changes that undermine harmful inequalities. Although in

---

[26] As an aside, Walzer does not provide sources for his arguments or give them substance with examples. A five-hour television series produced by Brian Lopping Associates for the BBC provides compelling documentation that the ethnic violence in Bosnia was less a function of historical cultural values and more a function of the tools of ambitious leaders, in particular Slobodan Milosevic of Serbia (Lewis 1996). See also John Bowen (1996).

[27] Like Hamlet for his mother, "the social critic similarly turns our eyes into our very souls" (Walzer 1988: 231). "The critic ... speaks to all those ... men and women ... who are uneasy with the mirror image" (Walzer 1988: 231n).

Thick and Thin, Walzer argues that uniformity and coercion are too high prices to pay for "human" values (1994a: 8), he assumes universal respect for life, liberty, and opposition to oppression. Further, coercion may be necessary to counter coercive attempts to limit the life or liberty (or the quality thereof) of some people.

Walzer has given us one account of the social critic's qualifications, one element of a critical method, and one role for the social critic. While these constitute a theory of social criticism, it is not a very good one because it leaves too much uncriticized. However, these are important parts of a more complete theory of social criticism. Although Walzer does not make adequate use of it himself, opposition to oppression leads to an important aspect of the critical method. The critic opposed to oppression scrutinizes all values, practices, and norms, even those seemingly shared throughout society for potentially harmful inequalities. Thus, if opposed to oppression, even relativists guide their social criticism by a universal value. Skeptical scrutiny is the aspect of the Third World feminist critical methodology that puts the value of opposition to oppression into critical practice. However, alone, skeptical scrutiny is not an adequate critical methodology.

Martha Nussbaum: internal essentialism as social criticism

Martha Nussbaum defends a set of standards that she argues are essential to, and should be shared among, human beings in order that they may live a fulfilling human life. She presents these as a philosophy of social criticism, arguing that anyone can be a social critic by recommending social change that would lead to more people living according to those standards. Nussbaum provides an important tool – a list of guiding criteria – for a social critic's method of promoting institutional change; however, alone that tool is an inadequate method of social criticism because it does not enable critics to hear all of the offstage voices of a society. Alone the guiding criteria are no better than skeptical scrutiny is alone as a method of social criticism. Rather, they are a necessary addition to it.

Nussbaum attempts to provide an important tool for relativist social critics who seem frozen by their very desire to be critical of all forms of oppression. Nussbaum wrestles free of that inaction by putting to critical use Aristotle's method of social criticism, internal essentialism.[28]

---

[28] She calls her approach "'internalist' essentialism" (1992: 208), the "Aristotelian procedure" (Nussbaum & Sen 1989), "internal criticism" (Nussbaum & Sen 1989), or the "Aristotelian approach" (1993a). Nussbaum's approach is a fresh perspective that

Nussbaum is both essentialist in that she recognizes that there are essential human values and relativist in that she argues that those values can be recognized only by studying them as they are manifested in the respective contexts of a variety of societies. Although this may appear to be an untenable position, she carefully argues that there are certain capabilities – to meet needs and enjoy rights – that are essential to a fulfilling human life, but she respects that those needs and rights may be differently recognized, although sometimes insufficiently recognized, in different societies. By advocating that all human beings should have the capacity to meet their needs and to enjoy certain rights, she avoids the paternalistic essentialism of approaches that mandate certain functionings, needs, or rights.[29] The responsibility of the social critic is to criticize social values of a given society if they are obstacles to some people's capability to live a fulfilling human life. Thus, all social values of a given social context are not valid. Although sensitive to the potential for misguided cultural imperialism, she nevertheless argues that social criticism should not be constrained by respect for unexamined social values. Thus Nussbaum's brand of essentialism appreciates that, though universally recognized, individual capabilities are differently realized in different contexts. Nussbaum uses internal essentialism to derive a list of human capabilities and with Amartya Sen argues that a society has a political and moral responsibility to make sure to enable all its people to have (though they may not choose to exercise) those capabilities. She means for the capability ethic to apply not just to a society's examination of its own political distribution, but to one's examination of any society's distribution (1995b, also 1995a; Crocker 1992, 1995).

By articulating a list of capabilities, Nussbaum further develops the capability ethic of Sen. Sen proposes the capability ethic partially in response to John Rawls's account of the primary goods that just institutions distribute in *A Theory of Justice* (1971). Whereas Sen defends the capability approach, Nussbaum develops Sen's approach by identifying its roots in Aristotle and by articulating specifically *which capabilities* are essentially human and morally compelling for public policy, thus demonstrating its application.[30]

Despite the appealing prospects of internal essentialism to reclaim from relativism the possibility of substantive social criticism,

---

is neither relativist nor, she asserts, essentialist in the sense of the negative connotation that word has acquired (1992: 243, fn. 6).

[29] For further discussions about what just institutions should distribute see Thomas Scanlon (1975), Sen (1984, 1985, 1990b), Ronald Dworkin (1981), G. A. Cohen (1993), and Rawls (1988).

[30] Knight & Johnson discuss the capabilities approach to assessing equality of political influence in the context of deliberative democracy (1997).

Nussbaum's methodology is flawed. Like Aristotle, Nussbaum inadvertently imports into her specific criticisms priorities that are different from those of her subjects. This methodological flaw, however, does not undermine the tremendous contribution that Nussbaum's development of the capability ethic makes to the philosophy of social criticism. My criticisms of Nussbaum consist primarily of modifications and developments of the capability ethic such that its methodology further mitigates imperialist and paternalistic critical perspectives. The specifics of the list that Nussbaum authors are an important contribution to dialogue among social critics, societies, and philosophers about what should be the content of such a list and my own list is a development of hers. However, the list is only a guideline and like skeptical scrutiny is only *part* of the Third World feminist method of social criticism.

As Nussbaum uses it, the capabilities ethic is both a philosophy of social criticism and a guide for social policy. It is based on a notion of justice that argues that a just society is one in which the principles of justice function to distribute capabilities fairly such that all within the society have a fair opportunity for a good quality of life. Nussbaum proposes a list of capabilities that should serve as "the basis for a global ethic and fully international account of distributive justice" (1992: 205). Part of the process of justifying the capability ethic is defending it as a historically familiar method of social study and defending the results of her application of this process. She claims that the capabilities and functionings she identifies can be universally recognized as the capabilities and functionings essential to being human. Nussbaum sets out first to defend Aristotle's methodology and then to use it to identify and further expand upon the capabilities and functionings that she argues are essential to a fulfilling human life.[31]

The Aristotelian method is based on identifying the basic characteristics or spheres of a human life and, from them, determining what functioning is prerequisite for the life one would call a good or fulfilling

---

[31] Although the parts of Nussbaum's argument were published in six papers over eight years, together they outline a coherent argument for the methodology and application of the capability ethic that is basically consistent across the papers. These six papers – "Human Capabilities, Female Human Beings" (1995b), "Aristotle on Human Nature and the Foundations of Ethics" (1995c), "Non-relative Virtues: An Aristotelian Approach" (1993a), "Human Functioning and Social Justice: In Defense of Aristotelian Essentialism" (1992), "Aristotelian Social Democracy" (1990), and "Nature, Function, and Capability: Aristotle on Political Distribution" (1988a) – are generally to be read together. The foundations of the arguments in these papers can be seen in earlier work (1986a and 1986b) and related arguments have been made in other articles (Nussbaum & Sen 1989 and Nussbaum 1995d, 1995e). "Non-relative Virtues: An Aristotelian Approach" (1993a) appeared in an earlier version in *Midwest Studies in Philosophy* (1988b). I refer to the later version.

human life. For example all human beings are mortal. They experience death of those they know and after a certain age know that they too will die (1995b: 76). According to Nussbaum, the corresponding basic capability that is part of a good human life is "being able to live to the end of a human life of normal length, not dying prematurely ..." (1995b: 83) and presumably, though she doesn't say so explicitly, not having a parent or child die prematurely. The purpose is to

retain the grounding in actual human experiences that is the strong point of virtue ethics, while gaining the ability to criticize local and traditional moralities in the name of a more inclusive account of the circumstances of human life, and of the needs for human functioning that these circumstances call forth. (1993a: 250)

In other words, Nussbaum intends for the capability ethic to be sensitive both to local values and to the essential values of human lives. According to Nussbaum, this method of social criticism is universally relevant because it is based both on accurate knowledge of the particulars of human lives and on variety in the ways in which they are lived and shared with others. While recognizing that Aristotle made mistakes in his application of the methodology, Nussbaum perceives the Aristotelian methodology to be a promising basis for a development ethic and social criticism.

Nussbaum asserts that internal essentialism is a methodology that is "historically grounded" and rooted in human experience (1992: 208). In a phrase that reminds me of Walzer's description of the connected critic, Nussbaum & Sen say the account is *"immersed rather than detached"* (1989: 308). Aristotle explains,

Here, as in all other cases, we must set down the appearances and, first working through the puzzles, in this way go on to show, if possible, the truth of all the traditional beliefs about these experiences; and, if this is not possible, then truth of the greatest number and the most basic. For if the difficulties are resolved and the traditional beliefs are left in place, we will have done enough showing. (Nussbaum & Sen 1989: 309, quoting *Nicomachean Ethics* 1145b)

For Nussbaum as for Aristotle, "the end [of philosophy] is not contemplation but action" (*Nicomachean Ethics* 1095a5).[32] Properly applied, the Aristotelian political ethic provides normative objective criteria for social criticisms that are culturally sensitive, respecting cultural values without reifying them by romanticizing the otherness of unfamiliar practices (Nussbaum 1992). Nussbaum proposes a list of eleven basic capabilities, emphasizing two functionings, practical reason and affiliation with others, that are essential to the others. Nussbaum

---

[32] Aristotle, *Nicomachean Ethics* cited by Nussbaum (1995d: 183). See also Nussbaum & Sen (1989: 308).

demonstrates the application of the capability ethic as a basis for political criticism and uses the capability ethic to suggest political and other institutional changes that are sensitive to cultural context, but not constrained by it (1988a, 1990, 1995a, and 1995b).[33]

Nussbaum uses the list as a basis for promoting legislation and public planning toward designing social and political institutions for the maintenance of the preconditions of those capabilities (1995b: 81–83) in much the same ways as human rights activists advocate states use UN Declarations and Conventions. Nussbaum acknowledges that there may be a low threshold of capabilities at which she would still recognize a person living such a life as human, but she argues that the political obligations associated with this list are based on "a higher threshold" than basic needs (1995b: 81–83, also 1990: 229). Nussbaum argues that securing for its population the capacity to have these essential human experiences is the purpose of social democracy (1990). She uses the list as a basis for criticizing and directing development policy. And she uses it in a more narrow way to guide specific recommendations for social and political institutions and development policy. In addition, one can see a development in her thought from treating the list as a set of foundational objectives for the lawgiver (1988a and 1990: 224), to a list of guiding criteria for the public planning process (1992: 221), to a list of political and social imperatives for any society (1995b).

Not only does the list guide a society's own self-examination or an individual's examination of her own society, but also it can guide an individual's judgments about other societies. Nussbaum & Sen assert that "objective value judgments can be made from the point of view of experienced immersion in the way of life of a culture" (1989: 308). By "using resources inside the culture itself," an outsider can be *"genuinely critical"* (1989: 308). However, just as the insider may fail to take under consideration all of the views in her society, so too an outsider, despite immersion in another society, may fail to recognize and take under consideration all the views in that society. While experienced immersion may be an important method of research and may yield insights of which insiders are unaware, alone it is an inadequate basis for social criticism, in part because immersion does not require that one solicit

---

[33] In "Aristotelian Social Democracy" (1990), Nussbaum provides a general account of the implications of the methodology for political criticism (with social implications for labor markets, property, political participation, and education). In "Human Capabilities, Female Human Beings" (1995b), she gives a more thorough account of the methodology and political implications of the capability ethic. She also describes the Aristotelian method as a process occurring across communities as in the criticism of national development policies (1993a and 1995b) and as a process occurring within a community (1995c).

and then *hear* the silent voices of those marginalized within a society. The lone immersed critic is not necessarily better at hearing extreme and unfamiliar views than an insider critic. Thus, after reviewing the content of Nussbaum's list, I turn to a discussion of its use as a method of social criticism before going on to demonstrate the role of the list in Third World feminist social criticism.

Nussbaum's capabilities list

The result of Nussbaum's application of the internal essentialist method is what Nussbaum calls the "thick vague conception of the good" (1990: 217) the basis of which are the eleven characteristics of the human life.[34] She intends the list to be universally applicable, yet open for further modification.[35]

1. Life. "Being able to live to the end of a human life of normal length, not dying prematurely, or before one's life is so reduced as to be not worth living."
2. Satisfaction. "Being able to have good health; to be adequately nourished; to have adequate shelter; having opportunities for sexual satisfaction, *and for choices in matters of reproduction*; being able to move from place to place."
3. Comfort. "Being able to avoid unnecessary and non-beneficial pain, so far as possible, and to have pleasurable experiences."
4. Use-of-mind-and-senses. "Being able to use the senses; being able to imagine, to think, and to reason – *and to do these things in a way informed and cultivated by an adequate education, including, but by no means limited to, literacy and basic mathematical and scientific training. Being able to use imagination and thought in connection with experiencing and producing spiritually enriching materials and events of one's own choice; religious, literary, musical, and so forth. I believe that the protection of this capability requires not only the provision of education, but also legal guarantees of freedom of expression with respect to both political and artistic speech, and of freedom of religious exercise.*"
5. Attachments. "Being able to have attachments to things and persons outside ourselves; to love those who love and care for us, to grieve at their absence, in general, to love, to grieve, to feel longing and gratitude. *Supporting this capability means supporting forms of human association that can be shown to be crucial in their development.*"
6. Practical-reason. "Being able to form a conception of the good and to

---

[34] Compare to *Thick and Thin* in which "thick" is the account of locally specific values, and "thin" is their general description (Walzer 1994a).
[35] The text, quoted from "Human Capabilities, Female Human Beings" (1995b: 83–85 *italics added*), is a developed version of the list Nussbaum gives in "Human Functioning and Social Justice" (1992: 222) and "Aristotelian Social Democracy" (1990: 225). In the latest version, Nussbaum added the passages I cite in italics. I add the titles – Life, Satisfaction, Comfort, etc. – to simplify referring to them in the following discussion. Note I change what Nussbaum numbers "10a" to "11."

engage in critical reflection about the planning of one's own life. *This includes, today, being able to seek employment outside the home and to participate in political life."*

7. Affiliation. "Being able to live for and [with] others, to recognize and show concern for other human beings, to engage in various forms of familial and social interaction; *to be able to imagine the situation of another and to have compassion for that situation; to have the capability for both justice and friendship. Protecting this capacity means, once again, protecting institutions that constitute such forms of affiliation, and also protecting the freedoms of assembly and political speech."*

8. Fellowship-with-nature. "Being able to live with concern for and in relation to animals, plants, and the world of nature."

9. Recreation. "Being able to laugh, to play, to enjoy recreational activities."

10. Freedom-from-individual-control. "Being able to live one's own life and nobody else's. *This means having certain guarantees of non-interference with certain choices that are especially personal and definitive of selfhood, such as choices regarding marriage, childbearing, sexual expression, speech, and employment."*

11. Freedom-from-social-control. "Being able to live one's own life in one's very own surroundings and context. *This means guarantees of freedom of association and of freedom from unwarranted search and seizure; it also means a certain sort of guarantee of the integrity of personal property, though this guarantee may be limited in various ways by the demands of social equality, and is always up for negotiation in connection with the interpretation of the other capabilities, since personal property, unlike personal liberty is a tool of human functioning rather than an end in itself."*

According to Nussbaum "a life that lacks any one of these [capabilities], no matter what else it has, will fall short of being a good human life" (1995b: 85). The content of Nussbaum's list is generally a development of Aristotle's list as articulated in the *Eudemian Ethics* and *Nicomachean Ethics* and she credits Aristotle with authoring the list. However, Aristotle and Nussbaum understand the list differently. Aristotle sees people as differing by nature and only citizens, only those with developed practical reason, that is, an elite all-male subset of the privileged population, will be able to be virtuous or to live a fulfilling human life (*Nicomachean Ethics* and the *Politics*). Nussbaum sees practical reason, the ability to guide one's own life, as a characteristic of being human whereas Aristotle sees it as a characteristic of only adult male citizens. Thus, Nussbaum interprets the capability ethic as guiding the distribution of capabilities to all people, whereas Aristotle only to citizens. Failure to explain how her version of the capability ethic prevents other forms of exclusion is a shortcoming of Nussbaum's account of the capability ethic as a basis of social criticism.

Nussbaum defends her account of the good human life as essential to all humans and universally applicable (1992, 1993a, 1995b: 63, 1995b and Nussbaum & Sen 1989). Nussbaum argues that if the capability theorist were to respect cultural relativism, she would lose the point of focusing on capabilities rather than preferences (1988a). According to the capability theorist, once all the capabilities are secured, the people can choose which to realize according to their personal and cultural preferences. Nussbaum is not, however, insensitive to the merit of what she generally views as alarming anti-essentialist views (1992: 203). Although she defends the universalist and nonrelative applications of the capability approach, she recognizes that the approach should not be hijacked and used as a means to defend imperialist or paternalistic ends particularly on the part of westerners toward nonwesterners. "This universalist, non-relative aspect of the [Aristotelian] view needs further development, however, if it is to prove possible to answer the legitimate worries of those who have seen all too much paternalistic imposition of some people's ways upon others" (1995a: 5). Although Nussbaum applies the capability ethic in criticizing social practices that inhibit women's ability to live a fulfilling human life, she (like Aristotle) understands that the Aristotelian method is open-ended and incomplete as currently formulated.[36]

By studying the particulars of how people live, the Aristotelian approach should yield an account of human life that is recognizably similar to life as people live it. But Nussbaum emphasizes that the account is not merely descriptive. It is "internal to human history and strongly evaluative" (1990: 217, also 1995c). "Ethical inquiry, [Aristotle] insists, must be what we call 'value relative.' That is, they are not 'pure' inquiries conducted in a void; they are questions about living asked by communities of human beings who are actually engaged in living and valuing" (Nussbaum & Sen 1989: 310).[37] According to this approach, the study of a society is partially guided by what is familiar. "What *we* desire to find, what *we* feel we can live with, enters heavily into practical wisdom's weighing of the alternatives" (Nussbaum 1986a:

---

[36] To be more precise, when Nussbaum refers to the list as "open-ended," she has three meanings. In "Aristotelian Social Democracy" she outlines two ways in which the list is open-ended (1990: 219). First, the natural environment can change causing what is necessary for a fulfilling life to change. Second, those who reflect on the list may change their views; "[w]e also want to leave open the possibility that we will learn from our encounters with other human societies ... recognizing, perhaps, that some features we regarded as essential are actually more parochial than that" (1990: 219). In "Human Functioning" and "Human Capabilities" she specifies that the list, while generally descriptive of a fulfilling human life, requires "local specification" which will lead to "plural specification" of the list in practice (1992: 224 and 1995b: 94).

Compare her view of the list to Walzer's view of thick and thin morality: "Minimal morality consists in the rules of engagement that bind all the speakers; maximalism is the never-finished outcome of their arguments" (1994a: 12).

[37] Bernard Williams (1995) has criticized Nussbaum for her evaluative interpretation of Aristotle's methodology.

320, *emphasis added*), but according to Nussbaum, it is not the exclusive guide.[38] Rather, she argues, the Aristotelian "strategy is to take each extreme view seriously as a genuine part of the appearances – that is to say as motivated by something that is really there to be preserved and taken account of" (1986a: 320).[39] This is not to say that the right evaluation of the extreme views is a median view, but rather that one must understand what of actual value the extremist has taken to valuing extremely and why. It is likely that a more moderate version of that value is a virtuous view.

The problem with the method is that nothing requires "we" – those who are doing the inquiry – consider how *all* people live or find something that *others* can live with. Nussbaum and Aristotle say that "each" extreme or unfamiliar view is taken seriously. However, neither explicitly or implicitly indicates her or his intention to seek out *all* unfamiliar views and to take them seriously. Consequently, the inquiry is biased toward what is familiar to those doing the inquiry, be they the entire society or philosophers within it. (By contrast, according to the Third World feminist method, deliberative inquiry and skeptical scrutiny insure that critics always assume that there are views as yet unknown that may reveal a form of inequality and exclusion.)

Applying Nussbaum's Aristotelian method

The Aristotelian method can be accused of being both liberal and illiberal. First, with practical reason and independence so central to the design and execution of one's life plan, the list seems to embody specifically liberal values. Bernard Williams criticizes Nussbaum's project for combining Aristotle's method with her own liberal values and in so doing claiming her values are foundational for ethics (1995: 196).

---

[38] Nussbaum frequently refers to "we." Generally, I think she means to refer to herself with other people who recognize their lives as human (1995c: 117). In this case, I think she means "we" who share local traditions (1990: 218), "we" in my society (1995c: 104), or "we" who share my views (1995c: 106), but she could also mean the larger human "we."

Sometimes "we" means just herself (1988a: 146), herself and her audience (1988a: 154) or the audience of Aristotle (1995c: 108). The use of "we" tends to obscure the fact that some people will not observe what she claims "we" observe. Defining who is meant by "we" is important for developing a coherent and useful philosophy of social criticism. In this book, I use "we" to refer to myself and my audience, presumed to be wearing the hat of political theorist.

[39] In this particular passage, Nussbaum is discussing how a philosopher determines the role of fortune outside the control of the agent in *eudaimonia*. In general, the method is to study "problem areas" and "Aristotle asks, what would good functioning be with respect to that problem?" (1988a: 178).

Susan Wolf questions the inclusion of Freedom-from-individual-control and Freedom-from-social-control in Nussbaum's list (Wolf 1995). While recognizing their practical value for contemporary criticism of oppression of women and other groups deprived of freedom, Wolf argues "they appear to assume a superiority of individualism over communitarianism at a level of theory that is, at least, controversial" (1995: 110). Although Wolf recognizes that these capabilities are important grounds on which to change the circumstances of women and oppressed groups, she is concerned that these capabilities explicitly prioritize liberal over communitarian values. Given that liberal values are "at least, controversial," she questions whether these capabilities belong in the list. Nussbaum responds that the open-ended list should embody no culturally specific values, but rather only those recognized universally as *human*. Although Wolf reads Nussbaum's list to be reiterating western values of autonomy, the ability to be the author of one's own life (Aristotle's practical reason) is its underlying value. For example, practical reason allows a critic to respect an individual's choice in the practice of religion while allowing her to be critical of the ways in which those entrusted to interpret religious texts or the intent of a higher power may base their dictates not on the will of the higher power but on mistaken or fraudulent interpretations of that will. Further, if this list *does* embody specific cultural norms, Nussbaum would ask that we modify the list not abandon the approach.

The criticism of the approach's illiberal exclusions or biases by contrast does lead us to question the approach. In a response to "Nature, Function and Capability," David Charles argues that Aristotle clearly did not intend for all women, slaves, foreigners, and laborers to receive the same benefits of political life as citizens (1988). Nor were they able to contribute to political life comparably. Therefore, Aristotle describes an elitist, not an informed and inclusive, distributive model. Nussbaum responds that although Aristotle did not intend for all to be citizens, he did intend for all citizens to be able to live a characteristically human life. Although Nussbaum identifies the problem of Aristotle's biases in *The Fragility of Goodness*, she does not go on to extend her analysis to identify the flaw in the Aristotelian method that allows Aristotle's cultural bias to emerge (1986a). She does not recognize that similar biases can be imported into her social criticism through the capability ethic.

In order to defend the Aristotelian approach against the exclusionary critique, Nussbaum needs to explain why Aristotle's version of the method allowed him to exclude those whom he determined were deficient humans (slaves, artisans, and all classes of women) and what is different about her version is that it does not allow the same exclusions.[40] In her own examination of Aristotle's application of his method with regard to women and homosexuals, Nussbaum finds that he imports his own judgments. Aristotle describes as natural those characteristics of women and homosexuals that were culturally reinforced in his time. She blames the misapplication of his method on "the tremendous power of sexual convention and sexual prejudice in shaping a view of the world" (1986a: 371). By my reading, however, that is not a mistaken use of the methodology. The assignment was "to find out what we deeply believe to be most important and indispensable." If certain conventions have "tremendous power," isn't it also true that they are part of what "we" deeply believe? Nussbaum's argument furthers her criticism of Aristotle's application of his method, but goes no further toward restoring confidence in the method. "Aristotle's own treatment of women and barbarians does not inspire confidence. We had better anticipate such abuses and guard against them" (1988a: 173).[41] However, Nussbaum does not offer a methodological "guard against them," but rather merely treats them as evidence of Aristotle's "defects as a collector of appearances" (1986a: 371). She acknowledges that the "father" of the capability ethic, Aristotle, "did deny women full membership in human functioning as [he] understood the notion" (1995b: 96). Nussbaum recognizes this flaw in Aristotle's execution, but she does not interpret this severe executional flaw as an indication that there is a severe methodological flaw. On what basis can the theorist be confident that Nussbaum's application does not have flaws that are different, perhaps more acceptable to a like-minded reader, but no less worrisome from the perspective of one concerned about the method in the hands of one less like-minded?

Her defense of the Aristotelian method rests on the assertion that Aristotle is mistaken and that such mistakes eventually get overturned. She claims that no people can deny the humanness of all those with whom they live without occasional "breakthroughs" of recognizing their humanness (1995b: 96). The argument seems to be that *eventually* in a society all people have to recognize their common humanity.[42] For evidence, she cites occasional "breakthroughs" such as Musonius Rufus's treatises from the first century AD on children's education, infanticide, marriage, and "That Women Should Do Philosophy" (1995b: 97). And she cites occasional "breakthroughs" by German

---

[40] Williams doubts that such a method can work (1995: 201–202).

[41] See also Nussbaum (1988a: 165–166, 1990: 239–240, and 1986a: chapter 8, 370–371, and fn. 51).

[42] Again, I am reminded of Keynes; see chapter 2.

citizens or citizens of Nazi-occupied territories against the "Nazi device of categorizing Jews as animals or inanimate objects" (1995b: 97).

Her defense is inadequate. History has counter-examples of groups' ongoing oppression at the hands of people in power who deny the full humanity of the oppressed. What Nussbaum has described as a "breakthrough" might better be described as deviant or aberrant behavior. Occasional aberrance does not bring about social change. The male-centered courses of western philosophy and political practice were not changed by occasional texts such as Musonius's. Nazism was not brought down by aberrant acts of sympathy and compassion for Jews as human beings. Looking at US history, breakthroughs such as the Emancipation Proclamation and the Civil Rights Act were part of significant challenges to discrimination, but they did not functionally eliminate discrimination against blacks and other minorities.[43] Discrimination, hatred, and racism still prevent many from recognizing their common humanity. Nussbaum's faith in a human tendency to recognize a common humanity, while attractive, is an insufficient defense of the Aristotelian methodology.

Aristotle's method is flawed because it allows him to import into his definition of essential human life judgments which are specific to the culture of leisured men of his time. Similarly, Nussbaum's method is flawed because it allows her to import into her definition of an essential human life the liberal values of autonomy and independence that may be more culturally specific than she treats them. The problem with the capability ethic is not that Nussbaum's list embodies liberal values, but rather that Aristotle's method allows her to. Though a universal list of guiding criteria is an important aspect of a critical methodology, Nussbaum's use of it is not.

Guiding criteria are integral to a critical methodology, but they do not constitute a critical method. Even if it were possible for there to be general agreement on the features of a fulfilling human life, and even if people the world over could follow good arguments to endorsing a list such as Nussbaum's, considerable disagreement about how to actualize the list in a given society would remain. One basis of disagreement is that the demands of the aspects of the list may conflict (1990: 225). When elements of the list suggest conflicting policies, people may disagree as to how best to solve the conflict or an individual may be internally torn about how to solve it (as Creon was conflicted, to use Nussbaum's own example, 1986a: 353). Further, in a pluralist society

---

[43] Susan Wolf in her commentary on "Human Capabilities" similarly recognizes the problem Nussbaum's approach faces in the real world (1995).

people will disagree also about how best to promote the capabilities of all because interest groups stand to gain from one method over another.

Either in the interpretation of the local understanding of the list or in identifying appropriate local means for promoting the list, someone can be mistaken. An example of this is in Nussbaum's repeated use of an adult literacy program as a model of how external critics can promote programs that develop basic capabilities. Based on *A Quiet Revolution*, Martha Chen's description of a literacy program started by the Bangladesh Rural Advancement Committee (BRAC), Nussbaum describes how development practitioners should make use of the list in social criticism and development programming.[44] According to Nussbaum, the BRAC workers who believed that literacy was essential to a woman's economic flourishing, autonomy, and self-respect sought to promote literacy among adult women in rural Bangladesh. After an initial failure of the program, the professionals worked with the women to give them a better sense of the value of literacy to their own lives. The workers did so in a cooperative way, learning about the women's lives and about the ways in which literacy might be useful to them.

Nussbaum inaccurately assesses the initial failure and the subsequent success of the program. She argues it initially failed because the village women, unfamiliar with the practice of educating poor women, did not appreciate the value of women's education. She argues the program was ultimately successful due to a dialogue between the BRAC workers and the village women in which the workers taught the women that literacy is valuable to them just as it is to women of other cultures because it enables their "economic flourishing, autonomy and self-respect" (1993a: 258).

Nussbaum's judgments are not, as she argued with Sen they should be, "made from the point of view of experienced immersion in the way of life of a culture" (Nussbaum & Sen 1989: 308). Instead they are largely based on her understanding of the capabilities list and her reading of Chen's analysis of BRAC's literacy program. Nussbaum oversimplifies the problems of illiteracy in Bangladesh. In her explanation of low female adult illiteracy, she puts too much emphasis on the women's lack of appreciation for the value of education (particularly the

---

[44] Nussbaum cites *A Quiet Revolution*, Martha Chen's description of a literacy program started by the Bangladesh Rural Advancement Committee (BRAC) (Chen 1983) (Nussbaum 1990: 215–16, 236–7; 1992: 225, 235–7, 240; 1993a: 258–9; 1995b: 91). BRAC is a development organization founded by a Bangladeshi businessman in February 1972 to provide relief and reconstruction to war-torn rural Bangladesh after its separation from Pakistan. From its beginning in Sulla, Sunamganj in Northeast Bangladesh, BRAC had grown to be the largest national nongovernment organization in the world in 1993.

education of women). The village women, Nussbaum believes, "may not even know what it means to have the advantages of education" (1995b: 91). Without having spoken to the particular women in the BRAC study that Nussbaum cites, but having spoken with over 800 rural Bangladeshi women, a third of whom had been involved in BRAC programs, I am confident that adult rural Bangladeshi women are aware of the value of education, generally, but consider their own education irrelevant now that they have children (and most adult women have children). In rural Bangladesh, land and education are the two broadly recognized sources of future income. Both are expensive. Children need school supplies and outside tutoring to be able to pass from grade to grade.[45] Bangladeshis see the education of their children as one of the best investments they can make for their children and for their own well-being, but it is an expensive investment.

While adult literacy is up from 24% in 1970 to 37% in 1993, it is still at the low end of all least developed countries and the lowest of its neighbors in the region (except Nepal). Illiteracy is a national problem that affects women disproportionately; compare 25% female adult literacy to 48% male adult literacy. Adult illiteracy is a function of inadequate education, not merely unequal education of men and women. Inadequate education in Bangladesh is a function of economic and social circumstances that affect the entire population, but affect women disproportionately. Because daughters are married off and are not expected to earn income for their natal family, when poor families can educate only one child, they frequently do not invest in the education of their girl-children.[46]

When wearing the hat of social critic, Nussbaum's method allows her to import her own values into her analysis of practices unfamiliar to her by inadvertently attributing to the essential list characteristics that are familiar to her through her own society's means of promoting the basic capabilities. In this case, she thinks that literacy promotes women's economic flourishing, autonomy, and self-respect (as did the BRAC workers) and thus enables women to have the same functional capabilities as their husbands and brothers (1993a: 258). However, "economic

---

[45] School teachers work part time as tutors to augment their income. In many places outside tutoring is necessary for students to cover the material necessary to advance grades.

[46] Statistics from *Human Development Report* 1996. Another practice that demonstrates the investment philosophy of poor parents is that those who are better off and can afford to educate one child educate the eldest son. He can then go to Dhaka or abroad, earn a salary, and bring his younger siblings or cousins to join him and be educated. In the process, the education of elder female siblings may be sacrificed, but younger female siblings may benefit. This is not a strategy available to those who are the poorer of the poor like the village women in the BRAC groups.

flourishing, autonomy and self-respect" have significantly different meanings (or are the wrong means to achieving full human functional capabilities) in the context of poor rural Bangladesh. If the local context were understood properly, the programmatic implications would be different from those identified by Nussbaum and the BRAC literacy project.

Although Nussbaum should not be expected to anticipate programmatic changes, the changes in BRAC programming reveal a flaw in Nussbaum's methodology. Since the study Nussbaum cites, the adult literacy program has been phased out of most BRAC branches. Credit for women, maternal and child health care, and nonformal primary education for girls are now the cornerstones of BRAC programming (BRAC 1992: 10). The village women and BRAC found credit to be a more effective means of promoting the economic stability of the poor and women's empowerment, women's health programming to be a better way to ensure that women live beyond their child bearing years, and getting girls started in school early to be a better way to promote female literacy.[47] The changes in program design were in part a function of an increase in Participatory Rural Appraisal as a means for planning development programs and changes in the focus of national NGOs and international funding sources on credit for poor women. The shift in development strategy reflects a growing belief that with increased economic means, women will better attend to the basic needs of their children, including the education of their daughters.[48] Interestingly enough, with credit and education for children has come increased demand for adult education. In 1995, BRAC started three adult literacy centers on an experimental basis in three villages in Manikganjas. In 1996 there were 63 centers. Each center has 25 adult students and one teacher. The adult students enrolled in a ten month long course which meets for two hours a day, six days a week and covers a curriculum of Bangla and Arithmetic principally. The course is complemented with two month-long sessions on health, nutrition, legal and social issues which are intended to help students retain their literacy skills by using them in addressing life-important issues. All centers have been opened in credit program areas and more than 50 percent of the adult students are borrowers.[49]

[47] The concept of empowerment has many meanings even within BRAC, but it is one of BRAC's two stated objectives: alleviation of poverty and empowerment of the poor (BRAC 1992: 9).

[48] The experience of SEWA is that once women have economic security and some autonomous control over family resources, they value literacy more (Selliah 1989: 21).

[49] The descriptions of changes in BRAC programming since 1993 are based on research by Mahmuda Rahman Khan.

Given the economic stress of rural Bangladeshi families, economic stability is an important component of economic flourishing. A credit program for women is potentially a more effective tool for extending economic stability to women and men equally (Ackerly 1995 and 1997). Similarly, interdependence is more desirable to Bangladeshi men and women than autonomy. For Nussbaum, autonomy means decreasing women's dependence on their husbands, but for Bangladeshi women, a more effective route to a valued quality of life is increasing husbands' dependence on their wives. Credit may also decrease women's dependence on their husbands; however, given the complexity of social and familial hierarchy reinforced through a broad range of practices, designing a program that does both is very difficult. Note, this is not a matter of semantics. In the economic and social context of rural Bangladesh, increasing a man's dependence on his wife does not increase that woman's independence from her husband. By giving access to credit only to women, credit organizations increase the dependence of poor men on their wives. Husbands have an economic incentive to encourage their wives' participation in the credit program. Women's increased earning potential increases their respect within the family and the income improves the family's well-being. Even considering the potential for men to appropriate their wives' credit, leaving the woman with a liability that provides her husband a resource, a credit program is more effective at achieving economic stability and interdependence than adult literacy.[50]

Nussbaum's specific criticisms of Bangladeshi practices and her recommendations do not reflect an adequate assessment of Bangladeshi circumstances and the problems related to the inequalities in the quality of life between Bangladeshi men and women. Therefore, Nussbaum inaccurately interprets the failure and success of the BRAC literacy program. As she has applied it, the Aristotelian method does not identify appropriate solutions. Nussbaum may argue that this demonstrates that she, like Aristotle, is capable of making errors in the application of the Aristotelian method, but that the method itself is not flawed. To the contrary, this example reveals a methodological flaw in Nussbaum's framework of social criticism that allows a critic to ignore the particularities of a society. While the idea of a list of human capabilities that is universally, though differently, recognized across cultural contexts is

---

[50] The problems of credit programs are beyond the scope of this comparison of adult literacy and credit programs. For favorable analysis of credit programs in Bangladesh see Syed Hashemi, Sidney Ruth Schuler, and Ann P. Riley (1996). For critical attention to the effects of borrowing on women see Ackerly (1995, 1997) and Anne Marie Goetz and Rina Sen Gupta (1996).

constructive for Third World feminism, the Aristotelian method Nussbaum uses to apply the list is not because of its exclusionary potential. Third World feminist social criticism is an alternative methodology that requires critics to listen to many critical views and to hear all of the silent voices and thus achieves a significant innovation over Nussbaum's capability ethic.

Reconciling relativism and essentialism in Third World feminist critical practice

Both Walzer and Nussbaum offer methods of social criticism, but these are too limited. Even if we consider Walzer's opposition to oppression as an important aspect of interpretation as social criticism (about which he is not as explicit as he is about life and liberty), it is a method of social criticism that lacks substantive guidelines or the means of its own assessment to avoid being inappropriately uncritical of accepted but oppressive values, practices, and norms. Nussbaum offers a list of guiding criteria but as a method of social criticism her list lacks the means of its interpretation in specific circumstances or its own evaluation to avoid importing the critic's values, be they liberal, exclusionary, or otherwise biased. The Third World feminist method, which employs skeptical scrutiny, guiding criteria, and deliberative inquiry, can be broadly critical and self-critical and thus provides a more effective model of social criticism.

Relativism urges us to recognize that different and multiple perspectives exist and it instructs philosophers, potential critics, and societies to consult that diversity in drafting social criticism. Some might argue that relativist critics *cannot* criticize a society that does not hold the value of relativism for not respecting diversity within its own or other cultures. Does the relativist perspective allow anyone to criticize a society that does not believe in relativism and rather believes in its obligation to impose a certain set of values on its own people and other peoples of the world? The version of relativist criticism I describe does. Third World feminist social criticism is *more* relativist than Walzer's social criticism as interpretation in that it encourages people to recognize diversity even if they are from a culture that does not and in that it asks critics to draw out that diversity.

Essentialism discourages relativism's uncritical embrace of cultural diversity. Nussbaum improves upon essentialism by suggesting that the criteria used to assess the values, practices, and norms of a society can be universal and not merely embody the critic's values or those of his society. However, Nussbaum's account of the Aristotelian method does not tell theorists or social critics how to avoid mistakenly doing so in our construction of a theory of social criticism and in its practical implementation. Third World feminist social criticism does. Third World feminist social criticism offers a method that uses guiding criteria but that subjects those criteria to skeptical scrutiny and deliberative discussion such that the criteria do not embody a narrow set of values. The inclusively meaningful list is used as a guide for critics' assessments of those values, practices, and norms identified through skeptical scrutiny and in the deliberations of those assessments.

Because it requires local interpretation, alone, the list is not an adequate critical methodology. Deliberative inquiry is necessary to help the critic interpret the list for a local context and to help society set priorities in its decision making. Skeptical scrutiny is necessary for assuring that the local interpretation of the list does not perpetuate or exacerbate existing inequalities, but rather undermines them. A complement to the other aspects of the methodology, the guiding criteria identify specific obstacles to certain of society's members' abilities to live a life they find fulfilling. The list provides a guideline (1) for criticizing certain values, practices, and norms and (2) for resolving conflicts between competing claims to oppression (that deliberative inquiry and skeptical scrutiny bring up for evaluation). I will propose a list and then show how it or a modification of it can be used to criticize values and resolve competing values.

In practice, critics have used guiding criteria that range from local and specific to universal and general. For example, the Bangladeshi and SEWA women articulate *local* and *specific* guiding criteria for social criticism and activism. The Bangladeshi women want not to be beaten by their husbands and they want to be able to send their daughters to school. They assert a right to equal consideration of their views by going collectively to two husbands' houses to make the wives' views heard. Similarly, the SEWA women assert a right to fair wages by collectively striking and negotiating with the employers. Further, the SEWA women identify other needs they have and either develop ways to provide them for themselves, or lobby the government and funding organizations for support. Both the Bangladeshi and SEWA women look to their own needs to identify their criteria for criticism and action.

Other feminists have tried to articulate women's demands in the form of *universal* and *specific* criteria for social decision making. The list provided by Martha Nussbaum, particularly its 1992 version, is such a universal and specific list.[51] It suggests that in all contexts of human life,

---

[51] The modifications included in her 1995 version make the list less universal (1995b).

people require the specific basic functional capabilities in order to live a life worthy of being called human. Other examples of universal and specific lists are those advocated by feminist human rights activists (to whom I turn in chapter 4) and made formal internationally in the Convention on the Elimination of All Forms of Discrimination Against Women (1979) and other UN documents. Women activists around the world have demanded that the violations of women's human rights be recognized and addressed by international and national policy.[52] International work formally led by the United Nations has yielded other universal and specific lists adopted by the UN General Assembly and ratified by many member states. These include the Universal Declaration of Human Rights (1948), the International Covenant on Civil and Political Rights (1966), and the UN Convention on the Rights of the Child (1989).

On a broader level, the scholars and activist networks I describe in chapter 5, Patricia Hill Collins, Women Living Under Muslim Laws (WLUML), and Development Alternatives for Women in a New Era (DAWN), articulate *universal* and *general* lists based on local needs and observations. Collins looks to the lives and writings of black women to identify their needs and interests. However, she articulates them in general terms as the freedom to draft their own politics of race, sex, and ideology and she does not define the specific criteria necessary for women to be able to draft such policies. On a still broader level, WLUML promotes a more generalized set of values that are a synthesis of those held by women living under Muslim laws around the world. They are that women have basic rights that the law, economy, and social practices should reinforce and that women are human beings of equal value with men. Riffat Hassan argues that women's inferior status in Muslim society is erroneously theologically defended, instead "according to the Qur'an, Allah created woman and man equal" (1991: 80). Hassan gives a thorough reading of Qur'anic and Hadith literatures to document her claim. Fatima Mernissi, in "Arab Women's Rights and the Muslim State in the Twenty-first Century," concurs (1995). Nazīrah Zein Ed-Dīn similarly appeals to Qur'anic texts and in addition historical accounts of pre-Islamic customs to demonstrate that the teachings of the Qur'an were improvements on the conditions of women (1982 [1928]). DAWN similarly endorses a universal and general set of values. As Sen & Grown write on behalf of the DAWN coalition,

[52] See Charlotte Bunch (1990) for an example, Elisabeth Friedman for a history (1995), and Saba Bahar for a critique of Amnesty International's review of women's human rights (1996).

beneath this diversity, feminism has as its unshakable core a commitment to breaking down the structures of gender subordination and a vision for women as full and equal participants with men at all levels of societal life. (1987: 70)

In dialogue with women working on local concerns, Collins, WLUML, and DAWN articulate universal and general standards for social criticism which address the specific local concerns of those who inform their work.

The universal and specific list I propose functions as criteria for social criticism intended to work together with deliberative inquiry and skeptical scrutiny as a cohesive method of social criticism. The list corresponds to a list of rights in international law in that it is meant to guide the design and reform of familial, social, economic, and political institutions. However, though informed by existing universal declarations in international law, in its language, form, and content, it does not follow a legal (or specifically an anti-discrimination) paradigm. Not unlike Nussbaum's list and consistent with Sen's account of capabilities as actual freedoms, this list is a set of criteria of what a human being born into this world should be able to choose to do in order to live a life worthy of being described as human and which the liver would describe as fulfilling. Just as skeptical scrutiny of coercive and potentially exploitative institutions leads the critic to defend freedom from oppression, exploitation, coercion, and discrimination, this universal and specific list of guiding criteria defends one's freedom to live a certain quality of life.

My argument here is that *a* list of guiding criteria is an important aspect of the critic's methodology. But not all lists are equally effective. My version is a work in progress offered in the spirit of continued dialogue about what it means to live a fulfilling human life. As we think about the content of the list, we wear philosophers' hats and use our collected understanding to modify it.[53] Nussbaum provides the skeleton for the list. Although her list embodies liberal assumptions about the value of individual autonomy, the list she proposes reflects significant thought about the basic requirements of a human being that is based in part on dialogues with philosophers and economists from around the world (1992 and 1995b). Consequently, her list is a good starting point. In addition, I incorporate universalizations of the local claims of some feminists (such as the Bangladeshi and SEWA women), and specifications based on the general claims of other feminists (such as WLUML and DAWN). I derive some elements of my proposed list from the collected knowledge implicit in multiple sources. These include the

---

[53] When someone uses the list as part of the method of social criticism, she wears the hat of social critic.

Universal Declaration of Human Rights (1948), the International Covenant on Civil and Political Rights (1966), the Convention on the Elimination of All Forms of Discrimination Against Women (1979), the UN Convention on the Rights of the Child (1989), and *The Global Vision Statement* compiled by Global Co-operation for a Better World, an organization that brought together representatives of the world's religions (1990). In addition, Susan Wolf (1995) and contributors to *The Quality of Life*, in particular Erik Allardt, Robert Erikson, and Paul Seabright have helped me develop my thinking about the list (1993). I derive certain elements from the criteria implicitly or explicitly articulated by feminists through their activism. Most of the contents of the list are affirmed by more than one of these sources.

Each person in the world should have the capacity to choose:

1. **Life** – to live a healthy life not cut short by accident, premature death, violence, or deprivation of basic needs (including food, drink, and shelter),[54]
2. **Painless** – to be reasonably free from physical pain,[55]
3. **Parents** – to know her name, nationality, and as far as is possible, her parents,[56]
4. **Security** – to feel secure that her needs will be provided for, that her interests will be represented in her youth and (when necessary) in infirmity, and that with reasonable effort she will continue to be able to live a life she finds fulfilling throughout her maturity,
5. **Community-Life** – to grow up and live in community with others,
6. **Trust** – to feel secure in her family, in her work place, and in her community and to trust the state, military, and police,[57]

---

[54] These are basically the same as Nussbaum's Life and Satisfaction criteria. She also includes opportunities for sexual satisfaction, control over one's own reproduction, and mobility in her list of basic human needs though she recognizes that these are less essential than those I mention (1995b: 77). Henry Shue argues that physical security and subsistence are basic human rights (1980). In application, while recognizing that a human life is not fulfilling if cut short, a society would likely prioritize cracking down on drunk drivers or implementing safety standards in industry over protecting people from their own carelessness.

[55] Less encompassing than Nussbaum's Comfort.

[56] Children may be adopted or cared for by legal guardians who are not their parents. Articles 7 through 12 of the UN Convention on the Rights of the Child (1989) assert that an identity including a name, nationality, and family relations are a child's fundamental rights.

[57] The aspects of this capability associated with liberal freedoms of association and unwarranted intrusion by the state are included in Nussbaum's Freedom-from-social-control.

7. **Participation** – to participate freely, fully, and equally in the full range of community life, including its familial, social, economic and political decision making,

8. **Resources** – to share in familial, social, economic, and political resources,

9. **Interdependence** – to develop relations of interdependence with others, to influence and to be influenced by others, to love and to be loved, to sympathize and to be sympathized with, to place demands on others and to feel obligations, to rely on others and to feel trusted, to value and be valued by others, to be generous and to accept generosity, and to be able to trust that her relationships of interdependence will continue over time,[58]

10. **Thinking** – to imagine, to reason and to plan, to exercise her senses, to form her own conception of the good, facilitated by education, access to information, and educative deliberation,[59]

11. **Planning** – to engage in critical reflection about the planning of her life, including the labor by which she supports herself, the management of labor and family obligations, owning and disposing of property, and entering or not entering a life partnership or marriage,[60]

12. **Doing** – to shape her own life in accordance with her own thoughts, plans, aspirations, and personal development objectives,

13. **Community-Integrity** – to be a part of a community which has the capability of self-determination regarding values, practices, and norms that are consistent with the individual capabilities of its members and those of other societies,[61]

---

[58] This criterion is different from a provision for autonomy. It is a capacity for autonomous critical thought combined with the recognition that critical thought is a collective project. Interdependence as I define it is more encompassing than Nussbaum's Attachments and Affiliation. Interdependence need not mean reciprocal relations. By putting interdependence on the list, I mean to capture both the communitarians' and postmodernists' recognition of human experience as collective experience, and the recognition by many liberals that preferences are not exogenously set but rather are formed and transformed through interaction with others.

[59] My account of Thinking combines aspects of Nussbaum's Use-of-mind-and-senses and Freedom-from-individual-control without denying the importance of Interdependence.

[60] My account of Planning combines aspects of Nussbaum's Practical-reason and Freedom-from-individual-control without denying the importance of Interdependence. According to Aristotle, a human life is a life that has things (nutrition, growth, and perception) in common with living plants and animals but it is a *human* life because it is organized by and around practical reason (*Nicomachean Ethics* 1097b25–1098a19).

[61] Community-Life and Community-Integrity are intended to reflect communitarian values.

14. **Spirituality** – to use religion and spirituality to fulfill her moral, ethical, and spiritual needs in ways that are consistent with her own capabilities and those of others,[62]
15. **Fun** – to make time for fun,[63] and
16. **Fellowship** – to live in fellowship with animals and nature.[64]

The list includes the needs of adults and children everywhere without excluding the needs of adults and children anywhere. In addition, the list includes competing criteria. For example, the need for authority over one's own life in Thinking, Planning, and Doing might compete with the need for Community-Life. As a result, the list can potentially be the basis for competing claims. However, the other components of the social critic's method – deliberative inquiry and skeptical scrutiny – are used to specify, interpret, and prioritize the list and to resolve competing claims for a given local context.

These criteria help direct the criticism of values, practices, and norms and adjudicate the competing claims to oppression that arise in practice. For example, from 1994 to 1998 the Taliban – Islamic fundamentalist students trained in refugee camps in Pakistan – rose to power in Afghanistan. In a country where factional fighting deprived many people of many of their essential capabilities, the order brought by the Taliban was partially welcome. The Taliban's strict ethical code ended the common practice of kidnapping and raping women that had been a legacy of the preceding struggle for power. However, the Taliban code has also meant closing girls' schools (and not allowing home schooling) and preventing women from going to work. So, though women's security has increased in one sense, the fulfillment of other capabilities is denied to the extent of constituting human rights violations (Rasekh et al. 1998). These are primarily health-related as women are not allowed to seek medical attention without a male escort. Women are not allowed to work so their ability to provide for themselves and their families and to meet their basic needs is curtailed. Women health workers have been allowed to go back to work. In Kabul since Taliban rule began women's employment has dropped from 62% of women to 20% of

---

[62] Spirituality affirms freedom of religion and conscience but is constrained in practice by respect for one's own capabilities and those of others. In other words one's capability for spiritual fulfillment should not be defended if it requires the denial of other capabilities for oneself or others.

[63] My account of Fun is similar to that of Nussbaum's account of Recreation.

[64] My account of Fellowship is similar to that of Nussbaum's account of Fellowship-with-nature.

women (Rasekh et al. 1998). Due to eighteen years of fighting, women had made up 70% of the work force and war widows, who have no alternative source of income, and their families, suffer severely from loss of income (Wali 1997). Although the Taliban originally asserted that when their power was secure and the risk of violence less they would lift some of the restrictions on women's mobility (Gannon 1996), in Kandahar 200 miles to the south of Kabul where the Taliban have had control since 1994 girls aged four to eight only are allowed only Qur'anic instruction and in Herat 300 miles to the west of Kabul which the Taliban have held since 1995 all girls' schools are closed (Selsky 1996).

The criteria guide Third World feminist social critics' inquiry about competing claims to oppression. Were the Afghanis oppressed by the post-colonial imperialism of the USSR or by their Afghani leaders after the Russian withdrawal? Are the Afghanis oppressed by the Taliban? According to human rights reports, the Afghanis have gained security from lawlessness at the cost of the loss of many other capabilities. In the Kabul study, women report a decline in mental and physical health due to both the trauma of war and the restrictions imposed by the Taliban. Eighty-four percent have lost one or more family members in war. Sixty-nine percent report that they or a family member have been detained or abused by the Taliban. For Afghanis who are not Taliban, Taliban rule has not secured the ability to participate in creating the rules that govern their lives. By prohibiting most women from working, Taliban rule has undermined women's ability to share in the community's economic resources, to plan their life, and to provide for their families. For girls denied education, Taliban rule has inhibited the ability to develop their thinking. For Afghanis, Taliban rule has denied them an ability to be part of a self-determining community; instead community values are determined and enforced by the Taliban. For Afghanis who are not Taliban, Taliban rule has created insecurity about life prospects. For Afghanis who are not Taliban, Taliban edicts have denied them the ability to make choices about their own spirituality. According to Laila al-Marayati, the Taliban form of Islam is perceived as foreign by most Afghanis (1998).

Drawing on Rasekh et al. and al-Marayati, I have made a cursory assessment of the effect of Taliban rule on the capabilities of the members of society. Given these observations, there is *no question* that the Taliban's practices and their impact on the Afghani people's ability to live lives they find fulfilling should be the subject of analysis and discussion by social critics. Other critics drawing on other sources could enhance this understanding of the Taliban-enforced practices. Certainly, proposals as to how best, and following what priorities, to restore the capabilities of the population will have to be derived from informed and inclusive deliberations drawing on the knowledge of many critics. The list provides a guideline for these assessments.

Although the list guides critics' assessments, during the process of using the list, the critic may also reconsider the list. For example, thinking about the Taliban, Afghani people, and the history of Afghanistan suggests that we might consider adding to the account of "Trust" a trust that other nations will not threaten the sovereignty of one's own nation or that one's government will be able to protect one's state. The criteria themselves can be the subject of deliberation even as they guide social criticism.

Although the Taliban have brought the prospect of security and stability necessary for economic development that the previous power struggle could not secure, the costs have been denial of other capabilities and explicit denial of women's capabilities. In order to assess the trade-offs, critics need to promote deliberative inquiry among the people affected by the change in Afghan rule. Those consulted should be the Taliban, those sympathetic to the Taliban, those who reject the Taliban's form of Islam as being foreign to the Afghan practice of Islam, non-Muslim minority populations, and (though it should not need to be said separately) the women of all these groups. In their study of women's health and human rights in Afghanistan, Zohra Rasekh, Heidi Bauer, Michele Manos, and Vincent Iacopino report that almost 96% of women who have lived in Kabul, the capital, for at least 19 years support women's human rights (1998). Except for the relativist who wishes to ignore the wishes of Afghani women or to deny their authenticity, the guiding criteria lead to a clear understanding that the Taliban values, practices, and norms are being accepted by some and forced on others. Except for the essentialist who wishes to ignore the appropriateness of local knowledge for assessing the Taliban values, practices, and norms, the guiding criteria provide a basis for discussions about setting priorities and appropriate means for changing them. Given Afghan history, part of the internal discussions will probably include to what extent and in what form locals would like to ask for outside help in securing their capabilities.

The criteria give the critical method specific guidelines for assessing the local values, practices, and norms that skeptical scrutiny helped the critic identify as harmful. Different critics with different sources of information will probably have different interpretations of whether individual practices violate or protect individual capabilities on the list.

Therefore, the critics promote deliberative inquiry about a society's values, practices, and norms such that strategically appropriate changes can be discussed. As part of the feminist methodology, the guiding criteria are not essentialist but they lead to social criticism that respects the essential personhood of everyone.

Conclusion

Anti-relativist and anti-essentialist social critics can potentially create a standstill over whether a given practice should be subject to social criticism. Third World feminist social criticism rejects that standstill and asserts that both anti-relativist and anti-essentialist critical perspectives should contribute to social criticism. The Third World feminist methodology of social criticism described in this chapter identifies the tools that enable social criticism to be respectful of diversity and yet offer substantive social criticism. Skeptical scrutiny, guiding criteria, and deliberative inquiry are foundational to such social criticism. As we saw in chapter 2, deliberation without attention to the inequality in ability to influence deliberations is not an adequate basis for social decision making. And as we saw in this chapter, neither skeptical scrutiny alone nor guiding criteria alone (however, universal or locally accurate) can be an adequate basis for social criticism. Where general discussion, concern over possible oppression, or perceived shortcomings against the guiding criteria lead critics to question given or proposed values, practices, and norms, critics need to employ all three tools in their analysis to avoid being only essentialist or only relativist. Where these tools lead them to criticize certain values, practices, and norms, critics cannot leave them unexamined. Confidence in the methodology's ability to articulate sensitive and substantive criticism comes from its successful use. For some a particular application may seem too relativist, for others a particular application may seem too essentialist, but together these divergent arguments provoke deliberation that will likely yield better informed and inclusive ideas.

Given the scope of questions uncovered by this methodology of social criticism, Third World feminist social criticism must be a social process. Thus, the Third World feminist method has implications for critics' roles and qualifications. In order to scrutinize all values, practices, and norms, in order to have social discussions about critical values, Third World feminist social critics do more than assess values, practices, and norms. They help other critics and societies join in the critical process with roles such as research and promoting inquiry, arranging deliberative opportunities, and facilitating or initiating institutional change. Any single critic's analyses and actions are insufficient. Inclusive social criticism requires multiple critics working with wide-ranging skills and qualifications. In the next chapter, I give a more thorough account of critics' roles and in the following of their qualifications.

4   Roles: social criticism and self-criticism

Introduction

The women activists in the preceding chapters are social critics using the Third World feminist critical methodology in a wide range of applications. The researcher in the anecdote from Bangladesh and the SEWA organizers inquired about the condition of women; Save the Children and SEWA hosted opportunities for deliberation among women who previously lacked such opportunity; SEWA and GAD scholars (in particular those documenting women's activism) represent those whose criticism is otherwise offstage and do so in order to promote institutional change including the institutional change necessary for the represented to be able to speak for themselves. Individually, each of these social critics' efforts to influence social change is significant; however, in combination, they are even more conducive to promoting informed, collective, and uncoerced social criticism. Through their own inquiry and provoking the inquiry of others, Third World feminist social critics foster better and more broadly informed deliberation. By promoting opportunities for deliberation they create occasions for deliberative inquiry and exchange thereby fostering public decision making that is more inclusive. By promoting institutional change they undermine the influence of existing power structures on social decision making. Given the scope of social criticism – all values, practices, and norms, including those of the critical enterprise itself – there is a necessarily broad range of the roles of social critics. Collectively, critics filling this range of roles promote more informed, collective, and uncoerced social change. However, individually or in groups social critics can themselves reinforce hierarchies.[1] Although in theory all of

[1] For example, using the exclusive language of academia, academic social critics can reinforce academic elitism even while challenging other hierarchies. See the theoretically interesting essays in Nussbaum & Sen's edited volume, *The Quality of Life* (1993), and Nussbaum & Glover's edited volume, *Women, Culture, and Development: A Study of Human Capabilities* (1995) that are inaccessible to most development practitioners and certainly to their target groups.

the roles of Third World feminist social critics are of equal and complementary value to social critics, in the real world, certain people because of who they are, where they are from, and how they speak are given more attention by their audiences and other critics.[2]

In this chapter after drawing on the examples of Third World feminist social critics and the work of deliberative democratic theorists to provide a description of the critics' many roles, I illustrate some problems with Third World feminist social criticism using the example of the women's human rights movement. The women's human rights movement demonstrates a range of critics' roles, multiple and various critics working together, and the impact that Third World feminist social criticism can have on making social values, practices, and norms more informed and inclusive. The example of the women's human rights movement also gives us an opportunity to look at the limitations of Third World feminist social criticism and its means for addressing its own shortcomings.

Third World feminist critics are not demigods. They participate in the world they criticize. Although they may not be successful at bringing about revolutionary change through a particular effort, each effort makes some progress at least in the form of increased awareness among some but not all of the participants. Regardless of their measured success, if they are promoting increasingly informed and inclusive deliberations, broadening the knowledge of their audiences, or creating institutions that enable greater deliberation and knowledge, then they are practicing Third World feminist social criticism.

My account of Third World feminist social criticism is a description of an existing practice of social criticism and a prescription for political theory (including feminist political theory), but it is not a prescription for successful social change. Successful social change depends on a broad range of conditions determined by the familial, social, political, and economic context of the criticism and activism. As a practice, Third World feminist social criticism must be concerned about the inclusiveness of the deliberations it promotes. As a complement to political theory, Third World feminist social criticism must promote theory that is broadly informed. Thus, as a practice and in its theoretical implications, Third World feminist social criticism is self-critical. Examining the women's human rights movement allows us to look at the range of social critics' roles including the essential role of directing critical attention to the critics' efforts and shortcomings.

---

[2] In chapter 2, I discussed Sanders (1997) and Tully (1995) who describe the problem of unequal command for attention in deliberative fora as a problem for deliberative democratic theory. It is a problem for all discursive practices, including social criticism.

Critics' roles

As demonstrated by the examples of SEWA and other Third World women activists, critics play important roles in bringing about valuable learning by promoting inquiry, deliberative opportunities, and institutional change. In order to increase community knowledge, social critics facilitate inquiry so that deliberation is maximally informational. Similarly, social critics promote deliberation so that people develop the skills of understanding and anticipating each other's reactions, of learning and cooperating, and of critical thinking and collective problem-solving. Finally, social critics facilitate institutional change, in order to facilitate inquiry, promote deliberation, and enable informed, collective, and uncoerced participation of all those in a society who are affected by its institutions. Where deliberative fora are imperfect due to lack of participants' self-respect, equal and mutual respect, equal opportunity to influence outcomes, and agreed-upon accepted modes of deliberation, social critics must promote society's self-examination. By fulfilling these roles, individual critics encourage other critics and society to listen to the silent voices.

According to the Third World feminist model of social criticism, the critic is a facilitator of society's self-examination. This includes examination of the critical process itself. Third World feminist social critics use their critical methodology to promote:

1. *inquiry*: A key role of critics is to question, research, analyze, and interpret values, practices, and norms, to solicit the variety of perspectives within a society especially the views of those who have been silent as a function of oppression or coercion, and to promote similar efforts by others within the society.
2. *deliberative opportunities*: A second role of critics is to promote or host deliberative opportunities among the different and multiple perspectives within society where society otherwise has no adequate fora for hearing those perspectives. This includes providing security for free expression where societies may have practices that inhibit some from sharing their perspectives.
3. *institutional change*: A third role of social critics is to represent the silent or to propose institutional changes that allow them to participate themselves and to propose institutional changes that impinge on the ability of the powerful to exploit inequalities or that promote equality.

These overlap in many respects; however, I describe them separately because each identifies certain roles that are not included in the others.[3]

[3] In the next chapter, I develop the qualifications, specifically the critical perspectives, necessary for critics to fill these roles.

Inquiry

In the real world, where equality is not a widely held value or a common practice, inquiry about values, practices, and norms is an important role of critics. A critic may conduct her own research, analysis, or interpretation. Or, like the researcher in the example from Bangladesh, the critic may ask a question that provokes further inquiry among a group, or as in SEWA's effort to have self-employed women recognized as workers, a question may provoke discussion of values within the society and the government. Inquiry is not a simplistic accommodation of facts. Social observations, whether the result of casual inquiry, collective discussion, or social science research, require analyses and interpretation (about which critics may disagree). Analysis and interpretation can be done by a Walzerian critic interpreting her own society's values, practices, and norms as in the Korean Women's Hotline's efforts to serve the Korea-town community in Chicago described by Lisa Sun-Hee Park (1998). In this example, a battered women's hotline struggles to support battered women in the Korean-American community without being perceived as threatening to Korean community values. Supporting women as mothers could be seen as supporting Korean-American families, but could also be perceived as undermining the patriarchal authority of the family (1998). Thus as social critics, the hotline organizers interpreted and reinterpreted their community's values and norms in an effort to support women in battering relationships and thereby to strengthen their community.

Analysis and interpretation can also be done by an outside critic as is demonstrated by Save the Children's efforts to address the high maternal and infant mortality rates in its areas of operation in Bangladesh. The reasons for the high mortality rates are more complicated than the nutritional deficiencies of expectant and nursing mothers alone, but nutritional differences between females and males are an important part of the story and were being perpetuated by unequal food distributions. Through its research and field work, Save the Children learned about local nutritional and prenatal care practices. In order to determine what information would be valuable to the society and would influence their practices, Save the Children analyzed and interpreted their findings and the values, practices, and norms of the community where they worked. In sharing with the community their findings, they gave mothers and fathers information about basic health, nutrition, and physiology that they thought would influence the parents' practices, for example that the size of a child's brain is affected by the health and nutrition of the mother carrying the child.[4] Because providing opportunity to one's children is a strong value in Bangladeshi families, Save the Children emphasized that in order for children to succeed in life, women should be better fed, particularly during pregnancy. This piece of information, complemented with suggestions for achieving a balanced diet within a family's means, was carefully disseminated in the 1970s through trained village women, at health clinics, and in women's groups. Of course, not all villagers changed their practices; however, the information has influenced the distribution of food and other medical resources to pregnant women in many village families for three generations.[5] Successful interpretation whether by an insider, outsider, or someone with a more complicated critical perspective requires intimate knowledge of the context under scrutiny and the ability to think critically about its values, practices, and norms. To fulfill the roles of inquiry, the critic must be self-conscious in her questioning, cast a broad net in her search for evidence, and provoke other critics' and societies' engaged consideration of the issue under scrutiny. Ideas developed in public deliberation guide decision making. Consequently, an essential step in provoking inquiry is asking the *right* question. Questions provoke intellectual ideas and emotional responses. Both attitudes and ideas affect the deliberative process. As Dewey noted,

Answers given in discussion are momentous in practice. For the attitude expressed and developed in public inquiry is inevitably a genuine part of the practical answer that will emerge. It is the initial stage of what appears later as more tangible and seemingly more overt activities. The preliminary phase in which belief-attitudes take shape is too commonly dismissed as if it were merely theoretical and contrasted with something else labelled practical. But nothing is of more practical importance than that the question constituting the issue to be dealt with be rightly put. (1946b: 210)

Since the agenda itself should be deliberatively determined, asking the question in the right way is as important as asking the right question. What asking the right way means will vary by context, but it means at least asking the question in a way that provokes broad contributions, promotes listening where some are inclined to ignore, and generally promotes inclusion. Asking the right way does not mean asking in a way

---

[4] Obviously, the physiology of brain development is more complicated than merely its size.
[5] Initially, I learned about the early teachings of Save the Children from a Tangail woman on the Kustia trip who explained to me why she made sure her daughter-in-law was well-fed during her pregnancy even though she had yet to produce a boy. For more on maternal and child health in Bangladesh see Blanchet (1991) and (1984).

that leads people to follow something suggested by the question, rather than to follow their own line of inquiry.

Part of inquiry is gathering new evidence and pointing out when old opinions are obsolete (Mill 1859; Dewey 1980 [1916a]: 294–299). By example, Pateman demonstrates the role of social critics in gathering evidence. She defends her argument for the possibility of participatory democracy in the workplace by gathering and reviewing evidence of participatory organizations in workplaces in the United States, England, and Yugoslavia (1970).

In addition to analyzing evidence themselves, social critics promote learning throughout society (Dewey 1980 [1916a]: 290–299). This means social critics promote civic education and promote the improvement of schools and other learning environments. It also means they question and pay attention to what people learn from their involvement with each other and with institutions in their daily life, including questioning the equality within institutions and society.

Finally, as Dewey notes, the roles of the social critic include the promotion of ongoing evaluation not just of values and practices but also of decisions (1983 [1922]: 144). Critics who inquire provoke the examination of values, practices, and norms that are commonly unquestioned either because people cannot question them due to some form of coercion, due to force of habit, or because they don't know another way is possible. They also promote the society's self-examination or at least its examination by a subset of the society. The social critic must not only question existing practices and values, research versions of practices and values from past or other cultures, analyze her own findings and those of others, and provide evaluation herself, but also promote the community's collective evaluation process. Where society faces collective moral difficulties, current inquiry and the study of past inquiries aid in its informed consideration of those difficulties (Dewey 1983 [1922]: 10–11). With this in mind, social criticism is as much an attitude as a practice. Critics manifest this attitude in their method through skeptical scrutiny. They also manifest it by encouraging the critical engagement of others through fostering deliberative opportunities. Critics may guide occasions of collective inquiry to become deliberative opportunities in which the voices of the previously marginalized are heard and become politically relevant.

Deliberative opportunities

Inquiry enhances the informed and inclusive nature of deliberative fora. However, where deliberative fora are lacking, social critics' roles are to promote deliberation throughout society. Creating deliberative opportunities is an important aspect of criticism of a society in which the moral and political communities are not congruent.[6] For example, within Bangladesh, many recognize that there are multiple moral communities and that there is a diversity of moralities even within some small village communities. For some, discrepancies between moral values are a matter of piety. For others, the discrepancies are disagreements about the appropriate status of women in their families and in society. Communities may be aware of their internal differences but lack the means to resolve them. More generally, when practices within moral communities impede deliberation about a community's own values, the critic's most insightful contribution to social change may be to create deliberative opportunities. By promoting deliberative opportunities, the critic enables those within the society to hear each other's perspectives. The size of mass society, the demands that participation places on individuals, and the competing extra-political demands people have in their lives make realizing society-wide deliberative fora challenging. But some activists and some deliberative theorists have taken on the challenge of promoting and hosting deliberative fora. These may be safe places for deliberation among the marginalized. They may also be fora created to address specific issues.[7] Or, they may be fora for ongoing deliberations. As we saw in chapter 2, due to social, economic, or political inequalities, participants in deliberative fora do not command or receive equal respect. Critics can foster deliberation by creating the conditions for those who are less likely to be heard to instead be listened to attentively.

Where coercion or habit prevent people from changing the values, practices, and norms of the community in which they live, a social critic may host or promote deliberation among those within that community who generally have no public voice or who have limited opportunities to talk with and learn from each other. For feminists who recognize that some people are left excluded from the political context explicitly and through the tools of ideology and language that operate in the dominant political context, it is important for critics to create new contexts that generate and utilize "countermeanings" and "counter discourse" with which to criticize the dominant political context, its ideology, and its language (Hirschmann 1996a: 58). As described by Belenky, Field, Bond and Weinstock, the story of Jan Peterson's work in promoting

---

[6] This is particularly the case when political boundaries have been recently flexible – as in the break-ups of Yugoslavia, Czechoslovakia, and the USSR – but it is also the case if we look within the political boundaries of the USA at the variety of political ideologies of US citizens.

[7] See for example the deliberative fora established by Fishkin to address public utility issues in Texas and crime issues in Britain (Kay 1996; Fishkin 1995).

community activism and the development of the National Congress of Neighborhood Women (Neighborhood Women) is a story of creating deliberative opportunities among those who are left out of public dialogue, of using those opportunities to create a space for them in the public dialogue, and of using achievements to create opportunities for others who have been excluded from public decision-making fora. As Sandy Schilen, an activist in Neighborhood Women, put it, "Jan could see that gender was left out of the civil rights movement, that women were left out of the neighborhood movement, and that grassroots women and the neighborhood were both left out of the [international] women's movement" (Belenky et al. 1997: 227). When Peterson was a social worker in an anti-poverty program in Brooklyn, she recognized women's activism in their community. As Belenky et al. describe it, "many ordinary 'housewives' were actually working very hard to sustain and enhance the life of the community through PTAs, block associations, tenants' groups in the projects, political clubs, and churches" (Belenky 1997: 206). However, these women were working in isolation. Peterson hired some of these women in order to offer them institutional support for their various activities. The women realized they could be more effective if they worked together and so they began the group that grew into Neighborhood Women. With Peterson's support the women created a deliberative opportunity among women leaders. In these fora Peterson encouraged the women to develop their leadership skills and not to hand off their projects to male community leaders when a project became substantial enough to require a budget and administration (Belenky et al. 1997: 207–8). Instead Peterson encouraged them to speak for themselves in public spaces; for example, to lobby City Hall to incorporate the women's account of their community's needs in budget decisions (Belenky et al. 1997: 208).

To share the success of the women leaders in Brooklyn, Peterson worked with others to sponsor a conference on women's grassroots leadership in the USA. The National Congress of Neighborhood Women was the resulting organization that continued to sponsor dialogue among grassroots women's organizations. Further, dismayed by the lack of grassroots women's participation at the 1985 United Nations Third World Conference on Women in Nairobi, Neighborhood Women networked with other grassroots organizations to facilitate grassroots women's participation in the 1995 United Nations Fourth World Conference on Women in Beijing. As in the community level organizing, the philosophy of the network was to foster safe deliberative opportunities among women such that they could develop their own knowledge, understanding, and confidence and then use those to assert their interests in the broader public arena in which their voices had been previously marginalized.

Save the Children's women's meetings in Kustia and SEWA's organizing strategies both reflect similar efforts to create safe deliberative opportunities in which women can learn about themselves and their obstacles so that they can then assert themselves in public ways despite persistent inequality. By hosting a deliberative forum such as the community leaders' groups of Neighborhood Women, the Tangail women's groups, or the employment-based cooperatives, critics create among equals the circumstances for exchanging and learning about common ground, differences, and the possibility of collective action.

Mansbridge notes the value of safe enclaves "in which the like-minded can make their own sense of what they see" and develop strategies of resistance (1996: 57–58).[8] Mansbridge argues that protected spaces, uninhibited by the dominant culture, language, and means of power in the public sphere, allow those marginalized in the public sphere a means to

understanding themselves better, forging bonds of solidarity, preserving the memories of past injustices, interpreting and reinterpreting the meanings of those injustices, working out alternative conceptions of self, of community, of justice, and of universality, trying to make sense of both the privileges they wield and the oppressions they face, understanding the strategic configurations for and against their desired ends, deciding what alliances to make both emotionally and strategically, deliberating on ends and means, and deciding how to act, individually and collectively. (1996: 58)

Mansbridge is not specific about how a democratic polity should and can maintain these fora of protected deliberation, but she argues it should. Given the extent of the exclusion or marginalization experienced by those who have faced the challenges of surmounting social, economic, and political obstacles to participation in public fora, the more conventional solution of fostering multiparty politics does not create adequate opportunities for those marginalized by traditional politics to voice their opposition. Similarly supporting the importance of safe deliberative opportunities, James Scott argues that under conditions of extreme inequality, people are more likely to voice their true views in a

sequestered social site where the control, surveillance, and repression of the dominant are least able to reach, and ... when this sequestered social milieu is composed entirely of close confidants who share similar experiences of domination. (1990: 120)

[8] See also Hirschmann (1996a, 1996b). From a more postmodern perspective, Nancy Fraser refers to these enclaves of deliberative opportunities as "subaltern counterpublics" (1992: 123). See the discussion of educative deliberation in chapter 2 and the discussion of deliberative inquiry in chapter 3.

Those who draw our attention to the value of enclaves are appreciating not only the value of competing views, but in particular the value of the views of the excluded.[9]

Multiparty politics in no way insures that views outside traditional politics get heard. Though not always sensitive to the problems of inequality and marginalization that concern Mansbridge, Scott, and Third World feminist social critics, deliberative theorists have proposed a number of ways to foster deliberative opportunities with the intent of making decision making more broadly inclusive. If modified to take into consideration the problem of creating deliberative opportunities for those who are so marginalized as to avoid public fora, these may be promising for fostering public participation in deliberative fora. For example, Joshua Cohen and Joel Rogers propose public support for associations (1992). Government support would be contingent on the associations' having internal accountability, centralized decision making, broad membership, broad responsibilities, a formalized relationship with the state, cooperation with other groups, the sole responsibility for representing the interests they represent, and effectively the same power across groups (1992: 428–430 and 441). If modified to include an account of critical evaluation of their internal accountability, inclusionary decision-making practices, inclusionary membership practices, constructive not exploitative cooperation with other groups, representation, and perhaps most challenging equality of influence across groups, associative democracy might redress rather than re-dress substantive inequality in political decision making.

Another deliberative theorist, James Fishkin, suggests another possible institution, the deliberative caucus (1991, 1995). A random sample of the population is chosen to learn about and deliberate about certain issues or candidates. The group comes together for an extended period of time and is given the opportunity to question experts and candidates directly and to demand corroborating research for their claims. Participation is subsidized so that wealthy and poor have an equal opportunity to participate. Participants meet in small moderated groups so that each gets an opportunity to speak and be heard despite inequalities in experience and comfort speaking publicly. At the end of the period, the participants vote for their preferred candidates. The forum is televised so that the rest of the population can share in, though not participate in, the forum. Fishkin argues that in the US national elections the deliberative caucus should take place before the primaries so that voters are influenced by its choice – the choice of people

[9] For a discussion in the context of women's rights see J. Oloka-Onyango and Sylvia Tamale (1995: 724–730).

representative of the entire population – rather than by the choices of the New Hampshire primary and the Iowa caucuses. Fishkin's proposal is do-able. In fact, he has done it. By creating conditions of political equality among otherwise unequal people, Fishkin provides a vision of what political decision making in an ideal deliberative forum populated with ideally informed citizens.[10]

The concept of hosting a discussion may seem more appropriate to negotiations between warring parties than to a society's discussion of its own values. However, creating opportunities for deliberation by bringing people together is an important aspect of criticism within a society with moral and political disagreement and especially in the context of inequality. Existing practices may impede people from coming together to deliberate about a community's values. Under such circumstances, the critic's most insightful contribution to social change may be to create a forum for deliberative exchange. In fulfilling the role of hosting deliberative opportunities, the critic enables those within the society to hear each other's perspectives including the views of the previously silent. Where other impediments exist, it may be necessary to help participants to listen to one another.

Institutional change

The existence of a deliberative forum does not guarantee that everyone will participate in it or that participants will listen to one another. As we saw in the preceding discussion, under circumstances where power inequalities are exploitative or, where institutions are vehicles for exploiting power inequalities rather than for mitigating them, some may not be willing or able to voice their criticism in public. Social critics make deliberative fora more inclusively informed through institutional change. As social criticism, institutional change takes three forms: (1) enhancing society's and critics' knowledge and deliberative opportunities; (2) altering existing power structures; and (3) representing those unable or unwilling to express their criticism publicly.

Social critics can fulfill their role of institutional change by expanding public knowledge (here the role of institutional change overlaps with the role of promoting inquiry) or by creating or facilitating deliberative

---

[10] For discussions of the theoretical import and the practical application of promoting public deliberation among representative samples of the population and civic groups see Fishkin (1995) and Mathews (1994). Though doable and the effects of deliberation on participants' views are notable, the effect of the televised National Issues Convention of nonparticipant voters has not been measured (Fishkin 1996; Luskin et al. 1996; National Issues Convention 1996).

opportunities (here, the role of institutional change overlaps with the role of promoting deliberative opportunities). When promoting institutional changes, the critic seeks out power inequalities and seeks to remedy them through information, deliberation, representation, or other means.

In *Strong Democracy*, Benjamin Barber has a list of concrete institutional proposals for making public decision making more deliberative (1984: chapter 10). These included proposals for promoting civic education, local dialogue and decision making, and mechanisms for making national decisions deliberative. Among these include a proposal for a national initiative and referendum process. Barber's proposal balances Madisonian concerns about the whim of popular rule and the desire to increase "popular participation and responsibility for government" (1984: 284). According to Barber, the referendum process would be tied into his other proposals for civic education so that televised deep discussions, not superficial advertising, would provide the public with information about the issue on the ballot. The voting mechanisms he recommends are perhaps his most innovative. Rather than a yea-or-nay voting format, Barber suggests a multiple choice format so that citizens can support the idea but object to a particular proposal's wording, extremism, or conservatism. The first round of voting provides legislators and the public with an understanding of the strength of the public's support for the initiative and a way to distinguish between those who support the measure generally, but don't like the proposed formulation specifically. In addition, Barber requires two stages of voting to put a check on the possibilities of elite control of the information through the media or whimsical voting behavior by the majority (1984: 286–288). A second vote after a period of six months allows for changes in public information and increased discussion spawned by the first vote (1984: 281–289). Barber's proposal enhances collectively informed deliberation.

Mansbridge has more concrete recommendations of institutional changes that will make Congress more deliberative.

(1) give the incumbents an even greater advantage than at present (through increased at-home staff for constituency services, let us say), thereby alleviating constituency policy pressure and allowing greater attention to national affairs; (2) limit tenure to two (or three) terms in the Senate and four in the House in order to bring in new ideas and curb some negative effects both of incumbency and wanting to matter (e.g. excessive commitment to legislation that bears one's own mark); and (3) drastically limit or abolish the funding that interest groups can give campaigns or use to pay lobbyists in order to increase the degree to which constituents' preferences will be represented in proportion to their numbers. (1988: 85)

While recognizing that such changes are politically infeasible, she argues that together they would make Congress more deliberative and its decisions better informed. Shapiro also offers proposals for increased deliberation among citizens and representatives (1996a and 1996b) that together with Barber's and Mansbridge's proposals described a more inclusively informed representative democracy.

Although such institutional changes can enhance deliberation (under conditions of inequality), people may not choose to or be able to participate. Social critics may work to alter existing power structures to enable broader sources of information through broader participation as described in the discussions of inquiry and deliberative opportunities. However, where critics are unable to change existing power structures, they may try to represent the silent.

Before they can accurately represent those who are silent, critics need to interpret the silence of possible participants. For every kind of silence there is an appropriate role for critics to address the silence and enable potential participants to have the views considered in the deliberative fora. When fulfilling any of these roles, social critics are changing formal and informal institutions.[11]

In thinking about representing the silent, the critic asks why they do not speak for themselves. In the case where some people choose not to participate because they have no criticisms, critics need to facilitate participation such that the society and its critics are confident that anyone could voice criticisms if they wanted to.

Under circumstances where silence is difficult to interpret, the role of the critic is to facilitate the free flow of information and to foster deliberative opportunities that enable the silent people and the rest of society to explore and to better understand how their own values, practices, and norms may reflect and perpetuate power inequalities. Where silence is difficult to interpret or there are no social problems, the critic fosters community discussion that does not lead to social change. Rather it leads to heightened self-awareness as a community and creates an institution that promotes ongoing community inquiry into potential exploitative inequalities.[12]

Another reason people do not speak out is that they are not fully aware of their circumstances and thus do not perceive they have grounds for criticism. If people are silent because they are unaware of their

---

[11] See chapter 1, footnote 4 on institutions.

[12] With less concern for inequality but similar interest in examining that which society accepts, Socrates proposes that there be an institution (himself as gadfly) to provoke discussion and likewise, John Stuart Mill proposes ongoing discussion and defense of values even when they are broadly accepted.

circumstances and the power inequalities that perpetuate them, then informing them is a form of institutional change. For example, Martha Nussbaum cites a study where Indians were interviewed about their satisfaction with their health and given health exams (1992). The Indian women were more satisfied with their health than the Indian men, although medical examinations indicated the health of the women was worse. After some "consciousness raising" about good health the women reported less satisfaction with their health than before although their actual health status had not changed (1992: 230). Informed, the women changed their opinions of their health.[13] Informed, some may become critical of certain social practices or values that allow the exploitation of power inequalities. By imparting information, the social critic promotes the expression of multiple and potentially competing perspectives. In the example cited by Nussbaum, the critics chose to teach the women to represent themselves. Where consciousness-raising fails, the critic may represent the interests of the silent publicly as Amartya Sen has done through statistics analysis in "More than 100 Million Women Are Missing" and more generally by aiding in the conceptual redesign of the United Nations Development Program's *Human Development Report.*

Most social critics worry about those who know their conditions but do not speak publicly against them even if deliberative opportunities present themselves because they fear those with power over them. This is the case of the poor rural women of Bangladesh Sarah White studies (1992) and of the serfs, slaves, and untouchables James Scott studies (1990). Of those afraid of the powerful, some people may not only criticize the values, practices, and norms of society publicly, but as Scott discusses, do so through various forms of offstage defiance and resistance (1985, 1990). Likewise, a critic may speak publicly but anonymously, in euphemisms, veiling her dissent, or through more elaborate forms of political disguise (Scott 1990: chapter 6). Under these circumstances, the critics' attempts to create more opportunities for the silent to speak and be heard by proposing changes to formal organizations or to informal rules of public deliberation and decision making seem misguided.

If extreme inequality is the problem, how can we expect people to

---

[13] Under conducive institutional circumstances they might also seek medical attention. Nussbaum & Sen also acknowledge that what constitutes "health" is a potentially relative concept but argue that medical facts can convince those "individuals who are in some way representative, attentive, [and] who have scrutinized the alternatives in the right way" (Nussbaum & Sen 1989: 311). See Sen (1984: 82–83) for a more thorough account of the same study by the All-India Institute of Hygiene and Public Health (Lal & Seal 1949).

speak for themselves against that inequality? Creating secure deliberative opportunities as discussed above is one way. In addition, institutional change can alter existing power inequalities by promoting equality. In Bangladesh, some credit programs seek to increase women's status in the family by providing them with an opportunity to produce income for the family. When credit programs work well (from the perspective of the borrower), the husband is supportive of the wife's activity because of the increased family income.[14] Women's access to formal credit is a relatively new institution in Bangladesh. Because credit enables women to contribute to much needed family income, credit programs have burgeoned throughout the country (with domestic and international support). Where these programs prioritize women's empowerment, they facilitate institutional change within the family. When women have improved their status within the family, their views are heard and given more attention thereby increasing knowledge within the family and within the community.

The problem of severe inequality might lead some critics first to represent the oppressed – how else would their views be heard? True, representation can be an important means of allowing silent voices to be heard, but it is (at best) a second-best option if the reason for the silence is oppression. When one wants to speak, there is nothing empowering in being spoken for. Third World feminist social critics have been innovative in finding ways to enable women to speak for themselves. They have also resorted to representing those silenced by power inequalities though obviously changing the power inequalities is preferable to allowing them to perpetuate.

However, representation may be empowering for those people who do speak publicly, but whose views are dismissed and for those who are unwilling, unable, or uninterested in taking the time necessary to participate. For some people, effective participation in deliberation itself is fulfilling (regardless of particular successes or failures). But as discussed in chapter 2 for some people deliberative fora create obligations not opportunities. Children, family illness, and economic demands are possible competing obligations. Spending time in remote places and working uninterrupted are possible competing desires. If people are not participating because competing obligations are inhibiting their participation, critics need to consider the competing obligations as sources of inequality. But where people don't want to participate, representation is empowering. One who accurately represents those who choose to be

---

[14] Some programs do not have empowerment of women as their primary objective. Even those that do can contribute to borrowers' exploitation by their families and by the lending institutions themselves (Ackerly 1995, 1997; Goetz & Sen Gupta 1995).

represented is an empowering advocate. Good representation frees people to attend to matters that require their particular attention or that they find particularly fulfilling. However, the assessment of the adequacy and accuracy of the representation poses an epistemological problem. How is a critic or her audience able to assess the representation of those who are silent? Thus, because representation allows for the continued silence of the represented, critics must direct critical attention to any practice of representation. However, for epistemological reasons, critics must strive toward institutional change which would enable the silent to speak for themselves.

However social critics fulfill their roles, they must exercise their critical practice with self-consciousness. Third World feminist critics must be aware of the likelihood that their criticism will be incomplete and possibly exclusive. The women's human rights movement illustrates that even while fulfilling the range of critics' roles, social critics need to examine critically the results of their criticism.

Women's human rights[15]

The accounts of the women's human rights movement, particularly at and leading up to the 1993 United Nations World Conference on Human Rights in Vienna and the 1995 United Nations Fourth World Conference on Women (FWCW) in Beijing but also at and leading up to the population conference in Cairo in 1994, portray a success story of women's organizing and networking locally, regionally, and globally.[16] With the phrase "women's human rights movement," I refer to activists around the world who raise awareness about both the ways in which the human rights of female humans are violated and the ways in which women may experience violations of rights that should be considered their human rights but which fall outside the purview of traditional interpretations of human rights law. These latter rights are sometimes called "women's rights" because due to gendered social practices in

[15] Please see chapter 1 for the explanation of my use of the terms "Third World," "western," "nonwestern," "Northern," and "Southern."

[16] For the history of the women's human rights movement see Margaret Keck and Kathryn Sikkink (1998); for a more detailed account of the women's human rights organizing around Vienna see Friedman (1995). For an account of the movement leading up to the Vienna conference and NGO sponsored Tribunal at Vienna see Charlotte Bunch and Niamh Reilly (1994). For an account of women's human rights activism as utilizing the Third World feminist method of social criticism see Ackerly & Okin (1999). See also Charlotte Bunch's foundational statement of the violence against women paradigm in "Women's Rights as Human Rights: Toward a Re-Vision of Human Rights" (1990). For a more critical account that also recognizes the achievements of the movement see J. Oloka-Onyango and Sylvia Tamale (1995: 715).

various forms around the world, women are commonly engaged in childbirth, childcare, subsistence farming, and other unpaid labor. They fall outside the traditional paradigm of human rights because they are experienced in the private sphere of family and local community. This movement is made up of local, regional, and international activists who practice Third World feminist social criticism. Working separately and collectively, these activists from the North and South have secured women's human rights on the international human rights agenda. Although this success is commendable, all social criticism, even successful Third World feminist social criticism, should also be the *subject* of social criticism if it is continually to promote increasingly inclusive social change. Thus, in this section after describing the movement, and its fulfillment of social critics' roles, I am going to give a critical account of the successes and shortcomings of the women's human rights movement.

In order to further the women's human rights movement, it is as important to take stock of its shortcomings as it is to take stock of its successes. The successes reflect the inclusiveness of the political dialogue at Vienna and Beijing, and the effective representation by those with political resources and skill of those who lacked either or both. The shortcomings are likewise a function of the limits of this inclusion and representation. My purpose is not to challenge the deservedly positive interpretation that most accounts offer of the networking, organization, and political strategies of the women's human rights campaign. Rather, I want to supplement that view with more critical perspectives. In so doing I mean to show not only women's human rights activists filling the critics' roles of fostering inquiry, deliberative opportunities, and institutional change, but also the self-criticism necessary to make social criticism increasingly inclusive. In fact, both the successes and shortcomings of the movement are a function of its organizing theme, political strategies, and achievements.

At the Nongovernment Organization (NGO) Forum held in Huairou at the same time as the FWCW in Beijing, Bella Abzug reiterated the Conference theme's call to action, "The last decade for women has been networking, and the coming decade for women is action" (Chow 1996: 189–190).[17] The critical assessment of the movement's organizing theme, political strategies, and achievements to date provides a foundation for planning that activism. Moreover, to the extent that the women's human rights movement is part of a larger international women's movement, Third World feminist social criticism can guide the

---

[17] The Conference theme was "Action for Equality, Development, and Peace."

action of the women's movement to be inclusive of all the world's women.

Organizing theme

The women's human rights movement faced two challenges: to change the way that human rights were conceptualized internationally so that the human rights of female humans were recognized and to change the way that women around the world thought about a social movement of women such that it could truly be a movement for all women. The importance of the second for the first was evident from the outset of the United Nations Decade for Women (1975–1985). At the World Conference of the International Women's Year in Mexico City in 1975, tensions emerged between generally western women who advocated equality and based their claims on an antidiscrimination paradigm and generally nonwestern women who were concerned about issues of social and economic justice and based their claims on critiques of militarist, capitalist, colonialist, and imperialist hierarchies within their countries and across the global political economy. Moreover, grassroots activists from around the world felt underrepresented. Despite these tensions and in part as a response to these exclusions, women recognized each other as resources and women's organizations around the world began to network globally. These networks were strengthened at subsequent regional and international meetings during and following the Decade for Women.

The organizations working around the world on various issues related to women's human rights began to coalesce as an international movement around the effort to confront violence against women (Keck & Sikkink 1998: 165–166). The idea of mobilizing against violence against women united those women concerned with discrimination and those concerned with social and economic justice. Women working against domestic violence, the international sex trade, dowry death, and the torture of political prisoners found a common agenda around which to mobilize and network. Leaders of the women's human rights movement based at the Center for Women's Global Leadership (Global Center) circulated a petition calling on the UN Conference in Vienna to consider women's human rights in every aspect of its work. The petition campaign helped unify Third World feminist activists and strengthened their growing international network. Seeing their own local work as part of a larger international movement gave women's rights activists international allies (Bunch 1990, Bunch & Fried 1996). Seeing their work as a form of human rights activism opened doors to local allies who were generally other human rights activists (Keck & Sikkink 1998: 165–166).

Women from a variety of experiences found they had a common strategy. Bunch and Fried assert that violence against women was an effective unifying enemy because it was based on the universality of justice not commonality of experience (1996: 203). Because human rights language already had legitimacy as an international legal norm, it was an effective paradigm for women's organizing and influencing international human rights policy (1996: 204).

Political strategies

The political strategies of the women's human rights movement were similarly unifying and intended to make the movement and its influence inclusive. They were the petition drive, use of personal testimonials, facilitation of media support, and caucusing. Leading up to the Vienna conference, grassroots activists around the world collected from 124 countries nearly a half million signatures (and thumb prints) to the petition calling on the conference "to comprehensively address women's human rights at every level of its proceedings" (Bunch & Reilly 1994: 5).

In order to focus the attention of the UN Conference and international media on the myriad of ways in which women's human rights are violated, organizers planned a Tribunal at which testimonials of the violations of women's human rights would be heard before a panel of judges who were in a position to influence public awareness and policy. Although the testimonials were real, the Tribunal was to be educative about the violations of women's human rights generally, not an effort to seek restitution for specific violations. An International Coordinating Committee formed at the Global Center in February 1993 was charged with selecting diverse and representative speakers. The Tribunal was a way to marshal the broad grassroots commitment revealed by the petition drive and to let women speak of their experiences *themselves* at the NGO Forum in Vienna. The seeking, supplying, exchanging, and gathering of information in preparation for the Tribunal strengthened the international network of women's human rights activists.

The women's movement and specifically the Tribunal stole the media show at the 1993 Conference (Friedman 1995). Organizers were prepared with media kits including background materials on each woman testifying. Tribunal organizers provided each speaker with a support person and facilitated each speaker's interaction with the media. Reporters were able to write informed stories such that US newspapers from Los Angeles to Dallas to Bridgeport, Connecticut carried stories about the Tribunal using examples from a variety of testimonies. In their use of testimonials and media, the activists made effective use of what Keck & Sikkink describe as information politics (1998: 18–22).

In addition to these innovations the activists also employed the more traditional political tools of lobbying and caucusing to make the human rights dialogue more inclusive of women's perspectives.[18] Governments were lobbied to include NGO representatives in their UN delegations.[19] Through briefings delegations kept their constituents informed of conference proceedings, and delegations caucused with their constituents on the following days' issues. In practice, the representativeness of delegations and their interest in caucusing varied according to the political environment of each nation (Busia 1996; Friedman et al. 1998).

Achievements

At Vienna, women took advantage of the political opportunity created by the World Conference on Human Rights to make the world's leaders and media aware of the ways in which the "human rights of half of humanity" were being violated and yet unaddressed by the UN and traditional human rights groups (Friedman 1995: 22). The success of the women's influence was made concrete in the several pages of the Vienna Declaration that support women's equal status and human rights. The tangible outcomes of the conference were not limited to language. The international women's network that brought into deliberative contact women from the grassroots around the world was now a resource for women, one that they mobilized in preparing for Beijing. Further, the breadth of participation at the NGO Forums, particularly at Huairou, demonstrates that the women's human rights movement is part of an international women's movement.

Roles of activists as social critics

These successful outcomes were the result of the women's human rights social critics' fulfilling the range of Third World feminist critical roles. In their preliminary organizing efforts through the Vienna and Beijing conferences, activists from around the world promoted inquiry. The Global Center, the Latin American Committee for the Defense of

---

[18] See Ackerly & Okin (1999), Abzug (1996), and Morgan (1996b). However, some NGOs rejected lobbying as "conforming to their rules" and chose instead to focus on networking with other activists (Alvarez 1997: 312).

[19] The UN required governments to involve NGOs in the official preparations for Beijing (Friedman et al. 1998).

Women's Rights, the Asia-Pacific Forum on Women, Law and Development, Women in Law and Development in Africa, and the International Women's Rights Action Watch were instrumental in facilitating inquiry through networking. Activists used existing networks to expand those networks, to expand their knowledge, and to share their knowledge of the ways in which women's human rights are continually violated around the world and of the means of activism women have employed to challenge them. As Esther Chow put it, this grassroots activism and presence at the NGO Forum in Huairou "expanded circles of inclusiveness" (1996: 186). Activists both conducted their own research and asked questions that fostered further inquiry among women about their societies and the world. International and grassroots activists analyzed and interpreted their observations, individually. And collectively, they found that violence against women was a unifying theme that described what they were opposing in their own countries though their specific experiences of violence varied. It seemed that questioning violence against women was the right question because it was unifying without undermining activism on specific issues and because it added the perceived legitimacy of a universal appeal to justice. Through this broad inquiry, these activists criticized the existing views of human rights as being primarily violated by governments. Their information showed that women's human rights were violated in their families, by their societies' cultural norms, and by their socioeconomic conditions. Governments were not generally the perpetrators of violations of women's human rights in these circumstances, but they were guilty of allowing such violations to continue and they perpetuated such violations by codifying them in law. The women's human rights movement asked governments and societies to examine critically their own social norms and laws for ways in which they allowed the violations of women's human rights.

The women's human rights activists also demonstrate the critics' role in promoting deliberative opportunities.[20] Both in the preparation for the conferences and at the conferences, activist critics brought women's activists together to learn from each other and to strategize together. The Global Center, The International Women's Tribune Center, and the regional activists were instrumental in bringing to fruition the Vienna Tribunal which was a deliberative opportunity for women from around the world who had been sharing their experiences through networks with other women to present their testimonials to the world. Since not all of those whose rights have been violated could speak at

---

[20] Ara Wilson (1996) and Bunch & Fried (1996) also note the value of deliberation. Abdullahi Ahmed An-Na'im proposes internal and cross-cultural dialogue for the examination of the cultural legitimacy of the international human rights system (1994).

Vienna, organizers sought testimonials from women whose experiences were collectively representative or at least suggestive of the various ways in which women's human rights are violated around the world. The Tribunal was a forum to address the specific and overlapping issues of women's human rights violations. These were considered by the Tribunal under five categories: human rights abuse in the family, war crimes against women, violations of women's bodily integrity, socioeconomic violations of women's human rights, and political persecution and discrimination. The participants in the Tribunal were both women who had experienced the violations they described and representatives of other women. In addition to being a deliberative opportunity in which women could share their knowledge, the Tribunal also opened the doors to ongoing deliberations among human rights activists and policy makers about women's human rights.

Likewise, through the lobbying efforts of the caucuses, activists created other potential deliberative opportunities between NGOs and the country delegations. Although not a uniform practice, in many instances, NGO representatives worked hand in hand with the government delegations to resolve the disputed language in the official documents.

The last critical role of Third World feminist social critics is promoting institutional change. Women's human rights activists were particularly effective at promoting institutional change from the building of an international women's network to the staging of the Vienna Tribunal to innovating with the western political tools of lobbying and caucusing. These institutional changes expanded women's knowledge, expanded public knowledge of women's human rights violations, and contributed to creating new, or improving existing, deliberative fora.

Self-criticism

Although these achievements are noteworthy, they also invite examination. In order to assess the women's human rights movement using Third World feminist social criticism, activists and scholars must evaluate its promotion of inquiry, deliberative opportunities, and institutional change *and* direct similar critical attention toward the movement. As a single critic, I can only propose a direction for such criticism and invite others to draw on their knowledges to join a discussion about how to improve upon or change the organizing theme, political strategies, and goals of the women's human rights movement.

First, the women's human rights movement promoted inquiry around its organizing theme of violence against women. The cost of the organizing theme was that by unifying around violence against women, women's human rights activists obfuscated the still important disagreements among women around the kind of changes envisioned and around what would be necessary to bring them about. Moreover, by embracing the Convention on the Elimination of All Forms of Discrimination Against Women (CEDAW) and advocating for its support in the Vienna Declaration, the women's human rights movement endorsed the antidiscrimination paradigm and accompanying analysis rather than an approach more appropriate for dealing with questions of national and international socioeconomic justice.[21] Although for strategic reasons it may have been an appropriate political choice to seek to strengthen existing international norms for women's equal human worth, there was a theoretical and substantive cost to strengthening the antidiscrimination paradigm.[22] In their self-criticism, Third World feminist social critics now need to direct their inquiry toward violence against women as a unifying theme and at the antidiscrimination paradigm it has been used to promote.

Noreen Burrows (1986) and Hilary Charlesworth (1994) blame the public/private dichotomy and the interpretation of human rights along a male model of life experience for the persistence of the violations of women's human rights and argue that recognizing women's human rights will require transforming human rights law generally. The accepted paradigm of three generations of human rights – (1) civil and political; (2) economic, social and cultural; and (3) group or people's rights – is based on male life experiences. All aspects of the human rights paradigm pose problems for women because "they are built on typically male life experiences and in their current form do not respond to the most pressing risks women face" (Charlesworth 1994: 59). Removing barriers to women's ability to live like men does not help them to the extent that they live women's, not men's, lives, meaning they experience child-birth, generally have the social responsibility for childcare, and perform other unpaid labor including subsistence farming.[23]

---

[21] Formalized in 1979 and coming into force in 1981, the CEDAW is a convention for women's rights. It has been signed by 131 countries though many of these have signed with reservations.

[22] An alternative choice may have been to strengthen the institutions and the mechanisms of the Human Rights Committee, which supervises the *International Covenant on Civil and Political Rights*, and the Committee on Economic, Social and Cultural Rights, which supervises the *International Covenant on Economic, Social and Cultural Rights*, for meeting their responsibilities for women's human rights violations (see Stamatopoulou 1995: 43–44).

[23] In her critique of the antidiscrimination paradigm in US civil rights laws, Kimberle Crenshaw argues that the discrimination paradigm yields an erroneous "but for" analysis of inequality. It assumes that women would not suffer the harms they suffer if

According to Burrows and Charlesworth, the antidiscrimination paradigm does not help change what it means to be a human woman. For corroboration Charlesworth quotes Burrows,

For most women, what it is to be human is to work long hours in agriculture or the home, to receive little or no remuneration, and to be faced with political and legal processes which ignore their contribution to society and accord no recognition of their particular needs. (Burrows 1986: 82 cited by Charlesworth 1994: 60)

If the dichotomy between women's and men's experiences of human life is such that men and women have a different quality of life by virtue of their sex,

A more fundamental treatment of the skewed nature of the international human rights system would redefine the boundaries of the traditional human rights canon, rather than tinkering with the limited existing model of nondiscrimination. (Charlesworth 1994: 60)

It may be, as Charlesworth suggests, impossible to address even equality and quality of life issues for women within the antidiscrimination framework.

In addition to being unable to address concerns about women's equality and quality of life, the antidiscrimination paradigm is unable to be effective against violations of women's human rights that are not within states' control but that are rather a function of global political and socioeconomic realities. The practical problems with the CEDAW demonstrate the theoretical problems with antidiscrimination for dealing with the concerns of national and international socioeconomic justice. The international convention with the most reservations by its signatories, the CEDAW is not a strong international convention. It is particularly weak as a tool for addressing problems of economic and social injustice nationally and internationally such as the sex trade and the sexual exploitation of women. Women frequently are victims of these crimes when not in their country of citizenship and those committing the crimes may not be residents of the country where the crime is committed. It may be difficult for either state to act. Moreover, even where governments can act, as Cynthia Enloe has shown, state interests may be at stake in international gendered issues (1989, 1993). Individual states may be unable or unwilling to act effectively against global actors or the local subsidiaries of global actors.

they were men (1989). They would live a good life "but for" the fact that they were born women. By, in some cases, eliminating differences between men and women and, in other cases, revealing the mistakes of gender-neutral language in a context of gender difference, there would no longer be such harm suffered. According to Crenshaw, the discrimination paradigm leaves no remedy for those whose sex is female but whose gender is not that of a white middle-class woman.

More comprehensive criticism that took on national and international socioeconomic issues could be heard at the NGO Forum during the Beijing conference (Chow 1996: 187). Also, at the FWCW NGO delegates from Southern nations asked the conference to consider more systemic questions of global capitalism, the debt crisis, militarization, and democratization (Friedman et al. 1998; Chow 1996). Increasing awareness of the differences between women concerned about "equality and quality of life issues" and women concerned about "basic rights, poverty, development, and human security" in a context of the struggles of their nation or ethic group (Chow 1996: 187), however, did not lead women's human rights activists to abandon the traditional rights paradigm (Bunch & Fried 1996: 203–204).

As a unifying theme, violence against women masked the differences between women's understandings of the causes of and solutions to violence against women. Clearly, however, further inquiry into the causes of violence against women – be they discrimination against women, the socioeconomic oppression of women, the socioeconomic or political circumstances of their families, or other causes as yet unappreciated by the women's human rights movement – needs to be the basis of future collective action. As a result, it may be that women's human rights activists work collectively and in mutual support against different sources of violence against women. However, it may also be that as women's human rights activists learn from one another, they will discover a paradigm that is more unifying both thematically and substantively.

Second, the women's human rights movement created new deliberative opportunities and made use of them in their political strategies. However, while the women's human rights activists' strategic use of petitions, testimonials, the media, and traditional western politics were effective at creating deliberative opportunities for many of those who previously hadn't been heard to share their knowledge with one another and the world, these were inadvertently also exclusionary strategies. Although the NGO Forums of both conferences enabled many women to contribute to the deliberations and although the Huairou forum improved on the Vienna forum not all of those voices were able to exercise political influence. Due to their experience and their infrastructural resources, western women had significant influence on the movement's strategies (Busia 1996). Oloka-Onyango & Tamale argue that nonwestern women were given a voice in the women's human rights movement, but their voices were heard as providing regional and national perspectives rather than as contributing to the theoretical framework that guided the movement (1995: 701). In the organizing for

Vienna and Beijing it was difficult for nonwestern women to influence the movement's political strategies though as petition assignees and as testifiers they were strategically important to the movement and contributed to the NGO Forums at both conferences.

Those who guided the NGO Conference planning and lobbying drew on significant resources of means and experience. Those lacking that skill set were less influential. Although the movement would have been ineffective in the hands of uninformed people with no political acumen (wherever they were from), because generally western women and women networked into international NGOs and the UN were most likely to have these skills and resources, other women lacking the knowledge and resources to be influential in international networks were less visible in the formal UN proceedings and relied more completely on being represented by western and well-networked women. (Note that the socioeconomic reasons for the differences in women's means may have sources in common with the socioeconomic violations of women's human rights.)

For example, in her account of the caucus on the girl child, Busia argues that African and South Asian women ceded the responsibility for finalizing the draft language and bracketed text of the Beijing Platform for Action because they were either not able to attend or not able to stay through the end of a preliminary meeting in March in New York (1996: 208).[24] In one sense, as long as the women attendees made the same arguments as those who were not able to participate, as long as they made good representative arguments, activists and scholars should accept their leadership and in this case their representation of nonparticipant women. But for two reasons Third World feminist social criticism leads activists and scholars to question the leadership and representation by participants of nonparticipants in these ostensibly deliberative fora. The first is a political reason because it ignores the content of what the representatives said, but it is the most familiar (at least to feminists): Third World women should speak for themselves and be able to participate despite resource disparities; being represented is not as empowering as speaking for oneself. The second is an epistemological reason and gets to the content of the arguments made. If Third World women are not invited to and able to contribute to dialogue directly, critics cannot be confident that their representation is accurate. Moreover, they and the deliberative fora miss out on the learning that would

---

[24] The bracketed text is the portion of the text that will be resolved during the conference. All proposals for discussion during the conference must be made prior to the conference and captured in the bracketed language.

take place as a result of deliberative exchange.[25] Further, if Third World women are unable to participate directly, they are unable to contribute to the theoretical context of subsequent discussions. Resource disparities and variety in abilities to be politically effective will continue to work against women's efforts to make such conferences and the women's organizing around them more inclusive.

Thus, Third World feminist social critics need to create new opportunities for deliberation or to change substantively the models of existing ones. For example, in order to correct for the lesser influence of women with fewer resources, wealthy and middle-class activists could seek financial support for nonwealthy women to participate in regional and preliminary meetings at which the agenda is set and not just for their participation in the conference.[26] In addition, because some governments prevented the participation of those most informed and concerned about women's issues if they were not in favor with the government (Busia 1996: 210), feminist action needs to include finding ways to include the views of those whose governments would like their views excluded. In sum, the critical role of creating deliberative opportunities leads to reassessment of the inclusiveness of activist fora.

Third and finally, the successes of the movement were won in part as a result of institutional changes including building an international network of women's organizations, scholars, and activists. In addition some of the achievements such as the recognition that women's rights are universal in both the Vienna Declaration and the Beijing Platform for Action were themselves institutional changes. Yet, if success is won by using western political tools and by using and therefore strengthening the antidiscrimination paradigm, what exactly has been achieved for women interested in global social and economic justice? What do these institutional changes mean for women's activism and political action of the coming decade called for by the Beijing conference theme: "Action for Equality, Development, and Peace"? Will the international women's movement work to bring nations into compliance with the CEDAW, the Vienna Declaration, and the Beijing Platform for Action by using these UN statements to influence their own countries' policies toward women? Or, will activists ask their countries to consider the ways in which their policies influence the human rights of women outside state borders? Or will activists seek to influence international institutions in

---

[25] Fishkin provides an account of the extent to which views change as a result of deliberation (1996).

[26] For example, Brazilian NGO participation in the regional preparatory meetings was funded by the Ford Foundation and UNIFEM (Friedman et al. 1998: 22).

order that they too promote equality, development, and peace around the world?

Before and during the Beijing conference feminists were aware of the differences among women (Basu 1995; Oloka-Onyango & Tamale 1995; Chow 1996). Such awareness led to the Huairou NGO Forum's being the most inclusive to date with women from around the globe and particularly grassroots organizations creating deliberative opportunities among themselves and in the public forum of the FWCW. Despite these institutional changes toward greater inclusiveness, Third World feminist social criticism suggests that activists and scholars need to continue to assess the achievements of the movement in order to recognize that the organizing theme, political strategies, and goals of the movement may have institutionalized exclusionary values, practices, and norms in the international women's movement.

All Third World feminist social criticism whether an individual or a collective effort cannot stand alone and unexamined. Each criticism is supplemented by other criticism and must also be the *subject* of criticism. The role of inquiry includes fostering ongoing inquiry; the role of creating deliberative opportunities includes fostering greater deliberative opportunities; the role of institutional change includes fostering future institutional changes.

Third World feminist social critics need to be self-consciously aware of ideological differences and the differentials in resources available to promote them. Although western women have been increasingly genuine in their use of violence against women as a universal value, demonstrated by directing their criticisms at their own governments and societies (not only at those of the Third World), the call to action by Abzug needs to be supplemented by a call to self-evaluation. Though the theme of violence against women may have universal appeal, in actuality it was used principally to promote the antidiscrimination agenda of the CEDAW and traditional human rights.

Thinking about ways to address concerns of social and economic justice may yield insights as to how the human rights framework needs to change in order to be able to address concerns about equality, quality of life, and social and economic justice effectively. Thus having Third World women actively deliberating (not just inaccurately or even accurately represented) will lead to epistemological advances in thinking about human rights. The solidarity of Third World feminism comes not from transcending the historical context of women's privilege or exploitation but rather from engaging the reality of the range of women's experience through social criticism. Thus, a self-reflective examination of the movement's unifying theme, political strategies, and achievements may yield its most promising avenues for future action.

Conclusion

Third World feminist social criticism is the task of promoting inquiry, deliberative opportunities, and institutional change. These roles enable other critics and a society to hear the silent voices that power inequalities might otherwise allow them to ignore. As demonstrated by the women's human rights movement, even Third World feminist critics, collectively filling the roles of Third World feminist social critics, may do so imperfectly. Thus, social criticism is an ongoing process and must also include self-examination.

Most probably, no single critic could promote inquiry, deliberative opportunities, and institutional change for all the values, practices, and norms a given society may need to evaluate. Even if she could, her work alone would lack the essential critical perspective gained from deliberative inquiry with other social critics. In practice, different critics fill the various aspects of the roles I describe. Although a certain critic may fill only one role (or one aspect of one role), Third World feminist social criticism relies on all the roles being filled so that social criticism and social decision making will be maximally informed by the experiences and knowledges of those previously silenced due to inequality and coercion. Critics from a broad range of critical backgrounds are necessary to fulfill these roles and to provoke ongoing criticism not only of societies' values, practices, and norms, but also of the very methods, roles, qualifications, and conclusions of social critics themselves. The next chapter looks at the qualifications of critics and the value of critics with multiple perspectives.

5   Qualifications: everyday critics, multi-sited critics, and multiple critics

Introduction

As we have seen, poor village women in Bangladesh and self-employed workers in India working to improve their lives or those of their families, women activists and feminist scholars of activism around the world working on the challenges of development in their communities, and international and local human rights activists working to change local, national, and international understandings of human rights such that they respect women's human rights have much more in common than their geography, resources, and immediate concerns would suggest. Using the Third World feminist method of social criticism, these women (and men) promote inquiry, opportunities for deliberation, and institutional changes that facilitate broadly informed and inclusive deliberations. Anyone can be a critic in her everyday or professional life. She may be an insider, outsider, or multi-sited critic, though critics with this last perspective are unique and frequently provide insights unavailable to inside or outside critics. The only qualification for Third World feminist social critics is that each critic acknowledge her criticism is an essential complement to criticisms from people with other critical perspectives. Because social change is ideally an informed, collective, and uncoerced process, social decision making needs to be informed by many and different critical voices.

Together, filling a range of roles, critics reveal and even anticipate potentially exploitative power inequalities. At the training of the Bangladeshi women's groups, the researcher, the women, and Save the Children program officer all had different critical perspectives. The discovery among the participants of collective action as a means of effecting change in their families happened because of the multiple roles played by different critics from a variety of critical perspectives. In this chapter, I discuss the critical perspectives that enable critics to fill those roles.

The multiple roles for critics cannot be filled by a single critic or from

150

a single critical perspective. Therefore, social criticism is very often a collective endeavor as demonstrated by the Bangladeshi, SEWA, Gender and Development, and women's human rights activists. However, in concert with other critics, individuals can also fill the roles of social critics. The most compelling requirement for Third World feminist social criticism is for each to recognize that her view is incomplete, but valuable in creating broad understanding.

As we saw in chapter 3, Michael Walzer offers only a narrow view of the social critic's qualification – having the critical perspective of the insider or "connected" critic. In feminist theory it has become popular for the author to situate herself *vis-à-vis* her subject matter and for others to be suspicious if she does not share the insider perspective of her subjects (e.g., Flax 1995). However, some feminists buck this trend. Susan Okin, in discussing the practice of female genital mutilation, challenges the view that only cultural insiders can be legitimate social critics and identifies the "inside-outside" critic as one who has the cultural familiarity of an insider and the ability to draw on evidence from outside the culture (1997). Okin, an outsider to cultures where female genital mutilation is practiced, uses the arguments of inside-outside critics to corroborate her own (1998). Debates over who can legitimately critically discuss certain social practices in academic circles are only academic. In the real world, questions of whose arguments have critical authority are political. Social criticism is the project of undermining, or mitigating the effects of, power inequalities on social decision making.

In my view the quality of the work of the social critic should be measured by what she does, not by the perspective from which she makes her arguments. However, given that exclusion as a function of power inequalities limits some people's ability to voice criticism, I argue that the *multi-sited* perspective – which many feminist critics develop – provides an important critical perspective from which to encourage the otherwise silent voices. But no single perspective is adequate for soliciting all of such voices, and thus no single criticism provides an adequate justification of social change. Rather each perspective has the ability to contribute productively to social decision making.[1]

A variety of critical perspectives and multiple critics are necessary to fill the range of social critics' roles described in chapter four. Different critical perspectives may be better suited to certain roles than to others.

---

[1] Some perspectives, typically those that espouse some form of exclusion, may advocate impediments to collective and uncoerced decision making. However, knowledge of that perspective will make deliberation better informed. Moreover, as Mill and Gutmann argue, the experience of articulating one's views leads to affirmation, rejection, or alteration of those views based on reasons rather than habit (Mill 1974 [1859]: 96–101; Gutmann 1995: 578).

In order for a philosophy of social criticism to take into account the reality of power inequalities in the imperfect world, it must describe a collective social process. Whether its practitioners work individually or collectively, Third World feminist social criticism is a collective social process.

The critical perspectives of insiders, outsiders, and multi-sited critics

I indelicately group the endless variety of critical perspectives into three general types: insiders, outsiders, and multi-sited critics. Less important than a critic's perspective (or how I have labeled it) is what she does with it. Does the critic promote inquiry, deliberative opportunities, and institutional change such that existing and potential power inequalities are mitigated and social decision making is more informed, collective, and uncoerced? Each critical perspective has produced examples of critics who do. Focus on the content of criticism rather than on the identity of the critic can help critics extricate themselves from the disempowering impasse between anti-relativist and anti-essentialists caused by identity politics in order that they take on the important work of social criticism.

An *insider* is generally but not always an endogenous critic, one whose origins are within the community that lives by the values, practices, and norms she criticizes. This is Walzer's connected critic; according to him she is "a little to the side, but not outside" (1987: 61). He gives a number of examples of inside critics in *The Company of Critics* including Ignazio Silone and Simone de Beauvoir (1988). In their women's groups, the Tangail women from Bangladesh are inside critics though their experience in Kustia may have broadened their critical perspectives. The members of SEWA are inside critics; however, through their participation in SEWA and as a function of educative deliberation, their critical perspectives may broaden and change. Many of the local activists in the women's rights and human rights movement are inside critics whose criticisms were heard around the world through their testimonials.

An *outsider* is generally an exogenous critic, one whose origins are entirely outside the community she criticizes. The researcher on the walk in Bangladesh was an outsider. Ela Bhatt, though Indian, was an outsider of the communities of self-employed women who formed SEWA (Viswanath 1991: 12). Many Gender and Development scholars live outside the communities they study and aim to help.

It is hard to distinguish between insiders and outsiders. The distinction is not always as easy to make as the distinction between endogenous and exogenous critics. An endogenous and an exogenous critic of a given society have different origins. An inside critic may be endogenous, sharing the origins of the society in question, or exogenous, from another origin but having lived under the values, practices, and norms of the society, adopting most of them. An exogenous critic may speak as an outsider, or she may seek ties and familiarity, language and experience that enable her to speak as an inside critic. Perhaps the best judges of whether the critic is an insider or an outsider are other insiders who assess the critic's local knowledge and ease with their values, practices, and norms. Given that insiders may disagree in their assessments of the critic's local knowledge and comfort, the characterization of an inside or outside critic is one of perspective and is generally a matter for discussion. The distinction of a critic as endogenous or exogenous is less difficult because it is dictated by origin, but given the possible socioeconomic and geographic mobility of people, such a distinction may also be vague or occasionally mistaken. Therefore, the characterizations are not rigid.

These distinctions are also not particularly useful from the perspective that it matters less what a critic's perspective is than what she does as a critic. In order for the social critic to promote inquiry, deliberative opportunities, and institutional change she requires knowledge of the silent voices of the society in question. The possibility that the difference between an insider and an outsider is measured in degrees or kinds of knowledge is heuristically useful. A critic may make a strategic decision to seek more local knowledge in order to facilitate certain forms of criticism, or more outside knowledge in order to strengthen certain critical arguments. There are an endless variety of critical perspectives based on the potential critics' knowledge and access to knowledge. I argue that critical perspectives that are more complicated than those of the insider or the outsider are extremely valuable to social criticism, particularly in order to hear or represent otherwise unheard voices and to promote their being heard and respected in broader public fora. I focus on what I term the multi-sited critic, but by way of introduction, I first discuss the outsider-within which is a form of multi-sited critic identified by Patricia Hill Collins.[2]

In *Black Feminist Thought*, the stance of the *outsider-within* is identified

---

[2] Shahnaz Rouse describes women in Pakistan as "outsider(s) within" but her account does not discuss the epistemological contribution to social criticism that their position in society affords them (1998). Roberta Spalter-Roth and Ronnee Schreiber describe women activists in the US during the 1980s as raising outsider feminist issues using insider political tactics and the challenges that presented to their political success at mobilizing their constituents and achieving political goals (1995).

by Collins initially as the stance of African-American women domestic servants working in white homes in the USA (1991). The servants are outsiders in the white households in which they work and as such they see the gender hierarchy in the white families that the white women may be unable to see. Collins then applies the label more broadly, describing the "outsider-within stance" as "a peculiar marginality that stimulated a special Black women's perspective" (1991: 11). African-American women scholars who resist the hegemonic nature of "white male epistemologies" are also outsiders-within academia (1991: 232).

Outsiders-within face the challenging problem of translating ideas developed from their critical perspective for those who cannot or do not share the "peculiar marginality" of the critic. As Collins notes, "the ideas themselves defy direct translation" (1991: 233). In addition to the challenge of translation, working at the margin, and trying to speak to two audiences also has a personal cost. "'Eventually it comes to you,' observes Lorraine Hansberry, 'the thing that makes you exceptional, if you are at all, is inevitably that which must also make you lonely'" (Hansberry 1969: 148 quoted by Collins 1991: 233). The perspective that makes the critical contributions of an outsider-within so valuable to social criticism, social decision making, and social change, in part relies on her not being a part of a single community. Collins's outsider-within moves between worlds of academia and kitchen tables and is self-conscious of her social position and its personal costs.[3]

The outsider-within is one kind of *multi-sited* critic. The multi-sited critic has the unique perspective of an individual who has been an insider or outsider *vis-à-vis* more than one group: she has acquired local knowledge about more than one group. She is able to move between the places and ideas of those groups. And she is generally self-conscious about her perspective. Susan Okin refers to this as an "inside/outside" critic and gives the example of Rosemary Ofeibea Ofei-Aboagye who, studying in Canada, writes about domestic violence in her native Ghana (Ofei-Aboagye 1994) (Okin 1998, 1997). Jane Mansbridge refers to this as "the straddling individual" for whom "spending time both in an oppositional enclave and outside it promotes weighing the lessons of each venue against the other" (1996: 58). Maivân Clech Lâm accepts Isabelle Gunning's idea of "world traveling" as an antidote for uninformed feminism from the perspective of privilege. "World traveling" requires being self-conscious of one's situation in postcolonialism and

---

[3] For a more concrete account of academics moving between the worlds of the academe and kitchen tables see Jaime Grant's "Building Community-Based Coalitions from Academe: The Union Institute and the Kitchen Table: Women of Color Press Transition Coalition" (1996).

that one listen to the complexity of women's lives rather than articulate a simplifying narrative about them (Lâm 1994). For María Lugones, world traveling is the flexibility to shift "among the mainstream constructions of life" and other constructions (1990: 390). According to Lugones the good world traveler is fluent in the language and cultures of the world she visits, she is happy when she is there, she feels a bond with others of that world, and she has a shared history with others of that world (1990: 397). Only the first, a fluency in the language and culture of the groups or worlds the critic moves between, is defining of the multi-sited critic. However, happiness, bonding, and a shared history often contribute to the ease with which a multi-sited critic can move between worlds. According to Lugones world traveling requires shifting who one is, being "open to surprise," "open to self-construction," and practicing "self-reflection" (1990: 396, 397, 400, 401). Although I suspect many multi-sited critics have the first two qualities of openness, they are not easily-observed qualities. Of these only the third quality, self-reflection, or as I have described it, self-consciousness, is defining of the multi-sited critic.

I do not introduce a neologism lightly; however, I find it necessary. The challenge is to find a way to refer to the critic who crosses boundaries. She may be an insider in two communities such as a scholar with training in western academia and in her natal family in an African country. Or, she may be an outsider to two communities as in a woman living in exile from Iran in the US (Afkhami 1994). I choose "multi-sited" to indicate that the critic's perspective comes from her having familiarity with multiple *sites* and from her ability to move between them or to stand metaphorically or practically with one foot in each. In her life she has played many roles, held affinity with multiple identity groups, and gained local knowledge of more than one social world. In *Thick and Thin*, Walzer argues that all people are "many-sided" because they have many roles, interests, identities, and ideals over their lifetime and at once (1994a: 55–56, 85, 98, 102). My view of the multi-sited critic is that she may be a many-sided person – that is, one with many facets to her – but more importantly she is one who has local knowledge of more than one social world, moves between them, and is self-conscious about her critical perspective. The multi-sited critic knows more than one community having participated in them as an insider. The multi-sited critic's unique perspective comes from the interaction of those communities' influences on her.

The multi-sited critic may cross boundaries by speaking to multiple audiences and promoting deliberation more broadly. For example, In "Women's Rights as Human Rights: Toward a Re-Vision of Human

Rights," Charlotte Bunch speaks to women's human rights activists, human rights activists, and human rights policy makers around the world (1990). In addressing multiple audiences, she provokes self-examination within each. For women's human rights activists she proposes a unifying theme. For human rights activists she provokes discussion about their activism and assumptions. And for human rights policy makers she provokes discussion of the norms of human rights conventions and policy. Moving between the worlds of women's human rights activists, human rights activists, and human rights policy makers, Bunch's criticism provokes skeptical scrutiny and deliberative inquiry of the values, practices, and norms of international human rights.

In addition to moving between worlds, the multi-sited critic is also self-conscious of her critical perspective.[4] Thus, for example, in her account of the Beijing conference, Abena Busia describes the experiences of being in US and Ghanaian educational institutions because she thinks they inform her critical perspective (1996).

I might have chosen "multigenic" meaning having multiple origins, but it seems more accurate to talk about the social environments that inform the critic's perspective and not to limit the description of the critic to her places of origin. "Transgenic" might mean having origins across communities, but that word brings from biology a connotation of a genetic mutation. The multi-sited critic is not a mutant of one or another community, but rather someone who has created her own critical perspective from a variety of influences. "Intergenic" might capture aspects of the meaning of multi-sited. It suggests a critic who has a perspective somehow between communities. Multi-sited captures the influence of more than one community, but suggests that the actual perspective that the critic puts forward is her own, not a perspective from nowhere.[5]

In my view, a critic can be endogenous, exogenous, inside, outside, or multi-sited. No critical perspective is privileged over another. However, the social critic's position *vis-à-vis* the society in question affects her ability to fulfill one or more of the possible roles of social critics. For these purposes criticism is enhanced by the perspectives of many critics who are differently able to promote informed, collective, and uncoerced social change. The multi-sited critic's perspective – her ability to move between worlds and her self-consciousness – is particularly valuable among them, because of its educative function in informing her criticism

---

[4] See also Ruth Behar's *Translated Woman* (1993: Preface).
[5] For the explications of the terms I might have chosen, I am grateful to discussions with Mark Solan, George Tolley, and Susan Okin.

and in the scope of her audience. However, no critic's perspective – even that of a collective multi-sited critic – is adequate alone.

Individual multi-sited critics

The multi-sited critic may be an individual or a collective critic. Individual scholars can develop interesting and unique critical perspectives as a function of their moving between the worlds of their subjects of study and their academic audiences. Two examples of these are Patricia Hill Collins who, in *Black Feminist Thought*, gives an historically grounded contemporary account of black feminist thought (1991) and Patricia Caplan who, in *Class and Gender in India*, gives a contemporary criticism of Indian women's social work organizations in Madras (1985). These scholars' individual critical perspectives have direct bearing on what each is able and unable to witness and analyze, but their perspectives do not dictate the quality of their work.

Collins articulates a coherent account of the history of black feminist consciousness. Collins analyzes the coercion of black women and the suppression of black women's identity in the USA. The politics of black feminist thought, she argues, emerges from an interaction between black women's experience of oppression and their activism against that oppression. "This dialectic of oppression and activism, the tension between the suppression of Black women's ideas and our intellectual activism in the face of that suppression, comprises the politics of Black feminist thought" (1991: 5–6). In developing her account of black feminist thought, Collins represents and analyzes black feminist thought drawing on the lyrics and writings of black women from past and present generations whose texts have been ignored by mainstream discourse.[6] Although to make her point, Collins admittedly exaggerates the monolithic character of black feminist thought (1991: xiv), by providing synthesis and interpretation, she provides a perspective that is as valuable to deliberation as each of the perspectives she joins together. By synthesizing the variety of analyses of black feminists, she simulates

---

[6] Other feminists have provided anthologies of work by previously forgotten or marginalized feminists. Examples of such anthologies include *Third World, Second Sex: Women's Struggles and National Liberation* vol. 1 and 2, ed. Miranda Davies (1983, 1987); *Making Faces, Making Soul/Haciendo Caras: Creative and Critical Perspectives by Women of Color*, ed. Gloria Anzaldúa (1990); *Third World Women and the Politics of Feminism*, eds. Chandra Talpade Mohanty, Ann Russo, and Lourdes Torres (1991); and *Race, Class, and Gender: An Anthology*, eds. Margaret L. Andersen and Patricia Hill Collins (1992); *Women in Exile*, ed. Mahnaz Afkhami (1994); *Faith and Freedom*, ed. Mahnaz Afkhami (1995); *The Challenge of Local Feminisms*, ed. Amrita Basu (1995); *Race, Class, and Gender: Common Bonds, Different Voices*, eds. Esther Ngan-Ling Chow, Doris Wilkinson, and Maxine Baca Zinn (1996).

deliberations among the otherwise suppressed voices of black feminists of different generations. By giving voice to those feminists, she enables them metaphorically to participate in contemporary deliberations. She is a black woman feminist presenting the collective thought of black feminists to other black feminist scholars, to other feminists, and to other social science academics.

Collins's critical perspective is unique. She is an insider of contemporary black feminist circles because she is a contemporary black feminist. She also considers herself part of the community of black women (1991: 17–18). She is also outside the societies of many of the women she discusses because these women are from many places and times. She defines her own critical perspective on mainstream society and academia as that which she shares with black feminist intellectuals: "outsiders-within," that is outsiders of mainstream academia, functioning within it and linked to other groups outside it (1991: 11–12, 35–36). However, because they have to some extent been successful in the white male intellectual world, black feminist intellectuals are also potentially "outsiders-within" black feminist circles – or perhaps insiders who spend a lot of time with outsiders.

Collins uses the experience of many black women from a variety of places, times, and critical perspectives, to develop a black feminist standpoint (1991: 17–18). The "full actualization of Black feminist thought," she writes, "requires a collaborative enterprise with Black women at the center of a community based on coalitions among autonomous groups" (1991: 36). The black feminist standpoint she articulates is a multi-sited standpoint – broader than that of any particular community of black women and informed by the variety of forms of expression and activism that black women have used over the ages to manifest their strength and resilience in the face of interlocking forms of oppression.

Collins claims a central place for black feminist intellectuals in black feminist thought (1991: 33). Black feminist intellectuals are central to advancing black feminist thought due to their multi-sited critical perspective. Collins herself moves between worlds of academic discourse and kitchen table discourse. She has educated herself in the economic, political, social, ideological, musical, and literary history of black women and has developed tools to enable her to communicate her knowledge to audiences beyond the circles of black feminists.

Finally, she is self-conscious about her critical perspective as an insider, outsider, and outsider-within of two communities. Collins works carefully on the project of identifying a collective black feminist thought from the variety of experiences of the variety of women and over time. In addition to the familiar critical functions of inquiry, analysis, and interpretation, Collins offers up her analyses as propositions and seeks corroborating evidence. Collins's critical perspective leads her in her research to listen to previously silent voices. Thus, she is able to recognize the theoretical contributions of black domestic servants to black feminist thought.

Collins's scholarly approach is similar to my own in this book: to find the political theory in political action and in action that is not political in a conventional sense but that is so nonetheless. In their searches for greater understanding of power, multi-sited academic critics of necessity go outside the boundaries of their discipline to address questions and use research materials that, though not technically political science, have political import. Such boundary crossing is familiar to feminists, many of whom are multi-sited critics.

Patricia Caplan provides a complementary example of the multi-sited critic. However, she is a less successful multi-sited critic because she is not as adept at moving between worlds or as self-conscious as Collins. These shortcomings help to demonstrate that the value of the multi-sited perspective lies not in the origins of the critic, but importantly in what she does with her critical perspective.

Caplan studies upper- and upper-middle-class urban women and their voluntary social work organizations in Madras, India. Caplan concludes that charity and voluntary social work function to perpetuate gender and class boundaries. Upper- and upper-middle-class women, confined to domestic activities, and with increasing free time because capitalism and wealth gives them servants, develop their own public arena through charity and voluntary social work. However, their charity work helps reproduce the working class and hierarchical gender ideology (1985: chapter 10, especially 191–200). According to Caplan, "charity defines and separates class" (1985: 223). She argues that through their voluntary social work, the Indian women perpetuate a class and gender ideology that reinforces the status quo of economic and gender inequality.

Caplan is a foreign anthropologist, the wife of a foreign anthropologist, and a friend to some of the women in the groups that are the subjects of her study. She describes herself as a self-conscious outsider whose research methodology requires her to be at times an outsider within urban Indian women's organizations and occasionally an insider in the women's organizations (1985: chapter 1). She also portrays herself as an insider in another sense, by analogy. She studies the way in which class reproduces itself by drawing parallels between the response of urban British upper- and upper-middle-class women to the creation and rise of a middle class in Britain during industrialization and the response of Indian upper- and upper-middle-class women in contemporary Madras to the social changes associated with industrialization (1985: 18–19, 218). She is both an outsider of the women's organizations she studies and an insider of the economic class of women she studies.

Like Collins, Caplan is self-conscious about her critical perspective. In particular, she is concerned that she will be criticized, not for what she says, but for studying a society that is not her own (1985: chapter 1). She answers that concern by treating her research as providing a mirror for her own society and its history. In her conclusion, she draws a parallel between contemporary Madras and Victorian England and then extends her findings by finding corroborating evidence in contemporary Britain, United States, Kenya, Sierra Leone, and Pakistan (1985: chapter 11). Her work enables a dialogue across generations and across continents and provides insights for other efforts to challenge gender and class hierarchies within capitalist and peripheral capitalist economies and around the world.

Caplan is conscious of being an outsider, but tries to be an insider as well. Her self-consciousness about how difficult it is to be both demonstrates her multi-sited critical perspective. However, Caplan does not move easily between her worlds as an anthropologist, a member of the British educated class, and a member of the Indian women's social groups. As a result, her insights about the worlds she describes are disappointingly incomplete.

Her multi-sited perspective itself does not do the work of social criticism for her. While valuable for her own project, her multi-sited perspective is inadequate for providing her with a critical perspective from which to criticize her own work (as Collins is able to do by moving from academic to kitchen table discourse and back). First, in her effort to paint a general picture of the function of the women's organizations in reinforcing class and gender ideology, Caplan does not explore the diversity of views within the organizations. She continually cites documentation of the dominant views of the organizations (1985: chapter 10), but only notes the disconnect between those views and the practices of some of the members rather than exploring the ideas of those dissident members. She sees contradictions in the upper-class Indian class and gender ideology and assesses that ideology as an obstacle to a process of social change that would be more inclusive of the poor. As a multi-sited critic, she sees what many of the upper-class insiders do not. However, Caplan fails to be an audience for, or representative of, the minority views of upper- and upper-middle-class women who do not join the organizations or who participate in them but challenge the gender ideology that volunteer social work perpetuates. She has not used her multi-sited perspective to reveal and discuss a variety of views that might help her to better understand her subject matter. Although moving between the worlds of an anthropologist and the Madras women's groups, she has not described the diversity within the latter.

Second, Caplan does not sufficiently address issues of colonial relationship. She mentions for example that social work training in India follows the US model that treats poverty as an individual pathology not a social ill (1985: 131). The similarities and differences between the practice of social work in the USA, the UK, and India, the transmission of values, and ways of demonstrating status cry out for an analysis of the colonial relationship. Do the upper-class volunteers model their behavior toward the lower classes on colonists' condescending behavior toward them? Have some Indian social workers challenged the US model of social work? Have US challenges to the pathology approach been heard in India?

Because they move between worlds and because they are self-conscious about the effect of their perspectives on their observations, Collins and Caplan have multi-sited critical perspectives. They take advantage of their critical perspectives to do the work of social criticism that others entirely within or outside a society cannot do. A multi-sited critic has the critical perspective necessary to ask certain questions. However, as the strengths and weaknesses of Collins's and Caplan's respective arguments demonstrate, the critic, not her perspective, does the work of social criticism. It is the critic's job to ask questions and then to promote dialogue with critics who are asking related questions and to promote deliberative opportunities for the society to discuss these questions such that each critic's individual perspective contributes to the social process of criticism.

Collective multi-sited critics

Although they too benefit from dialogue with other critics, collective critics by virtue of the multiple critical perspectives of those within their network are frequently able to fill many of the roles of social critics. Educative deliberation within the group provides the resources of knowledge and confidence for members and the group to promote in the broader society deliberation that is inclusive of their views. Successful inclusiveness depends on the network's ability to move between worlds – to speak among themselves, to gather information from those not in the network, and to promote broad deliberation – and its self-consciousness – meaning its members' awareness of those whose views are included or excluded in their internal deliberations.

I chose to use Women Living Under Muslim Laws (WLUML or the network) and DAWN (Development Alternatives with Women for a New Era) as my examples of collective critics primarily because the work of their spokespeople, Farida Shaheed and Gita Sen and Caren Grown, is known among feminist and development scholars and because it is likely not known by political theorists. Feminists will hopefully use their familiarity with Shaheed and Sen & Grown to evaluate my assessment of the multi-sited perspectives used by collective critics. Political theorists will hopefully use the examples of these multi-sited and collective critics to broaden their conception of the perspectives appropriate and essential for social criticism.

WLUML is an international network of generally educated women that brings together grassroots leadership and scholars throughout the Muslim world.[7] The network was founded around issues and continues to exist as a function of its members' activism. WLUML began in 1984 in response to several international incidents involving women in conflict with Muslim laws. Three feminists were jailed for seven months in Algeria for discussing a government-proposed new family code. An Indian Muslim woman petitioned the Indian Supreme Court to protect those rights as an Indian citizen that were denied her by the religious law which the Muslim minority within India is allowed to use to adjudicate matters of family law. In Abu Dhabi, for alleged adultery, a Sri Lankan woman was sentenced to death by stoning. The sentence was to be carried out once she carried her pregnancy to term and nursed the child for two months. In Europe, divorced women whose children were in the custody of their Algerian fathers sought visitation rights or custody of their children.

In 1986 the network of women responding to these crises got together and drafted the network's First Plan of Action. Their general purpose is to inform women in various parts of the world of the great variety in Muslim law as it is practiced around the world, to reclaim for women the right to interpret Islamic texts, to clarify as a point of law and human rights the difference between Islamic law and Muslim practice, and to use that distinction to advocate for interpretations of Islamic texts, enactment of Muslim law, and changes in Muslim practices that are respectful of women as equal to men.

The difference between Islamic law and Muslim practice is important for Muslim feminists and for understanding the work of the network.

---

[7] The description of WLUML is based primarily on Shaheed 1994 and 1995.

Mahnaz Afkhami and Shaheed note the political importance of distinguishing between Islamic practices set forth in the Qur'an and Hadith (the narrative record of the sayings and actions of Muhammad) from Muslim practices which are more general social, cultural, and economic practices of followers of Islam (Afkhami 1995b and Shaheed 1994). Riffat Hassan distinguishes between the teachings of the Qur'an and the later interpretive texts, arguing that the latter contain faulty scholarship and ideas imported from Judaism and Christianity (1991). In theocracies Islamic and Muslim practices are linked by the unified religious and political authority.

Islamic law is religious law as practiced either by the Prophet (according to Sunnites), or by the Prophet and his family (according to Shi'ites). Muslim law and practices are more generally the laws and practices of those who are followers of Islam. However, Muslim laws and practices vary by country. They are based on practices in place before the people in a given place adopted Islam, for example, the practice of female genital mutilation in parts of Africa. They are laws and practices that come from colonial rule; for example, in South Asia, British colonial laws deprived Muslim women of their religiously sanctioned right to own and inherit property (Shaheed 1994: 1000). And practices change over time, as in Bangladesh the switch in marital contracts among Muslims from the practice of paying bride price to the bride's family to what had been generally the Hindu practice of the bridal family's paying dowry to the husband. When laws and practices are defended as ordained in the Qur'an, feminist Muslims ask for the right to interpret the texts. Such scholars include Fatima Mernissi, a sociology professor in Morocco who has reinterpreted classic Islamic texts and studied the legal status of women in Morocco, Algeria and Tunisia (1995), Riffat Hassan, a Pakistani feminist theologian (1991), and Nazīrah Zein Ed-Dīn, a Lebanese-born Muslim scholar whose writings incited controversy during her day and are informative today (1982 [1928]).

An example of the network's effectiveness is the success of the Collectif '95. Women have been marginalized in different and similar ways in Arab states and have had difficulty putting their interests on the national agenda (though the Arab nations give a lot of attention to women's place within society). When Arab states organized to create legislative coherence in family laws across Arab states, women formed the Collectif '95. "Fearing the implications of legislation that would further reduce women's rights in the family, activists networked to preempt this by producing a counter-draft proposal for a uniform code of the family based on gender equality" (Shaheed 1995: 97). WLUML members recognized that the proposed new code would codify some of the most oppressive laws affecting women in each of these countries. As the Collectif '95, they mobilized to propose a counter-draft drawing on those aspects of existing family law that recognized women's equality. As a result of their efforts no uniform code passed. The network used the knowledge gained through educative deliberation among themselves to generate better informed public deliberations in the broader society.

By virtue of being a network, WLUML captures the views of women from many cultural and experiential backgrounds. Collectively WLUML members are multi-sited critics. WLUML offers multi-sited criticism as a function of the range of religious, cultural, and national backgrounds of its members and, by creating deliberative opportunities, enables its members to be more multi-sited. Further, through their participation in WLUML, members can develop their multi-sited perspective. Through the network, a WLUML member can move between the worlds of many Muslim women and be self-conscious of her own situated knowledge. WLUML provides resources and fora for Muslim women to participate in international dialogues about Muslim practices and laws. WLUML has facilitated networking and information sharing among women living under Muslim laws around the world. By drawing on each other's cultural particularities, women can advocate for laws which are less oppressive for women, yet which can still be considered Muslim (Shaheed 1994 and 1995).

Through WLUML and other networks with a similar purpose such as the Global Network for Reproductive Rights, International Women's Rights Action Watch, Women's International Cross Cultural Exchange, ISIS International, and Sisterhood Is Global, women have been able to improve their understanding of obstacles to women's participation, their understanding of women's interests, and thereby, their ability to represent women. Perhaps exemplified by their experiences in mobilizing for the 1993 UN World Conference on Human Rights and for the 1995 UN Fourth World Conference on Women, women have developed means of networking internationally and locally so that the criticisms put forward by individuals or certain groups have benefited from educative deliberation within the broad community of women activists. Such extensive deliberations better enable feminist critics within the collectives to move between worlds and to be self-conscious about their unique critical perspectives.

Collective critics may collect and share diverse views and information as demonstrated by WLUML, or they may collect, synthesize, and disseminate views and information. DAWN synthesizes insights from a variety of Third World feminists in order to "shape a counter-knowledge, an alternative feminist epistemology" for development strategy (AWID 1991: 82).[8] In order to offer a counter-knowledge, DAWN draws from the "realities at the grassroots level" to challenge development norms (Stamp 1991: 64).

Subordinate economic and social status, and restrictions on women's activity and mobility are embedded in most traditional cultures, as our research over the last fifteen years has shown. The call to cultural purity is often a thinly veiled attempt to continue women's subjugation in a rapidly changing society. But traditions and cultures also divide women themselves, since traditions and practices vary across classes in the same society. (Sen & Grown 1987: 76)

DAWN, like WLUML, is a multi-sited critic, incorporating and representing the many views from women of varied critical perspectives. DAWN grew out of the 1985 Nairobi Conference at the end of the United Nations Decade for Women and discussions initiated by an Indian economist, Devaki Jain, leading up to the conference. DAWN facilitated the continuation of educative deliberation among Third World feminists and between Third World and western feminists.[9] DAWN is a collective of Third World feminists, researchers, advocates, and practitioners. This diversity contributes to recognizing common ground. As Sen & Grown write on behalf of the DAWN coalition, "beneath this diversity, feminism has as its unshakable core a commitment to breaking down the structures of gender subordination and a vision for women as full and equal participants with men at all levels of societal life" (Sen & Grown 1987: 70). With their commitment to a unifying policy agenda, Sen & Grown synthesize the views of DAWN members and years of research to represent women around the world. Women's organizations have asserted women's right to participate in decisions about social change and have given women a means through which to put certain social changes on the agenda where they were not.

Sen & Grown's book *Development, Crises, and Alternative Visions* had a moderate to significant influence on those working in the field of women in development (Parpart 1993). However, their attempt to synthesize women's vast and varied experiences and knowledge into a condensed policy agenda brought criticism from some feminists (e.g., Hirshman 1995). Among those sensitive (or trying to be sensitive) to gender issues

[8] Sen & Grown give the account of DAWN on which I rely (1987). Jane Parpart provides some background (1993). Mitu Hirshman (1995) and Parpart (1995) offer criticisms of Sen & Grown's synthesis. For a more recent account of DAWN's role in facilitating the inclusion of perspectives from the Third World see AWID (1991).

[9] Eastern European and Russian feminists are still struggling to be heard in international feminist dialogues (Posadskaya 1995; Matynia 1995). The issues that these feminists raise regarding formal equality, informal inequality, and institutional marginalization of women are important for all women's economic, social, and political functional equality and effective participation.

and to women in development, their work influenced thinking and policy. However, within the large development organizations, gender issues are discussed in segmented and under-funded departments devoted to women. In many development organizations, the gendered impact of development proposals has yet to become an integral part of organizational decision making (Kardam 1991; Razavi & Miller 1995a, 1995b).

As a strategy, then, one might argue that DAWN's collection, synthesis, and dissemination method of activism may not have been effective. Their work used educative deliberation among those working in women, gender, and development to promote further educative deliberation among themselves and with a sympathetic audience. DAWN continues to be a resource for those seeking the input of grassroots experience in the Third World (AWID 1991: 1). But, it is less obvious that it promoted educative deliberation in the broader society as WLUML did in the case of the Collectif '95. However, as demonstrated by how often it is cited, *Development, Crises, and Alternative Visions* continues to be a resource and an eye-opening introduction for those working in development and may strengthen their efforts to promote educative deliberation about women, gender, and development more broadly.

Although gender-conscious approaches to development are only now becoming mainstreamed in certain development organizations, gender-awareness has made significant inroads. The multi-sited perspective of DAWN's members contributes to its influence. The DAWN authors move between academia and development practice. Sen & Grown's book bridges those worlds by being accessible to both academics and practitioners. And because of the diversity of women's experiences reflected in DAWN, the authors were self-conscious about being inclusive and respectful of that diversity.

As discussed in chapter 3, DAWN's critics argue that in presuming to synthesize the learning of women around the world, Sen & Grown obfuscate the differences among women's worlds (rather than move between them). Moreover, they are accused of privileging a false universal perspective (rather than being self-conscious of their own perspective). Whether they prove correct or not, these criticisms are worthy of consideration. DAWN's multi-sited perspective is a function of the national and professional diversity of its contributors. Particular members of DAWN may also be multi-sited as a function of participating in deliberation through DAWN depending on whether they use the resultant learning as a means to move between worlds and develop their self-consciousness of their own perspective. Collective critics are as multi-sited as the diversity within the collectivity. Individual and collective critics need to engage in dialogue with other critics. If social criticism is to be informed, collective, and uncoerced, it must invite inquiry and deliberation among multiple critics.

Critics at work: listening where they live and where they don't

A particular critical perspective can be enabling, but it does not do the work of social criticism. Regardless of their critical perspectives, in order to promote informed, collective, and uncoerced social change, social critics need individually and collectively to listen to the voices within the society in question – those they are used to hearing and those they have never heard. In the previous chapter 1 grouped the roles of social critics into three categories: promoting inquiry, deliberative opportunities, and institutional change. A variety of critical perspectives, but particularly multi-sited perspectives, are valuable for filling these roles. Parenthetically, whether a critic is effective at listening to the silent voices and making those voices heard in the broader society is not only a function of her critical perspective, but also a function of the distribution of power within the society. The following arguments about the work of social critics are based on the former, but I recognize the possibility that where inequalities are great, much social criticism is silenced.

Inquiry

Inquiry makes public information that has been kept private either by choice, fear, or exclusion. Good inquiry requires asking the right questions in the right way and casting a broad net in the search for evidence. The insider has two strengths in promoting inquiry. First, she may be able to conduct her inquiry by phrasing questions such that they are comprehensible to the previously silent and such that unheard voices are made audible. The insider critic may be able to ask the right question. Second, the insider can expose an "insider" secret. Collins cites an interview by Claudia Tate of Ntozake Shange.

In her chorepoem *For Colored Girls Who Have Considered Suicide*, Ntozake Shange (1975) creates the character Beau Willie Brown, a man who abuses his lover, Chrystal, and who kills their two young children ... Tate asked Ntozake Shange, "why did you have to tell about Beau Willie Brown?" (1991: 186–187)

Collins notes that with this question Tate invokes the bond of a "collective family 'secret.'" In her response, Shange rejects the harmful silence of keeping such a secret. "I refuse to be a part of this conspiracy of silence. I will not do it. So that is why I wrote about Beau Willie

Brown. I am tired of living lies" (Collins 1991: 186–187 quoting Tate 1983: 158–159). Concurring, Collins argues that self-criticism needs to be a part of black feminist thought going forward. Alice Walker and Audre Lorde have also helped make black women's abuse visible (Collins 1991: 188). An insider may be well-positioned to know the family secrets and unrevealed inequalities. The challenge for an insider is that she may not hear the critical perspectives of those who are generally unheard or heard only on the margins of her society. Or, she may be familiar with values, practices, and norms that perpetuate harmful inequalities but she may not recognize them as harmful or be able to be critical of them. Thus, the insider may be the only critic familiar enough with local values, practices, and norms to recognize that they should be scrutinized. Moreover, although the insider may be unable to inquire about certain values, practices, and norms, her perspective is invaluable in understanding them. Note that the knowledge of the insider can only be fully appreciated by the insider herself and thus no representation can ever be unquestionably accurate and adequate.

An outsider, by contrast, may not see harmful inequalities because she only sees what is revealed to her. She may identify some harmful inequalities, but ignore others. Or she may recognize harmful values, practices, and norms as obstacles to informed, collective, and uncoerced social change, but be unable to ask the question or phrase it such that it sparks inquiry. As we saw in chapter 4, when writing as a social critic, Martha Nussbaum makes mistakes of interpretation due to her incomplete observations and inquiry as an outsider of rural Bangladesh. By contrast as in the study cited in chapter 4 by Save the Children of maternal and child health in Bangladesh, the outsider can ask questions and bring important information about health that enables learning. Thus although the outsider's inquiry may be mistaken, the outsider provides an invaluable perspective.

The successful inquiring multi-sited critic sees a problem, asks probing questions, and phrases them right. Multi-sited critics do not replace critics with other perspectives. However, where inside critics are not critical and outside critics are unable to see a problem, multi-sited critics may be able to promote inquiry such that a critical dialogue begins to which other critical voices can then be added.

Despite its advantages, the multi-sited critic is not infallible. Collins is a multi-sited critic who is both an outsider-within white academia and an insider who travels outside black feminist circles. Her history and interpretation of black feminist thought provides both the nonmarginal academic community and the otherwise marginalized black feminist community with an articulation of black feminist thought which is accessible to both. Her effort gives voice to black feminists previously unheard in the nonmarginal academic community and furthers the efforts that the marginalized group had been doing alone. Caplan is less successful. She uses her multi-sited perspective to inquire about and to interpret the practice of voluntary social work through private organizations among upper and upper-middle class women in Madras. Like Collins, she promotes awareness within the nonmarginal academic community. But Caplan is less successful than Collins at moving between worlds and leaves unexplained the perceptions of those women who do not share in the dominant practice of upper-class women's social.

Collective critics can use their multi-sited perspectives to promote internal inquiry and inquiry in the broader society. WLUML promotes inquiry among women within and across countries and uses this knowledge to influence and support public dialogue more broadly. DAWN promotes inquiry among women by collecting research from around the world and conducting its own. Sen & Grown furthered inquiry in the broader academic and professional development communities by writing *Development, Crises, and Alternative Visions*. DAWN continues to conduct its own research and to participate in the deliberative fora of others (AWID 1991).

Like other critical perspectives the multi-sited critic's perspective itself does not do the work of social criticism, but it does enable critics to see the diversity of human experience. For example, although the multi-sited critic sees the problem that neither the insider nor outsider sees, she may not be able to voice her observation. The black women working in domestic service discussed by Collins see the inequality between white women and men that those women cannot see. "When you come right down to it, white women just *think* they are free. Black women *know* they ain't free" (Nancy White in Gwaltney 1980: 147 quoted by Collins 1990: 208). However, they do not express their criticism of white gender hierarchy to the nonmarginal society they are outside; nor do they necessarily use their observations to draw attention to gender hierarchy in their own circles. In addition others may dilute the message of the multi-sited critic. Although DAWN has had an impact on development, as we saw in chapter 3, Sen & Grown's contributions as critics of development have been overlooked by postmodern critics (Hirshman 1995; Parpart 1995: 236). Finally, the multi-sited critic may make mistakes or errors of omission. Alone, even the multi-sited critic offers unreliable social criticism.

Social critics interpret the practices that have arisen to accommodate competing values and they ask whether the values arose to justify existing practices. They ask, do these values or practices rely on or reinforce an exploitative power inequality? In addition, they promote the community's collective evaluation process. The familiarity of inside critics may make them better at pointing out the ways in which seemingly noncoercive values reinforce oppressive or potentially oppressive practices. However, under circumstances where power inequalities inhibit free expression – think again of those living in the water, afraid to argue with the crocodiles – inside critics may be less able than outside critics or multi-sited critics to ask, or to speak, about the oppression. Individually or collectively, inside, outside, and multi-sited critics through questioning, research, analysis and interpretation solicit the variety of views within the society on the institutions in question. The multi-sited critic has unique local knowledge of multiple social worlds, the ability to move between them, and self-consciousness about her critical perspective that may make her better able to promote inquiry than other critics.

Deliberative opportunities

Whereas inquiry is essential to an individual's and a society's recognition of practices that are potentially exploitative of inequalities, the deliberative forum is where society's multiple perspectives on those values, practices, and norms can be shared. Without such a forum, it is hard for people to *hear* the views of one another. Where such a forum is lacking, an important role of critics is to promote opportunities for the deliberative exchange of views. Although an inside critic may have the knowledge necessary to offer an invitation to deliberation that is accepted and to structure a forum for deliberation that is effective, insiders, particularly if they are oppressed, may be unable to fill that role. Multi-sited and outside critics may have the resources to arrange and secure deliberative fora for previously unheard people and to enable their voices to be heard in the broader society.

Alone, an insider may not feel safe enough to promote a deliberative opportunity. But collectively, insiders may be able to surmount the oppression that leaves each individual silent. For example, alone, the Tangail women's savings group member who was beaten by her husband and the member who wanted her daughter to continue in school were unable to influence their husbands' decisions. However, when the Tangail women went collectively to the homes of the two husbands, they were able to promote a deliberation between husband and wife in which the wife's view was heard. Acting collectively, the women created a safe forum for themselves to voice their criticism.

Collins gives a slightly different example of black women creating a safe place in order for them to find their individual and collective voices (1991: 95). Collins's examples of "[e]xtended families, churches, and African-American community organizations are important locations where safe discourse potentially can occur" (1991: 95). Not only are these places for safe discourse, but also they are places where their discourse can be heard by their community. Because in mainstream discourse, black voices are marginalized, they need a secure place to deliberate with each other.[10] Deliberative inquiry among equals provides a safe context in which to develop a strategy of collective action for future deliberative exchange with those who are more powerful. The voices that they identify in the security of their own spaces may later be used to develop social criticism of the broader society.

The outsider may be able to promote deliberative opportunities by creating a safe forum for the previously oppressed or unheard to share their views before a safe audience. In this way they learn to express their own ideas, gain recognition and affirmation from others, and collectively develop strategies for bringing their concerns to the broader society. For example, in holding organizational meetings, SEWA organizers promoted deliberative exchange amongst the self-employed women of Gujarat in which they identified common needs.[11] By forming women's groups in Tangail, Save the Children formalized and gave formal strength to existing networks among women. By bringing together the Tangail and Kustia women in a protected environment apart from their husbands and other social influences, Save the Children promoted deliberative exchange amongst the Bangladeshi women during which they identified collective action as a potentially effective strategy for social change. These outsider organizations use their status to create secure environments for deliberation. Educative deliberation in a secure forum can be a springboard for bringing those views to the broader, public deliberative forum.

Although in general I emphasize that critics' resources are more important than their critical stances for promoting deliberation, in the case of deliberations where multiple views are in dispute, the critical distance of an outsider, or someone perceived as impartial, may itself be a resource which helps promote deliberative exchange. Research in psychology shows that the presence of an impartial third party can lead

---

[10] See also Belenky et al.'s account of the Mother Center movement in the USA (1997).

[11] One might argue that the SEWA organizers were outsiders with more education and political experiences than the self-employed women. Initially, this was true and it continues to be true when SEWA expands into new rural areas.

disagreeing parties to a more advantageous outcome from both of their perspectives (Ross & Ward 1996). One of the strategies of women's rights activists was to have the judges at the Vienna Tribunal be participants in the UN Plenary and, though impartial, sympathetic.

Collective multi-sited critics may be able to provide deliberative opportunities for people to exchange ideas with those to whom they would otherwise not have access. WLUML creates such opportunities through the network. Multi-sited critics can create deliberative opportunities by bringing otherwise marginalized perspectives to public fora. The women's human rights movement demonstrates some political strategies for promoting deliberative opportunities for previously unheard voices. Using less political strategies, DAWN creates such opportunities by sharing their work in public fora, publishing and distributing their work, and participating in the deliberative fora of conferences. An insider, outsider, or multi-sited critic may be successful at promoting deliberative opportunities that offer the security necessary for the previously silent to speak up. Less important than identifying the critical perspective of each is noting the ways in which each critic's perspective enables her (and them collectively) to promote deliberative opportunities.

Institutional change

Of course, by creating deliberative opportunities social critics are creating institutional change. Other forms of institutional change include making existing fora more deliberative either by changing them, by representing the silent, or by encouraging their participation. Again, these can be done by inside, outside, or multi-sited critics, but the last may be particularly effective.

WLUML promotes changes in laws and practices such that they are less oppressive to women. In so doing the network also promotes a general set of values: that women and men are human beings of equal worth and that women have basic rights which the law, economy, and social practices should reinforce. The values they promote are a synthesis of those held by many women living under Muslim laws around the world and consistent with feminist readings of the Qur'an (Hassan 1991; Mernissi 1991).

DAWN promotes institutional change by providing analysis of global crises such as the linked problems of food, fuel, and water; the balance of payments and debt crisis; militarization and violence; and social movements of "national chauvinism, racism, and sexism" (Sen & Grown 1987: 50–77). In addition, DAWN promotes institutional change by offering alternative visions for societies including women's roles in social change. Specifically, they articulate collective strategies for women's social and political activism. DAWN represents the values of Third World women "in breaking down the structures of gender subordination and a vision for women as full and equal participants with men at all levels of societal life" as essential and shared and proposes changes to help realize those values (Sen & Grown 1987: 70).

In their efforts to promote social change, WLUML and DAWN do not reiterate or reinforce the dominant values of the society. Rather, these multi-sited critics challenge many of those values. These networks move between social worlds and are self-conscious of which worlds inform their arguments. They defend their views by appealing to an essential value, the equal worth of female and male human beings, appreciated around the world in a variety of contexts. Through their practice of social criticism, they try to promote inclusive social decision making that is respectful of that equality. They want the participants in decision-making fora to be able to hear all of the previously silent voices. To do so, they sometimes represent the unheard voices as spokespeople. Each member uses her participation in the network as a source of learning from others in order to complement her own singular perspective and as an avenue of sharing her perspective.

Another form of institutional change comes through representation. Collins discusses black women who are outsiders-within the African-American movement because they are women and black women who are outsiders-within public service because they are heads of social service agencies (1991: 157, 159). Both are multi-sited critics who use their strength and knowledge fostered through their community with other black women to make institutional changes in the broader society such that society comes to address black women's concerns. By representing the marginalized within the African-American movement and social service system, black women enable the views of those marginalized to be heard in decision-making fora. Because Third World feminist critics worry about the adequacy and accuracy of their representation and the disempowering effect of being represented rather than of speaking for oneself, they also seek to enable the marginalized to represent themselves. The women's human rights movement's effort to arrange the Vienna Tribunal is an example of some critics' using their political skill to enable other critics, who had gone unheard, to speak for themselves and to be heard. Because not every woman whose human rights had been violated could speak in the forum of the Tribunal, organizers attempted to select a spectrum of women whose collective experiences would be representative of other women's experiences or at least indicative of the variety and extent of the violations of women's human rights. Through different mechanisms SEWA's trade groups have had the same institutional effects of both representing women and changing institutions so that women can represent themselves.

Obviously, the range of roles requires a range of critics. Although no critic is unqualified and each brings a valuable contribution to social criticism, multi-sited critics are particularly good at fulfilling many of the critics' roles. The multi-sited critic in particular is able to use her own unique combination of familiarity and critical distance in promoting values, practices, and norms which do not protect or foster power inequalities that can be exploited to the advantage of the powerful. The perspective of the multi-sited critic can be lonely as Lorraine Hansberry said (1969). It can also be perceived as elitist as Uma Narayan worries (1997). Some multi-sited critics achieve their ability to move between worlds through the advantages of education, travel, and funding. Others have their multiple worlds forced on them and become multi-sited critics to cope. The black domestic servant and her relation to her employer that Judith Rollins describes in *Between Women: Domestics and Their Employers* (1985) and the experience of living in exile that Mahnaz Afkhami describes in *Women in Exile* (1994) are examples of forced conditions for developing a multi-sited perspective. How self-conscious and how able to move between worlds the woman becomes are matters of the critic's own development. Self-consciousness is the multi-sited critic's tool against her potential elitism or obscurity. Self-conscious and in dialogue with other critics, critics are better able to fill all these roles.

Multiple critics

Within a society, there may be differences of opinion. In order for social criticism to reflect the views of the vocal and the silent, critics need to promote inquiry, deliberative opportunities, and institutional change in the society. But as we have seen, no single critic can fill all these roles. No critic alone could adequately provide an account of a diverse reality. The broad scope of social criticism requires a broad social effort. As Walzer argues in *Interpretation and Social Criticism*, "[s]ocial criticism is a social activity ... social critics are individuals, but they are also, most of the time, members, speaking in public to other members who join in the speaking and whose speech constituted a collective reflection upon the conditions of collective life" (1987: 35).

No critic alone is capable of promoting broad adequate public dialogue about existing or potential oppression. Social criticism instead invites all within and outside the society to be critics.[12] Critics may be academics such as Collins and Caplan. They may be local activists like SEWA and the women on the walk in Bangladesh or international activists like the members of WLUML, DAWN, and the women's human rights movement. They may be heroes, writers, artists, and philosophers. They may be individuals and they may be organized groups.

There are legitimate concerns about inviting all people to be critics. As Walzer warns, "once one begins including all the people who are touched or affected by a given decision, and not just those whose daily activities are directed by it, it is hard to know where to stop" (1983: 292). The concern about inviting too many people to join in the critical endeavor is legitimate only if it is logistical. Logistics are an important challenge and increasingly so in modern nation states with large populations ostensibly sharing a political community, even more so in this view which broadens the base of those who participate to include outsiders and multi-sited critics. Multiple perspectives provide multiple sources for scrutiny of exploitative or potentially exploitative values, practices and norms. Organizing deliberative fora so that they allow for a wide range of critical input without having political influence be the prerequisite for being heard is a political challenge, but it is not a political obstacle like power inequalities are. Benjamin Barber is particularly concerned with how the institutions of broad political participation can assuage elite fears of the supposed whim of popular rule (1984) but we might read most deliberative theorists as being concerned with making popular deliberation more reasoned.

Third World feminist social critics are not concerned with managing the multiplicity of critical voices if having those voices means that social criticism is better informed, more inclusive, and unaffected by power inequalities. Regardless of her critical perspective, no single critic is able to promote access to the public forum for all of the many silent voices. Even multi-sited critics seek the contributions of other critics. For example, Collins seeks colleagues among other black activists and scholars and in fact builds her arguments around them. Caplan seeks colleagues among other anthropologists. SEWA seeks out the views of its membership and others interested in women, gender, and development; WLUML and DAWN seek out the views of those within and beyond their networks. Feminists generally recognize the value of critical dialogue among critics. However, as the examples of Caplan's discussion of Indian upper-middle-class women's social work and Martha

---

[12] This is not to say that all critics' methodologies will promote informed, collective, and uncoerced social change or that all criticisms are equally valid.

Nussbaum's discussion of the BRAC literacy project show, a singular critical perspective, nuanced or not, is generally inadequate for full information.

Educative deliberation is powerful for critics and society. The implication is that the broader the participation and representation in deliberative dialogue, the more information will be shared and the greater the opportunity for learning and discovery for all. Having multiple critics raises a logistical challenge similar to those generally discussed in the context of political fora. Despite the logistical and political obstacles to multiple critical perspectives, societies can wrestle with, rather than accept, those obstacles. Some institutional changes proposed by the deliberative theorists and Third World feminist critics are mechanisms for dealing with the obstacles of, and challenges to, creating participatory deliberative fora, but may apply to promoting discussions among critics as well.

Conclusion

As the variety of social critics described in this chapter reveals, the critic's perspective is an important tool for her drafting social criticism, but it is not a method. One's critical perspective cannot do the work of social criticism. Rather, each critic from her own perspective applies the critical methodology developed in chapter 3.

Given my respect for the diversity in critical perspectives and in the ways in which Third World feminists practice the feminist methodology, it may appear that I have catalogued an existing practice of social criticism, but not identified a direction for feminist social criticism. In fact, I would very much like to give credit for developing this theory of Third World feminist social criticism to those who have authored it – to the women on the walk, to SEWA, to GAD theorists and practioners, to black feminists, to women's human rights activists and theorists, to Collins, to Caplan, to WLUML, and to DAWN. However, while appreciating their individual contributions to Third World feminist theory, I have also encouraged us to learn from them. Bringing together their practice of social criticism into a coherent theory of feminist social criticism, I have offered a practicable solution to the theoretical problems with deliberative democratic theory and a vision of a theoretical solution to what has become a practical problem in much feminist theory. Third World feminist social criticism offers an account of how to bring about social change toward deliberative democratic theory's ideal deliberative conditions – using deliberation among multiple critics from multiple perspectives, especially those of the multi-sited critics to make deliberations more informed, inclusive, and uncoerced. Third World feminist social criticism offers a theoretical exit to the practical impasse between anti-relativist and anti-essentialist feminists. Listening to the critical observations of inside, outside, and multi-sited critics who exercise the feminist methodology of skeptical scrutiny, guiding criteria, and deliberative inquiry, feminists can participate in substantive social criticism that is respectful of, and informed by, diversity.

6   Third World feminist social criticism as feminism

Introduction

In the real world, inequalities are exploited by those better positioned in social, familial, political, and economic hierarchies such that the views of the less powerful go unheard. At the beginning of this book, I promised to present a Third World feminist theoretical and practical account of social criticism that resolves a problem in deliberative democratic theory, that meets and exceeds critical theory's standard of theory, that respects both sides of the relativist–essentialist schism in feminist theory, and that situates Third World feminism as the heir of feminism because Third World feminists listen to the otherwise silent sources in a given society and are critical of the inequalities that silence them. Third World feminist social criticism is critical where other theories are not.

In order to be critical, a theory of social criticism needs to be more than actionable, coherent, and self-reflective. It also needs to identify the critics' method, roles, and qualifications such that critics listen to otherwise silent or unheard voices and are critical of exclusive, elitist, or coercive social decision-making fora. Based on the activism of women around the world, I have offered Third World feminist social criticism as not only theoretically important to democratic theory, critical theory, and feminist theory, but also as the realizable complement to their theoretical ideals.

In chapter 2, I present an overview of Third World feminist social criticism including a sketch of the method, roles, and qualifications it proposes for critics. In chapter 3, I provide details of skeptical scrutiny, guiding criteria, and deliberative inquiry that comprise the method and argue that all three are essential to a critical method that provides solutions to the problems in contemporary political and feminist theory of both respecting diversity and offering trenchant social criticism. Because the subjects and task of social criticism are so broad, the critics' roles are also broad. In chapter 4, I describe the range of critics' roles summarized as promoting inquiry, deliberative opportunities, and institutional change. In addition to criticizing society by fulfilling these roles, critics must turn their critical attention also to their own work such that the practice of social criticism itself becomes increasingly inclusive and informed by an ever-increasing range of experiences. In chapter 5, I argue that there is no exclusive qualification of social critics, but that the multi-sited critical perspective is particularly important for social critics' ability to listen to the silent voices in their own societies and in others. Moreover, each critic's voice joins that of others in order that social decision making and social change are inclusive of *all* the silent voices. This chapter concludes the account of Third World feminist social criticism by situating it in the context of some contemporary feminists' efforts to address the theoretical problems I have argued Third World feminist social criticism solves.

Not only does Third World feminist social criticism offer a theoretical insight into how deliberative theorists, critical theorists, and feminist theorists might address problems in their fields, but also Third World women activists have shown us that the theoretical solutions they propose are doable in practice. As a theory of social criticism, Third World feminist social criticism is better than the alternatives I have acknowledged because Third World feminist social criticism explicitly engages the problem of inequality that deliberative theory, critical theory, and feminist theory have been able to sidestep through rhetorical devices or by framing their arguments such that the problems associated with inequality are outside the scope of their projects. This is not to say that Third World feminist social criticism is a prescription for political success. It can and has failed to achieve its goals (though intermediate ends of the development of participants' skills and resources may be directed toward future goals).[1] Even if critics view each effort as bringing about some progress toward ultimate goals, the method of Third World feminist social critics may not be politically expedient especially when facing extreme power inequalities.

In addition to the practical problems that Third World feminist activism must confront, there are theoretical challenges. These theoretical challenges are inescapable because the theory itself requires the critic to engage them. First, in their use of the method, feminists can make mistakes that perpetuate inequalities or create new ones. For example as we saw in the discussion of the women's human rights movement, Third World feminist social critics may reiterate certain hierarchies even while they work to change others. Though problematic

---

[1] See the discussion of the women's human rights movement in chapter 4. See also Belenky et al. and their discussion of the Mother Center movements in the USA and Germany (1997).

in practice, such failures of social criticism are not problems for the theory. Rather they invite a broader range of critics discussed in chapter 5 and ask those critics to fill the broad range of roles discussed in chapter 4. Second, in their execution of roles individual critics may intend to represent some women in their challenge of inequality, but in fact create a new inequality between themselves as representatives and the women they represent. Again, the failures of individual critics are failures of the practice, not the theory. The practical antidote is to increase the range of critics' critical perspectives and roles. Third, though no qualification or critical perspective is decisive for social criticism, I have emphasized the critical value of the multi-sited critic who moves between worlds self-consciously. Such a critical perspective is possible because the critic has the experience of being an insider and an outsider, of being included and excluded. If critics are successful at bringing about more inclusive social, familial, economic, and political life, the critical perspective of the multi-sited critic will change – she will no longer be subject to harmful inequalities. As with the other two potential theoretical problems, this is a problem for the practice, not the theory. Instead of yielding an experience of inequality and exclusion, multi-sited world traveling will yield the knowledge associated with crossing real and imaginary boundaries between groups, experiences, and knowledges. Even under conditions of perfect equality, the multi-sited critic promotes valuable exchanges of knowledge and thereby helps anticipate and prevent future experiences of inequality. As a theory of social change Third World feminist social criticism attempts to deal with the problem of inequality in practice by recognizing that social criticism and social change are ongoing processes.

Despite its practical shortcomings as a critical practice, Third World feminist social criticism advances deliberative democratic theory, feminist democratic theory, feminist critical theory, and postmodern feminist theory. In that light Third World feminist social criticism is feminist democratic theory. John Gunnell has argued that because politics is a function of history and convention, there cannot be a general theory of politics (1997). Ian Shapiro has come to the same view about resolving tensions that exist within democratic theory: "there is little that is general to be said about the democratic management of tensions internal to the democratic ideal" (1994: 147). Although we may not be able to say anything generally predictive of social change, we can say something normatively prescriptive. In the process of responding to the criticisms I have directed at others throughout this book, I have been presenting a general theoretical account of social criticism designed to encourage critics and theorists to appreciate the history and convention of their time, and also to imagine possible greater achievement of what they as democrats value. I do not presume that political theory and political life are on an inevitable trend toward greater realization of democratic values, but rather offer an account of how those who wish to promote the democratic values of inclusiveness, self-respect, mutual respect, and equality of political influence can do so in the context of inequality and disagreement in a changing world.

Other feminists have wrestled with the problems of contemporary theory. With different emphases and solutions, they consider problems of inequality, of identity and representation, and of boundaries between public and private issues and spheres of life. After recapping my criticism of deliberative democratic theory from chapter 2, I look at some attempts by feminist theorists to address problems in contemporary democratic theory. I choose to discuss Anne Phillips, Seyla Benhabib, Chantal Mouffe, and Nancy Fraser because they are theorists of democracy who have made feminist analysis and critique part of their work and as such contribute to democratic theory and to feminist theory.[2] These feminists have helped develop feminist critique of liberal, critical, and postmodern theory;[3] yet, their proposals are theoretical solutions that, like the theories they criticize, lack an account of how they can be realized. Although I might have chosen others (some of whom I discuss in previous chapters), here I focus on these few theorists because they seek to address theoretical problems that Third World feminist social criticism addresses more effectively.

Feminist democratic theory and criticism

Deliberative democratic theorists propose models and means of public decision making in order to promote public understanding, consensus (in some cases), and political agreement despite moral disagreement (in others). Their deliberative fora require the participants' self-respect and mutual respect, their equality of influence, and their agreement on what constitutes appropriate arguments. Though there have been disagreements among them, for example as to whether deliberative democracy meets or sets an epistemological standard, they have been collectively working to construct a model of public decision making that is more

---

[2] Many feminists who contribute to democratic and feminist theory are not included in the following discussion. For a broad discussion of the implications of feminist work for democratic theory see Mansbridge (1993) and Carol Gould (1993).

[3] According to Stephen Leonard, feminist theory generally shows the most promise for outlining political theory that is practically relevant and can fulfill the promise of critical theory (1990). I have argued Third World feminist social criticism in particular fulfills that promise.

inclusive and better informed than liberal democracy and not merely the compromise of competing interests. However, in trying to design deliberative fora that enable people to learn from one another, they rely on substantive and procedural constraints that exclude those who cannot participate according to that model.

Ostensibly, deliberative democratic theory deals with two problems in contemporary liberal democratic theory: (1) how to increase legitimacy of political decisions through participation and broad popular input without introducing Madisonian tyranny of the majority or unworkable mayhem and (2) how to respect participants as equal individuals when individuals are discriminated against or advanced based on perceived group affiliation and where interests of minority groups may be continually ignored by an active majority.

Deliberative theorists address the first problem by increasing legitimacy through participation in deliberative fora. Participation may be direct, through elected representatives, or through randomly selected representatives. In the first case participation is open to all those affected by the issue (Manin 1987; also Cohen 1989a). As discussed in chapter 2, this can be elitist because some people who ought to participate don't have the requisite will or time, some with the will and the time will not be heard due to various forms of discrimination, and some will not be heard because they are unable to present their views according to the terms of appropriate content of deliberative fora. Lynn Sanders (1997), Iris Young (1996), and James Tully (1995) have advocated that a broader range of modes of speech be considered legitimate in deliberative fora. While these suggestions accompany cogent criticisms of deliberative democratic theory, introducing a range of acceptable modes of speech in the legislative deliberative forum may render that forum unworkable and illegitimate as participants no longer agree on the appropriate content of arguments presented in the legislative deliberative forum. Deliberative theorists generally prefer to sustain a narrow understanding of what constitutes a reasonable agreement because the reasonableness of deliberants' arguments provides the legitimacy of the outcomes of deliberation. Thus, in trying to address the problem of legitimacy, the deliberative theorists have allowed either the problem of tyranny of the meeting or tyranny of the method.[4]

Some deliberative theorists suggest representative participation, instead of direct participation. Whether deliberation takes place among elected representatives (Mansbridge 1992, 1988; Bessette 1980) or among a random sample of the population (Fishkin 1991, 1995, 1996),

---

[4] See the discussions of tyranny of the majority, tyranny of the method, and tyranny of the meeting in chapter 2.

those who do not participate in these deliberative fora may get an epistemological benefit in the sense that the political decisions that affect their lives may be better informed. However, nonparticipants will not get the educative benefit of direct participation in public life that Dewey attributes to public deliberations (1980 [1916a], 1983 [1922]).

One might consider multiple kinds of deliberative fora. Some deliberative fora, such as those described by David Mathews in *Politics for People* (1994) and by Benjamin Barber in *Strong Democracy* (1984), are designed to increase citizens' direct participation. Others are designed to use the learning that takes place in representative fora to influence public decision making in the broader society (Fishkin 1991). However, this and related proposals merely strike different balances between tyranny of the meeting and tyranny of the majority.

The second problem – how to respect citizens as individuals and yet respect that they may experience discrimination due to their perceived group affiliation or that they may have interests as a minority group that they are unable to have the majority recognize – is solved by deliberative theorists' assumptions. By stipulating that the deliberative forum is a place of self-respect and mutual respect on the part of the participants, where participants have equality of influence and where all agree on the forms of argument that are appropriate to the forum, deliberative theorists have assumed away much of the problem of minority participation or representation. Whether or not they (or others) identify them as members of a given minority group, participants will be able to speak, have their views respected, and be able to influence outcomes without discrimination. If they can present their interests in such a way as not to be contrary to other group interests (easier still if we assume common ground), then their needs will not be marginalized continually by majority interests.

The strength of these assumptions in sustaining the legitimacy of decisions made in deliberative fora suggests that the next step of deliberative theory needs to be to relax these assumptions or to tell us how to bring them about deliberatively. In the hands of deliberative theory's proponents, relaxing the assumption of equality comes first (Bohman 1996; Dryzek 1996; Knight & Johnson 1997).

Some feminists have relaxed some of these assumptions. Phillips, Fraser, and Mouffe try to include inequality in their assumptions of political context. Benhabib, Fraser, and Mouffe think about how deliberative fora might be organized such that they are conducive to self- and mutual respect. All think about redrawing the boundaries between public and private so as to challenge the exclusion of arguments on the basis of their being considered private concerns by public standards. But none of these feminists relaxes all of the deliberative theorists' assumptions. Third World feminist social criticism relaxes them all and offers ways to enable self-respect for all, to make mutual respect credible, and to make the definitions of acceptable content and form of contributions to deliberative fora more inclusive using a deliberative method of social criticism. Third World feminist social criticism makes deliberative theory a critical theory: actionable in the real world, coherent in that deliberation is used to set the standards for deliberative fora, and self-reflective in that deliberation is used in a process of reflecting upon the standards of legitimacy in deliberative fora. Thus, Third World feminist social criticism advances both deliberative democratic theory and feminist critical thinking about democratic theory.

Feminists have used feminist theory or a feminist perspective to further liberal democratic theory. Sanders and Young (discussed in chapter 2) are two among many who have tried to advance the "next steps" of democratic theory.[5] Less critical of liberal democratic theory, Anne Phillips ask us to think critically about liberal democracy's ability to change to accommodate feminist concerns and about whether feminism offers anything that other critics of liberal democracy don't (1991, 1993b).[6]

Phillips defines liberal democracy broadly but focuses on the same two problems I identify. In thinking about the first question – how to make democracy inclusive and participatory while manageable – Phillips does not think that feminism can take democratic theory beyond the problem of trading off equality of participation and direct participation (1991: 163). The more participatory democracy is, the less direct democracy can be. Increasing equality of participation means moving toward representative democracy where each person is equally able to cast a vote and (setting aside the issues associated with funding campaigns and elections) the ability to draw on personal or other resources to influence public decision making is undermined. Thus, increased equality reduces the quality of participation. Phillips argues that feminists should recommend increased participation cautiously because the cost of participatory democracy is equality – the interests of those with more and less time to participate or more and less experience in participating will be unequally defended in deliberative fora (as Young and Sanders emphasize).

To the second question, Phillips also responds that feminists have not done a better job than liberal democratic theorists at responding to the problem of discrimination and group exclusion. Critical of Young's

---

[5] Given the range of Young's work, it is inappropriate to label her a liberal feminist.
[6] See also Mansbridge (1993), Gould (1993), and Carmen Sirianni (1993).

model of group representation (1990a), Phillips argues that within liberal democracy theorists such as Kymlicka have done a comparable job at representing group rights (1993a).[7] Phillips does not offer a reading of Kymlicka or others who have wrestled with the question,[8] and is clear that she does not know how to address the associated problems of marginalized groups' interests, but she thinks that liberal democracy is as able to solve the problem as feminism (1991, 1993b).

According to Phillips both feminism and liberal democracy have been asking questions about political equality and about oppressed and dominant groups. She sees feminism as offering a modification to ongoing critical dialogue within liberal democracy (1993b: 119). Those modifications are (1) a need to challenge inequality; (2) a way of dealing with individuals as individuals and in groups; and (3) the exploration of the politics and power of any proposed delineation between public and private (1991).

Other feminists are not as confident in liberal democracy's ability to modify itself in ways that address these concerns. Seyla Benhabib (1989, 1991, 1996b) and Nancy Fraser (1992) explore solutions from the perspective of Habermasian critical theory and Chantal Mouffe (1992) and Fraser (1995) seek postmodern means to address them.

As discussed in chapter 1, according to critical theory, social criticism should guide human action; it should be coherent and consistent; and social criticism should be "reflective," that is, critics should be able to criticize the values, practices, and norms of a society according to principles which are themselves open to criticism (Geuss 1981: 1–2, 55–95).[9] Seyla Benhabib argues that Habermas's ideal speech situation, discourse ethics, and account of the public sphere have implications for his critical theory in which he emphasizes "political participation and the widest-reaching democratization of decision-making processes" (1991: 86).[10] Through public participation, through action and discourse, people participate in creating the norms that shape their lives. In

---

[7] Phillips references Kymlicka (1989). Jodi Dean argues that group representation has political risk; "shoring up the boundaries" between groups and will cost political communities possible larger interconnections among people and groups (1996: 7). Anthony Appiah's criticism of group representation is that it gives people a political identity rather than allowing them to choose for themselves how they will identify themselves politically (1994b).

[8] See Charles Taylor (1992) and Walzer (1990b, 1992).

[9] Some theorists give deliberative democratic theory similar qualities. In *The Dialogue of Justice*, James Fishkin argues that deliberative democratic theory should be self-reflective (1992: 124). In "Beyond the Republican Revival" Sunstein argues that deliberation is a critical idea (1988: 1549).

[10] In *Situating the Self*, Benhabib distinguishes her model of discourse ethics from that of Jürgen Habermas (1992).

"Liberal Dialogue Versus a Critical Theory of Discursive Legitimation" Benhabib proposes that the Habermasian model of deliberation provides a better basis for the legitimation of power than the liberal account of deliberation (1989; see also 1991). She criticizes Bruce Ackerman's liberal account of legitimacy through dialogue in the liberal state which is a model based on a "transcendental perspective" and offers instead a deliberative model based on "egalitarian reciprocity" (1989: 146, 150). According to Benhabib, the Habermasian account of public deliberation offers procedural not content constraints (1989: 149), and she is critical of Ackerman's approach which she argues relies on content constraints. The difference between Ackerman's model and Benhabib's is like the difference between Gutmann & Thompson's model and Cohen's. Gutmann & Thompson offer three principles of deliberation and three constraints on outcomes (1996). Cohen outlines a procedure he expects to yield legitimate outcomes (1989a). Cohen and Benhabib do not think that their constraints on deliberative procedures constitute content constraints (as Gutmann & Thompson's and Ackerman's clearly are). Yet, while they do not explicitly constrain outcomes, they implicitly constrain outcomes by limiting those ideas that can be considered.

Like Cohen, Benhabib argues that in order to be justified in bringing an argument to a deliberative forum, the speaker must show why the argument is justifiable by showing that her audience could come to agree with it. Deliberants must present their arguments in ways that satisfy their society's "idea of a fair debate" by recognizing and affirming participants' mutual respect, equality of influence, and the value of creating further deliberative opportunities (1989: 151). Although ostensibly rejecting the liberal model of the deliberative forum in favor of the Habermasian ideal speech situation, in "Toward a Deliberative Model of Democratic Legitimacy" Benhabib specifically associates her model with that presented by Cohen (Benhabib 1996b: 69; Cohen 1989a). Despite appearing to reject substantive constraints in her critique of Ackerman (1989, 1991), by embracing Cohen's model of deliberation, particularly by reaffirming the importance of constraining content to conform to society's "idea of fair debate," Benhabib rejects the inclusion of nonconforming modes of speaking in the legislative deliberative forum though she does think they may be appropriate for other public deliberative fora such as social movements (1996b: 83–84). Although excluding nonconforming modes of speech, she does assert that those affected by the norms in question have an equal right to question the rules of deliberation (1996b: 70). She attempts to reconcile the need for substantive constraints on the process of public discourse with the demands of discourse ethics by arguing that "the constraints can be subject to discursive critique and clarification, even if they can never wholly be suspended" (1991: 97 fn. 26). Thus, Benhabib's model of deliberative democratic legitimacy assumes that a community (and those at its margins when they are affected by its policies as in resident aliens or those sharing its ecological environment) have common norms of fair debate and can use those to guide their discussions about the rules of deliberation. In order for this not to be a circular argument, the assumption of the norms of fair debate must be strong enough that the norms of fair debate are not the subject of deliberation for such debate would constitute their suspension.

Benhabib's embrace of constraints on the content of deliberation (though she considers these procedural constraints) demonstrates the similarities between the constraints on participant participation in the ideal speech situation and the constraints on participation in a legislative deliberative democratic forum. Although in her defense of the deliberative model she seems to put up for public discussion the nature of power in the deliberative fora, the appropriate boundaries between public and private, and the appropriate subjects for deliberative fora (1989: 153, 155; 1991: 90–95; 1996b: 70), the model she describes in fact respects society's norms of "fair" debate (1989: 153, 155, 151; 1996b: 83; also 1991: 97 fn. 26). In her 1989 version of the argument, Benhabib shares Young and Sanders's interest in including in the subject of deliberative fora the very topic of what forms of discussion should be admissible:

[A]s a critical theorist I am interested in identifying the present social relation, power structures, and sociocultural grids of communication and interpretation that limit the identity of the parties to the public dialogue, that set the agenda for what is considered appropriate or inappropriate matters of public debate, and that sanctify the speech of some over the speech of others as being the language of the public. (1989: 155–156)

However, in her 1996 discussion of deliberative theory, Benhabib rejects the idea that multiple forms of discursive content should be admitted. Addressing her comments to Young's argument specifically, Benhabib answers,

Greeting, storytelling, and rhetoric, although they may be aspects of informal communication in our everyday life, cannot become the public language of institutions and legislatures in a democracy for the following reason: to attain legitimacy, democratic institutions require the articulation of the bases of their actions and policies in discursive language that appeals to commonly shared and accepted public reasons. In constitutional democracies such public reasons take the form of general statements consonant with the rule of law ... some moral ideal of impartiality is a regulative principle that should govern not only our *deliberations* in public but also the *articulation* of reasons by public institutions. (1996b: 83)

The two arguments seem to conflict; yet, Benhabib reconciles them by arguing that there are multiple publics and that in public speech outside of the legislative or constitutional forum such as in social movements, greater examination of participation, the agenda, and the rules of deliberation are necessary (1996b: 70), whereas in the legislative forum "general statements consonant with the rule of law" are universally recognized (1996b: 83). Benhabib uses the norms of acceptable arguments in a constitutional forum as the standard for acceptable arguments in any legislative deliberative forum thereby occluding the possibility of discussion about whether liberal constitutional norms of argument are appropriate to a legislative deliberative forum whose scope is public decision making more broad than constitutional decision making. Compared to the range of constitutional discursive mechanisms described by Tully in *Strange Multiplicity* (1995), Benhabib has a narrow view of what norms of constitutional deliberation are appropriate for legislative deliberation. According to Benhabib, for the development of public opinion, there may be many institutional fora that allow heterogeneous forms of expression, but in the legislative forum arguments must conform to more restrictive norms (1996b: 83–4, 87).

It seems that in Benhabib's account the critical theorist should reflect on power relations in deliberative fora, but the participants in legislative deliberation should conform to them (1989: 155–156, 151; 1996b: 83). Participants conform to them because they agree on what are acceptable modes of discussion before beginning those deliberations. Such agreement presumes prior deliberation which she acknowledges in a footnote (1991: 97 fn. 26).

Benhabib is confident that participants agree on appropriate modes of discussion because intolerant views that embody inequality are outside of the ideal speech situation and instead part of "historical struggles for recognition, battles, and debates" (1989: 153). Thus, according to Benhabib, problems associated with heterogeneity of values, practices, and norms are resolved through social movements and corresponding public-opinion-forming deliberative fora such that in legislative deliberative fora there is homogeneity of values of fairness, of deliberative practices, and of norms of debate.

Benhabib offers solutions to two of the problems identified by Phillips – identity and representation and the public/private boundaries – by relying on deliberation. In multiple publics, identity and group representation as well as the boundary between public and private will be the subjects of deliberation.

However, Benhabib does not take up Phillips's first concern, inequality. Benhabib brackets inequality with two moves. When describing the public sphere in "Models of Public Space," although she challenges Habermas's designation of public and private, her notion of a public sphere is a modest modification of his (1991). The public sphere is not the state, nor the economy, but the realm of democratic, discursive deliberation about common affairs. Her first move that introduces the problem of inequality is the assertion in "Toward a Deliberative Model" that there can be multiple deliberative fora of social movements and associations that are distinctly different in their norms of procedural constraints from the legislative deliberative forum (1996b). As Fraser argues in "Rethinking the Public Sphere," Habermas ignores the multiplicity of publics such as those of women's activism (1992). In Fraser's analysis, Habermas's single sphere is problematic because it reinforces the hierarchy of the liberal, bourgeois, male-dominated public sphere over women's spheres of public activity. However, merely recognizing the public nature of other spheres of activity, as Benhabib does, does not in itself undo the social norm that puts greater value on the liberal-bourgeois-male-public sphere of legislation. In fact, by placing the legislative deliberative fora above and apart from the others, Benhabib reinforces this hierarchy. As Fraser argues in her critique of Habermas, "there is a remarkable irony here ... A discourse of publicity touting accessibility, rationality, and the suspension of status hierarchies is itself deployed as a strategy of distinction" (1992: 115). By giving the legislative realm distinction, Benhabib exhibits this same irony.

The second move that brackets inequality is in assuming that all are able to participate in the legislative deliberative forum according to its procedural constraints which follow collectively accepted norms. In the real world, precisely because the norms of what is appropriate for public deliberation and what is worthy of public respect have not been those things associated with the traditional private sphere of life, such procedural constraints are in effect substantive constraints. Accordingly, women and the work that women do in the public and private spheres are devalued in the public sphere. How, then, can deliberation alone be a tool for determining the bounds of public and private appropriate for various issue areas and most importantly for the legislative deliberative forum? Under conditions of inequality, during deliberation about the norms of deliberation those with the ability to influence the procedural norms of public deliberations can use them to declare certain content private and therefore inappropriate. During deliberation about the boundaries between public and private, deliberants can refer to the procedural norms of deliberation to declare certain content inappropriate for the legislative deliberative forum. In the context of critiquing Habermas's account of the public sphere, Fraser writes, "declaring a deliberative arena to be a space where extant status distinctions are bracketed and neutralized is not sufficient to make it so" (1992: 115). The same critique can be leveled at Benhabib's reconstruction of Habermas's discursive public sphere. Further, when Benhabib moves away from Habermas to Cohen and considers the procedural norms for the legislative deliberative forum and the wider and divergent norms for the deliberative fora of social movements (1996b), she also moves away from her earlier improvement upon Habermas's understanding of the public sphere where the norms of deliberative discourse including the boundaries of public and private are determined (1991).

In chapter 1, I cited Fraser's criticism of Habermas, that his critical theory does not adequately wrestle with the struggles of the contemporary era (Fraser 1991). The same criticism can be directed at Benhabib. If (as Benhabib suggests, 1989: 153) the historical struggles against inequality and for recognition are outside of the scope of her discursive model, how relevant is her model to social criticism? Either these struggles should take place (as she suggests) outside of the legislative deliberative forum or we need to find a way to make the legislative deliberative forum a place of dealing with the important struggles, principally those related to power inequality. I am arguing for the latter. As Benhabib recognizes "public dialogue is not external to but constitutive of power relations" (1989: 155). For critical theory to be relevant to today's struggles, it must recognize that struggles around inequality are both the content and the context of deliberative fora. Due to differences among participants, setting procedural constraints on public discourse yields substantive constraints. Because power inequalities provide the context of deliberative fora, discussing the constraints themselves will also not yield more inclusive deliberation.

Nancy Fraser takes a less liberal, more postmodern turn in her feminist reading of Habermas's public sphere, though her theoretical proposals seem more akin to Phillips's liberalism than to Mouffe's postmodernism. Fraser reviews the history of the public sphere and argues, like Benhabib, that there are not one but many publics. According to Fraser, the liberal, male, bourgeois public sphere which Habermas treats as *the* public sphere – the sphere Benhabib calls the legislative deliberative forum – historically asserts primacy over the others (1991). In her analysis the postmodern and "postliberal" solutions to the problems of inequality, individual, and group identity and representation, and the public/private split are (1) not to bracket inequality; (2) to promote and recognize a multiplicity of publics; and (3) to admit what the liberal model considers private interests and issues into public fora for deliberation (Fraser 1992: 295; 1992). These three proposals echo Phillips's proposals (1991). Although Benhabib and Fraser both contribute to critical theory, they offer competing theoretical solutions to the problems of democratic theory.

Postmodern feminist theorists are not satisfied that either liberal or critical theory has the means to challenge inequality, deal with individuals as individuals and as members of groups, and explore the politics and power of delineations between public and private as Phillips argues liberal democratic theory can and as Benhabib trusts critical theory will.[11] Chantal Mouffe draws on anti-essentialist criticism of liberal democratic theory to propose a feminist alternative vision of citizenship and political community to deal with these three problems. She rejects the liberal model of citizenship (1992: 324) in favor of an anti-essentialist radical democratic model in which citizens form a common identity and a political community based on recognizing the equivalence of their identities (1992: 317–318, 326).[12] Although from some anti-essentialist perspectives any form of recognition constitutes an identification with one another and thus an obfuscation of difference,[13] Mouffe asserts that people can recognize their differences and still identify themselves as part of the same political community.

Mouffe's anti-essentialist reconceptualization of citizenship and political community addresses the concern over inequality and the concern over individual and group identity by proposing "equivalence" among individuals regardless of their differences as a solution to the problems of inequality that are a function of difference. I interpret equivalence as a moral and political notion that affirms the human worth of each individual while recognizing cultural differences across individuals within a political community. Equivalence does not require affirming the equal moral worth of the belief systems associated with all cultures and subcultures. So equivalence does not require a political community to respect and condone cultural practices of racism, sexism, or other forms of discrimination. If equivalence required moral and political

---

[11] Note that the range of concerns of feminists associated with the postmodern or poststructural perspectives is greater than concern about these three issues. See for example Judith Butler (1995), Drucilla Cornell (1995), and Mouffe (1992). As explained in chapter 1, I generally discuss "anti-essentialism" as it is that aspect of this range of work that is the object of my critical attention and upon which Third World feminist social criticism can improve. Here I use the term postmodern in order to follow the auto-identification of Fraser and Mouffe and the convention used in *Feminist Contentions* (Benhabib et al. 1995), *Social Postmodernism* (Nicholson & Seidman 1995), *Feminism/Postmodernism* (Nicholson 1990), and *Feminism/Postmodernism/Development* (Marchand & Parpart 1995).

[12] See also "Democratic Citizenship and the Political Community" in which Mouffe further develops her account of citizenship (1991).

[13] See for example, Mohanty's critique of Robin Morgan's *Sisterhood is Global: The International Women's Movement Anthology* (Mohanty 1995: 77).

relativism, it would endorse inequality and obstruct efforts at building political community across differences and thus be inconsistent with Mouffe's argument. As I have interpreted equivalence, it is a political norm that requires universal (or near universal) acceptance in order to be effective. However, even in her account of political community, Mouffe recognizes that people do not respect all difference always (1992: 326). Thus, while intending to deal with inequality, Mouffe essentially brackets the problem of inequality because she does not deal with the real perception and circumstances of inequality that often exist in contexts of heterogeneity.

Mouffe's alternative model of citizenship recognizes citizenship as neither the source of one's identity nor an aspect of one's identity. Instead identities are determined through interaction with others and may vary according to context and those present (1992: 326). Thus, questions of identity are deliberatively determined, not given and static.

Finally, Mouffe's view of citizenship has implications for community and the boundaries between public and private activity. In the context of interaction with others, citizens negotiate the appropriate boundaries of public and private, "because every interaction is private while never immune from the public conditions prescribed by the principles of citizenship" (1992: 325). Mouffe reads the feminist critique of the public/private dichotomy in liberalism as correct, but argues that rather than adding in those values associated with femaleness as Phillips and Fraser do, the very dichotomy, the boundary itself must be the subject of deliberation. According to Mouffe, the boundaries between public and private are changeable and vary as a function of people's interactions.

Mouffe's proposals, like Benhabib's, bracket inequality, treat identity as formed deliberatively, and appreciate the boundaries of public and private as deliberatively determined. However, her theory differs from Benhabib's in that Mouffe also recognizes the ongoing nature of defining the political community. Because people will always identify themselves as a group – in this case a political community – by juxtaposing those who are "we" with those who are "they," the ideal of a political community is always being revised to be more inclusive (1992: 326). Accordingly, inclusive political community is the unrealizable ideal that is nevertheless the appropriate goal (1992: 326). Thus, Mouffe's account differs from Benhabib's significantly in that Mouffe allows for the boundaries of the legislative deliberative forum to be continually redefined from within that forum.

Mouffe's suggestions differ from Fraser's in significant ways. First, neither Fraser nor Mouffe means to bracket inequality, but Mouffe functionally brackets inequality by redefining citizenship such that difference translates into equivalence rather than inequality. While theoretically suggestive, Mouffe's proposal is practically irrelevant because it lacks an account of what society should do when people don't respect their equivalencies across differences and do not desire greater inclusiveness. Fraser has no theoretical solution, no plan for dealing with inequality theoretically, but she recognizes that inequality is a practical problem and thus needs to be dealt with by theory. Social and economic inequalities impact the distribution of political power and consequently, as a theoretical matter, they cannot be assumed away and, as a practical matter, they cannot be assumed not to influence political equality (1992). Second, Fraser wants a multiplicity of publics, whereas Mouffe envisions one political community in which citizens continually renegotiate questions of identity. These are very different solutions. Fraser's multiplicity of publics leads to questions about how to deal with the problems of listening across multiple publics. It seems that there would be the same problems of listening and inclusion in each public as exist in one public, plus there would then be the added problem of communicating among publics. By recognizing multiple publics, Fraser does not mean to suggest that enclaves or "subaltern counterpublics" as she calls them should be considered public. That would only redefine "public" without dealing with the substantive problem underlying the definition. Enclaves are not publics in her view but they are places where members can regroup, train, and strategize in order to influence effectively "public arenas" or "the public at large" (1992: 124). Third, both Fraser and Mouffe want to be able to include some liberal "private" interests and issues in the public arena. Fraser does this by adding them in wholesale (as Phillips does),[14] whereas Mouffe wants continually to renegotiate the boundaries of public and private as they are appropriate for each interaction (as Benhabib does). While both contribute to postmodern democratic theory, Mouffe's and Fraser's solutions are substantively different.

Neither is particularly effective at dealing theoretically and practically with the problems of inequality, discrimination, and inclusion. Thinking back over Phillips and Benhabib as well, it seems that feminist theory, while provoking us to think better about problems of inequality, discrimination, and inclusion, has not been as successful at providing the theoretical advances necessary to deal with these problems construc-

---

[14] This is perhaps an unfair simplification of Phillips as she is not clear what she means by renegotiating the boundaries between public and private, but it seems that once renegotiated according to Phillips, they would be static again. Thus the significant difference between Phillips and Fraser is that Phillips thinks there should be a boundary. Fraser seems to remove the boundary entirely.

tively in practice. Third World feminist social criticism is such an advance; whether its roots are in liberal, critical, or postmodern theory, democratic political theory needs a complementary account of social criticism. No democratic political theory will get institutions right for all people in all times in all places in part because actual peoples, times, and places complicate things and in part because theorists are fallible. Therefore, democratic political theory needs a complementary account of social criticism to tell society and theorists how to move in the direction of increased equality and greater inclusion when in any given time and place communities fall short of the ideal. Like Mouffe, I expect that no community can permanently attain the ideal. Third World feminist social criticism guides society and theorists in the interim.

Third World feminist social criticism

Third World feminist social criticism wrestles with inequality. It sees identity as a function of individual choice in the ideal world and a function of associations that others make about an individual based on apparent group affiliation in the imperfect world. And it sees that the public/private dichotomy has been problematic for women and others whose private issues have been made public issues without their consent and for those who are trying to have their private issues treated as public ones. In addition to these three problems that feminists have drawn our attention to, Third World feminist social criticism is able to deal with other theoretical problems that are not neatly captured by these. Because Third World feminist social criticism is a means for assessing outcomes, it enables critics and societies to deal with those problems that societies may anticipate and others that they do not. Social criticism can help theorists and societies improve theoretical suggestions, institutional designs, systems of representation, even methods of social criticism because it is a means for assessing anticipated and actual outcomes. Social criticism is an ongoing project and thus it is able to pick up where political theory leaves off.

First, instead of bracketing inequality, Third World feminist social criticism envisions using skeptical scrutiny, guiding criteria, and deliberative inquiry to move toward equality. Critics continually assess existing and potentially exploitative inequalities. Because inequalities can manifest themselves in so many ways – different economic and social resources, different natural abilities, and luck – it is difficult for a democratic political theory to deal definitively with inequality generally, though it can certainly address specific inequalities with certain institutional design choices. Third World feminist social criticism complements democratic theory because it is a means to social change that is guided by democratic values of equality and inclusion, and that is appropriate to a given context. For example, Phillips draws our attention to the problem facing democratic theorists who wish to increase the quality of democratic participation without increasing inequality. Third World feminist social criticism outlines a means for assessing particular outcomes and institutional remedies so that through deliberative processes society and theorists can assess a given tradeoff they made. As a result of their evaluation they may modify institutions of participation to bring the effects of those institutions in line with the society's agreed-upon tradeoff, discuss changing the tradeoff, or reject the tradeoff and try to increase participation and equality of participation through as yet unimagined institutions.

Likewise and second, Third World feminist social criticism can guide our assessment of other theoretical proposals and of the outcomes that those proposals yield. For example, I describe above two proposals for dealing with the problem of individual identity and minority group interests – (1) creating or recognizing multiple publics (Phillips, Benhabib, and Fraser), and (2) making identity an appropriate subject for the one public sphere (Mouffe). Further, although Young, Phillips, and Fraser think about the problem more narrowly as one of minority group representation, the problem is also one of identity formation, chosen group affiliation, and forced group affiliation (as in discrimination or Young's form of group representation).[15] Third World feminist social criticism has many resources for dealing with this set of questions. According to Third World feminist social critics, individuals are the authors of their own lives and should be able to choose how to identify themselves and which identities will lead to political affiliations. However, where a society decides to recognize certain groups as having interests that need representation that their minority status prevents from being heard in one-person-one-vote democracy, Third World feminist social criticism assesses society's choice of groups and the appropriateness of assuming homogeneity of interests among group members. Multi-sited social critics can be invaluable in these assessments because they can move between multiple publics. Where a society chooses to entrust one public forum with the challenge of respecting individual rights including the individual rights of minority group members, Third World feminist social criticism provides ongoing assessment of public decision making and its effects on all members. Secure enclaves for deliberative opportunities among those excluded under

---

[15] For a rich discussion see the contributions to Amy Gutmann's edited volume *Multiculturalism*, especially the chapter by Appiah (1994b).

either the practice of multiple publics or the practice of one public may enable the excluded to develop the knowledge and resources necessary to influence public decision making.

Third, Third World feminist social critics are able to include private interests in public fora with more theoretical guidance than either Phillips or Fraser offer. They are also able to provide the necessary assessment of public choices about which private interests to make public concerns and which to leave to personal privacy. Benhabib and Mouffe entrust that decision to the public forum without providing those who wish to keep some interests private the theoretical resources to make such a suggestion. Third World feminist social criticism is such a resource. Third World feminist critics include private interests in public decision making by treating testimonials as information and by fostering adequate and accurate representation. Like Mouffe, they recognize that the boundary of public and private will vary by context. Generally, Third World feminist social critics expect people with different experiential backgrounds to disagree about where to place and how to negotiate the boundaries of public and private. Third World feminist social critics use skeptical scrutiny, guiding criteria, and deliberative inquiry to assess the political, social, and economic outcomes of society's choices about which interests and issues to consider public and private.

In addition, there are other problems for political theory and life that are not neatly covered under these three questions. For example, related to questions of inequality and the boundary between public and private issues, is the question of the allocation of time to politics. People are unevenly willing and able to participate directly due to logistical challenges and personal priorities. Although their domestic activities have historically left women with less time for politics, there is variability among women and among and between women and men as to their willingness and ability to allocate time to politics. Thus, based on individuals' and groups' circumstances, their choices may lead them to have unequal influence in political decision making. Third World feminist social criticism asks theorists and societies to evaluate outcomes that are a function of the socially constructed institutional demands on citizens' time.

Similarly, there is variability in people's ability to make themselves heard which also yields unequal influence on political decision making. A society's goal will likely not be to make all participants equally able to participate. Even if that is the chosen goal, there will likely always be periods of inequality due to individual life changes such as illness or a desire to spend more time at work or with one's family. If a society chooses the minimum political participation possible in order to ensure equality, social criticism is necessary to assess the quality of political decisions and to contribute to informed and inclusive decision making by promoting accountability of representatives by seeking means of efficient dissemination of information. If a society chooses a more participatory model of democracy then Third World feminist social criticism guides the assessment of whether people are unequally able to participate due to their nature, social vulnerability, or reasons that are not morally arbitrary (like having committed a crime). Where representatives are necessary to promote the interests of those less able to participate, social critics will have to assess the accuracy and adequacy of the representation. Finally, social critics can examine the outcomes – the various values, practices, and norms that are sustained by the society for patterns of inequality that should be corrected.

Though liberal democratic theory, critical theory, and postmodern theory expect self-respect and mutual respect, in the imperfect world such conditions are lacking. Third World feminist social criticism enables the assessment of values, practices, and norms that potentially promote self-respect and mutual respect. This includes directing critical attention to social criticism itself such that its practice does not undermine self-respect and mutual respect through for example hegemonic assertions of representation.

In all of these cases, Third World feminist social criticism is an ongoing process that complements democratic political theory and promotes democratic norms where actual institutions fail. Unlike deliberative democratic theory and critical theory, Third World feminist social criticism does not rely on agreed-upon modes of contributing to decision making. In fact, among Third World feminist critics there is a broad understanding of what constitutes acceptable forms of argument, but even that understanding is the subject of critical attention.

Third World feminist social criticism – in theory and practice – shares much with other feminist theory. It is critical of dominant discourses and ideologies. It promotes revolutionary criticism and incremental social change. It is practically grounded, relational, and contextual. It links everyday, national, and international political life. It searches for common ground while appreciating diversity. It is interactive with the subject of its criticism. It respects that some social change needs to take place in protected enclaves. Finally, Third World feminist social criticism continues the "unnamed tradition," as Belenky et al. refer to it, of women's activism, leadership, and power that has been sustained by women such as Ella Baker who fostered the leadership skills among African-American students through the Student Nonviolent Coordinating Committee (1997), Ela Bhatt who fostered the activism of the self-employed women of SEWA, Jahanara from Tangail who recognized collective action as a means of challenging unequal power in the family, the founders of the Korean Women's Hotline, and the thousands of development and women's human rights activists and the scholars who document their work and achievements. For Third World women activists, deliberation is a critical tool to make women and their societies better informed and better able to understand and articulate their interests.

What really makes Third World feminist social criticism *feminist* is that it is a theory and a practice by women (whether they call themselves feminist or not) who believe that human beings – regardless of sex, sexuality, ethnicity, class, caste, religion, country of origin, national identity, aboriginal status, immigration status, regional geography, language, cultural practices, forms of dress, beliefs, ability, health status, family history, age, and education and regardless of how these are socially constructed in various societies – are equally worthy of human dignity and respect. Feminism in its theoretical and practical forms is activism but, given the problems of silence, power inequalities, and the methods of offstage defiance or anonymous public resistance that subordinate people employ, we need not expect their behavior and thoughts to conform to a particular view of activism in order to recognize their feminism. To return to an idea from chapter 1, "Feminism supports the proposition that women should transform themselves and the world" (Soares et al. 1995: 302). An observer may appreciate that certain women are engaged in transforming themselves and the world and thus that they are feminist even if they have not demonstrated their feminism in a way the observer can recognize the women's belief in equal human worth. Observers who are thorough in their research (and perhaps confident in the human potential of their subjects) help us appreciate the critical activity of those who are subordinate.[16]

Of course, not all social criticism is Third World feminist social criticism. As I showed in chapter 3, Walzer's and Nussbaum's approaches to social criticism define the method, role, and qualifications of the social critic such that they are too limited to enable social criticism to be adequately critical and to make adequate use of all critical perspectives. Walzer's critic may make use of deliberation to the extent that the critic engages in dialogue with a society about its values, but he makes no use of guiding criteria and inadequate use of deliberative

[16] See Scott (1985, 1990), White (1992), and Belenky et al. (1997) for anthropological and psychological research techniques for identifying how and what people know and think.

inquiry. Thus his critical method is inadequate for criticizing dominant and accepted values, practices and norms. The role of Walzer's critic – interpretation – is narrow and doesn't capture many activities in which social critics engage in order to bring about social change. The critical perspective of Walzer's critic – a little to the side, but not outside – is limiting and excludes critical perspectives that may be useful in challenging dominant and accepted institutions. Although in *The Company of Critics* he describes the activities of critics who seem more multi-sited than connected, he emphasizes the value of the connected critic for social criticism (1988). Further, the Walzerian critic's method, role, and qualification do not direct him to think critically about his social criticism. Thus, he lacks the means and necessity of evaluating his own work.

Nussbaum's critical method is also incomplete; she makes rich use of guiding criteria, defining them and applying them to criticize political, social, and economic policies and programs. In defining the guiding criteria, Nussbaum makes some use of deliberative inquiry, but in applying them she makes inadequate use of it. According to Nussbaum, a broad range of perspectives, including the perspectives of outside and multi-sited critics, are valid for social critics, but she does not appreciate the importance of multiple critics for making social criticism broadly informed. As with Walzer, the critic's role according to Nussbaum is also narrower than that defined by Third World feminist social criticism. Nussbaum's critic applies the guiding criteria. Criticism following the guiding criteria may lead to institutional changes, but it does not promise the increased information and inclusiveness which accompany inquiry and deliberation. Third World feminist critics expand the scope of critical dialogue through promoting inquiry, deliberative opportunities, and institutional change. Finally, Nussbaum does not direct critical attention to her own criticism. Like Walzer's account, Nussbaum's account of social criticism lacks a mechanism for self-criticism.

Third World feminist social criticism provides a better account of social criticism as a *social* project, broadly informed by perspectives that include the silent within a society. Contrast the social criticism of the women on the walk in Kustia, animated by their self-discovery and sisterhood with the marchers in Walzer's *Thick and Thin* carrying words such as "Truth" and "Justice" on placards through public places. The latter demand to participate in politics. The former are anticipating less grand political change, but are cautiously hoping to realize significant changes in their daily lives. Both are social critics and both can use Third World feminist social criticism to make their criticisms more informed and inclusive. Contrast the Kustia women, conscious of their priorities and limitations, with Nussbaum's outside social critic using a list of guiding criteria to recommend greater social justice in development planning. It seems that both are social critics, but that neither is adequately informed. The Kustia women need more information about what is possible and the outside critic needs more information about the needs and priorities of those within the society in order to design the most effective development plan. Third World feminist social criticism provides an account of how both social critics can make their criticism informed by, and inclusive of, otherwise unheard critical voices. Third World feminist social criticism provides the means of making social criticism an informed *social* practice.

While clearly a valuable feminist practice, Third World feminist social criticism also contributes to feminist theory. I share Benhabib's concern about the ability to do feminist theory and feminist social criticism without philosophy. "Social criticism without philosophy is not possible, and without social criticism the project of a feminist theory, which is committed at once to knowledge and to the emancipatory interests of women is inconceivable" (1995: 25). Benhabib is concerned that postmodernism is not an ally of feminism because it undermines philosophy as a resource for social criticism. As I have argued in discussing feminist liberal, critical, and postmodern democratic theorists, while helping to make democratic theory more democratic (specifically inclusive of all women), these theorists perpetuate certain of the anti-democratic features of democratic theory (though not the same ones). In their hands liberal, critical, and postmodern theorists retain certain theoretical features that make them weak allies of feminism.

A theoretical and practical solution, Third World feminist social criticism is both a practice for promoting political transformation and the solution to the problems in democratic, critical, and postmodern theories that make those theories uneasy allies of feminism. Not only is Third World feminist social criticism the necessary complement to deliberative democratic theory, but also it does a better job than feminist liberal, critical, and postmodern theories at dealing with the problems associated with unrealized democratic values including inequality, exclusion, and defining what issues and information should be public.

It would be enough for Third World feminist social criticism to strengthen the feminist critiques of democratic theories, but Third World feminist social criticism also strengthens feminism itself by helping to close the gap between anti-relativist and anti-essentialist feminisms.

Anti-relativist feminists (for example, Nussbaum) use a critical method that emphasizes guiding criteria (though their criteria may differ substantially from those I outline in chapter 3). They give minimal attention to the critic's critical perspective allowing an outsider to represent the experiences of insiders perhaps to be inattentive to the potentially exclusionary effects of her representation on those marginalized. They are critical of the critical paralysis brought on by anti-essentialism.

Anti-essentialist feminists (for example, Mohanty and Flax) use a critical method that emphasizes skeptical scrutiny. They are attentive to the influence of the critic's perspective on her argument and analysis and thus feel more comfortable analyzing the mechanisms of influence rather than assessing the content of the argument from multiple perspectives.

Third World feminist social criticism is neither anti-relativist nor anti-essentialist. The guiding criteria and skeptical scrutiny are only effective as a critical method when together they are part of a method that applies them both through deliberative inquiry about the values, practices, and norms skeptical scrutiny brings under review and deliberative inquiry about the content and priority of the guiding criteria that should be used to assess them. Moreover, for Third World feminist social criticism no critical perspective is privileged though diversity of critical perspectives is sought. Thus, Third World feminist social criticism uses categories and critical attention to those categories to offer social criticism and to direct critical attention towards its own findings.

In asking whether there can be postmodern feminist theory, Fraser & Nicholson offer a general description. It would be "pragmatic and fallibilistic. It would tailor its methods and categories to the specific task at hand, using multiple categories when appropriate and forswearing the metaphysical comfort of a single feminist method or feminist epistemology" (1990: 35). Judith Butler adds to their expectations for a feminist social theory: "A social theory committed to democratic contestation within a postcolonial horizon needs to find a way to bring into question the foundations it is compelled to lay down" (1995: 41). In sum, postmodern feminist theory is a fallible process of multiple methods and categories of analysis such that its arguments reflect the democratic disagreements that are internal to any inclusive argument. In one sense, Third World feminist social criticism is postmodern feminist theory as Fraser & Nicholson and Butler define it.[17] Third World

---

[17] To be accurate, I should refer to postmodern "feminisms" because there is much variety among them as demonstrated by the differences between Mouffe and Fraser above. Postmodern feminists' differences include different perspectives on the critical value of essentialism. Jane Flax reads feminism as a type of postmodern theory (1990). Jodi Dean sees the possibility of common bonds forming as a function of continued engagement around differences (1996). See also Butler (1995: 39), Cornell (1995b: 145), Mouffe (1992), and those Mouffe cites: the journal *differences*, 1 (September 1989) and Diana Fuss, *Essentially Speaking* (1989).

feminist social criticism embraces the variety in individual and collective critics' qualifications and roles. Like postmodern feminist theory, Third World feminist social criticism "is a practice made up of a patchwork of overlapping alliances" (Fraser & Nicholson 1990: 35) that is devoted to giving critical attention not only to the society it critiques but also to its own critical practice.

But in another sense, Third World feminist social criticism is post-postmodern because it does offer what is in a sense a postmodern metanarrative. Whatever else may be part of a method of social criticism, to be adequately critical, it needs to have all three aspects of the Third World feminist critical method: deliberative inquiry, skeptical scrutiny, and guiding criteria. Like postmodern feminisms, it is anti-essentialist if the effort to identify essential human capabilities is attempted without deliberative inquiry and skeptical scrutiny. But it is also opposed to skeptical scrutiny of essentializing (or any other practice) if that scrutiny takes place without deliberative inquiry and an effort to then consider what such a practice should entail. As I have shown in chapter 3, any single aspect of the method can lead to one form of exclusion or another. Third World feminist social criticism is an ally to democratic theory, its feminist critics, and to feminism itself.

Although the traditions in political theory that Third World feminist social criticism advances are western, Third World feminist social criticism is not. As Kumair Jayawardena says in the introduction to her book in which she counters those who would assert that feminism is western,

... feminism, like socialism, has no particular ethnic identity; further, any movement for liberation and social change in the Third World can be strengthened only by the participation of the women at all levels and, in so doing, they are able to free themselves from exploitation, oppression and patriarchal structures. (1986: ix)

Although certain feminisms embody aspects of the ideological context in which they are put forward, feminism (understood as a collection of feminisms) has no ethnicity, national origin, or other identity. I prefer to say just the opposite, Third World feminist social criticism has every identity. It recognizes the local uniqueness of individual actions and analysis and demonstrates that they are globally relevant to feminist theory. In this sense it provides what Oloka-Onyango & Tamale seek: a way for women's experience to "feed into the evolution of international feminist theory" (1995: 701).

Because Third World feminist social criticism goes beyond liberal democratic theory, critical theory, postmodern theory, and the feminist critiques of these, we might label it post-liberal, post-critical, and post-postmodern feminist theory. But Third World feminism treats political philosophy as an ongoing theoretical project and social criticism as an ongoing practical project. Thus, Third World feminist social criticism is best thought of as furthering liberal democratic, critical, postmodern, and feminist theories. Remember the latter part of Soares et al.'s definition of feminism: "the political action of women: as agents effecting change in their own condition. Feminism supports the proposition that women should transform themselves *and the world*" (1995: 302 *emphasis added*). Third World feminist social criticism is not only the practical complement to existing theory, but a practically realizable (indeed, realized) theoretical advance. It holds out a promise of people able to make their worlds more informed and inclusive and less influenced by inequality. It identifies a means for people to be critical without obviating important differences among people. It identifies a means for people to promote democratic values despite living under undemocratic conditions. Moreover, it celebrates that women have been doing so all along.

Bibliography

Abzug, Bella. 1996. "A Global Movement for Democracy." In *Beijing and Beyond: Toward the Twenty-first Century of Women. Women's Studies Quarterly* 24, 1–2: 117–22.

Ackerly, Brooke. 1995. "Testing the Tools of Development: Credit Programs, Loan Involvement, and Women's Empowerment." *IDS Bulletin,* 26, 3 (July): 56–68.

——— 1997. "What's in a Design? The Effects of NGO Choices on Women's Empowerment and on Family and Social Institutions in Bangladesh." In *Getting Institutions Right for Women in Development,* ed. Anne Marie Goetz. London: Zed Books, 140–58.

Ackerly, Brooke and Susan M. Okin. 1999. "Feminist Social Criticism and the International Movement for Women's Rights as Human Rights." In *Democracy's Edges,* eds. Ian Shapiro and Casiano Hacker-Cordón. Cambridge: Cambridge University Press.

Afkhami, Mahnaz ed. 1994. *Women in Exile.* Charlottesville, VA: University Press of Virginia.

——— 1995a. "Preface." In *Faith and Freedom: Women's Human Rights in the Muslim World,* ed. Mahnaz Afkhami. Syracuse, NY: Syracuse University Press, ix–xi.

——— 1995b. "Introduction." In *Faith and Freedom: Women's Human Rights in the Muslim World,* ed. Mahnaz Afkhami. Syracuse, NY: Syracuse University Press, 1–15.

——— ed. 1995c. *Faith and Freedom: Women's Human Rights in the Muslim World.* Syracuse, NY: Syracuse University Press.

Afshar, Haleh, ed. 1996. *Women and Politics in the Third World.* New York: Routledge.

Ahmed, Leila. 1982a. "Western Ethnocentrism and Perceptions of the Harem." *Feminist Studies* 8, 3 (Fall): 521–34.

——— 1982b. "Feminism and Feminist Movements in the Middle East, a Preliminary Exploration: Turkey, Egypt, Algeria, People's Democratic Republic of Yemen." *Women's Studies International Forum* 5, 2: 153–68.

Alarcón, Norma. 1990. "The Theoretical Subject(s) of 'This Bridge Called My Back' and Anglo-American Feminism." In *Making Face, Making Soul/ Haciendo Caras: Creative and Critical Perspectives by Women of Color,* ed. Gloria Anzaldúa. San Francisco, CA: Aunt Lute Foundation Books, 356–69.

Alcoff, Linda. 1988. "Cultural Feminism Versus Post-structuralism: the Identity Crisis in Feminist Theory." *Signs: Journal of Women in Culture and Society* 13, 3: 405–36.

Allardt, Erik. 1993. "Having, Loving, Being: an Alternative to the Swedish Model of Welfare Research." In *The Quality of Life*, eds. Martha C. Nussbaum and Amartya Sen. Oxford: Clarendon Press, 88–94.

Allen, Paula Gunn. 1986. *The Sacred Hoop: Recovering the Feminine in American Indian Traditions*. Boston: Beacon Press.

1992. "Angry Women are Building: Issues and Struggles Facing American Indian Women Today." In *Race, Class, and Gender: an Anthology*, eds. Margaret L. Andersen and Patricia Hill Collins. Belmont, CA: Wadsworth Publishing Company, 42–6.

Alvarez, Sonia E. 1997. "Latin American Feminisms 'Go Global': Trends of the 1990s and Challenges for the New Millennium." In *Cultures of Politics, Politics of Cultures: Re-visioning Latin American Social Movements*, eds. Sonia E. Alvarez, Evelina Dagnino, and Arturo Escobar. Boulder, CO: Westview Press, 293–324.

Andersen, Margaret L. and Patricia Hill Collins, ed. 1992. *Race, Class, and Gender: an Anthology*. Belmont, CA: Wadsworth Publishing.

Anzaldúa, Gloria, ed. 1990. *Making Faces, Making Soul/Haciendo Caras: Creative and Critical Perspectives by Women of Color*. San Francisco, CA: Aunt Luce Foundation Books.

Appadorai, A. 1955. *The Bandung Conference*. New Delhi: Indian Council of World Affairs.

Appiah, Kwame Anthony. 1994a. *Identity Against Culture: Understandings of Multiculturalism*. Berkeley, CA: Regents of the University of California, 43–9.

1994b. "Identity, Authenticity, Survival: Multicultural Societies and Social Reproduction." In *Multiculturalism: Examining the Politics of Recognition*, ed. Amy Gutmann. Princeton, NJ: Princeton University Press, 149–63.

Aristotle. 1984. *The Complete Works of Aristotle: The Revised Oxford Translation*, ed. Jonathan Barnes. Princeton, NJ: Princeton University Press.

AWID (Association for Women in Development). 1991. *The Future for Women in Development: Voices from the South*. ed. Nancy O'Rourke. Ottawa: The North-South Institute/L'Institut Nord-Sud.

Bachrach, Peter and Morton S. Baratz. 1970. *Power and Poverty: Theory and Practice*. New York: Oxford University Press.

Badran, Margot and Miriam Cooke. 1990. *Opening the Gates: A Century of Arab Women's Writing*. Bloomington, IN: Indiana University Press.

Bahar, Saba. 1996. "Human Rights Are Women's Right: Amnesty International and the Family." *Hypatia* 11, 1 (Winter): 105–34.

BRAC (Bangladesh Rural Advancement Committee). 1997. *BRAC Report 1996*. Dhaka: BRAC.

1992. *Empowering the Poor: BRAC Report 1991*. Dhaka: BRAC.

Barber, Benjamin. 1984. *Strong Democracy: Participatory Politics for a New Age*. Berkeley, CA: University of California Press.

Barriteau, Eudine. [1992] 1995. "Postmodernist Feminist Theorizing and Development Policy and Practice in the Anglophone Caribbean: the Barbados Case." In *Feminism/Postmodernism/Development*, eds. Marianne H. Marchand and Jane L. Parpart. London: Routledge, 142–58.

Bartlett, Katharine. 1990. "Feminist Legal Methods." *Harvard Law Review* 103, 4 (February): 829–88.

Basu, Amrita. editor. 1995a. *The Challenge of Local Feminisms: Women's Movements in Global Perspective*. Boulder, CO: Westview Press.

1995b. Introduction. In *The Challenge of Local Feminisms: Women's Movements in Global Perspective*, ed. Amrita Basu. Boulder, CO: Westview Press, 1–21.

Beauvoir, Simone de. 1945. *Les Bouches Inutiles*. 14th edn. Paris: Gallimard.

Behar, Ruth. 1993. *Translated Woman*. Boston: Beacon Press.

Belenky, Mary Field, Lynne A. Bond, and Jacqueline S. Weinstock. 1997. *A Tradition that Has No Name: Nurturing the Development of People, Families and Communities*. New York: Basic Books.

Belenky, Mary Field, Blythe McVicker Clinchy, Nancy Rule Goldberger, and Jill Mattock Tarule. 1986. *Women's Ways of Knowing: The Development of Self, Voice, and Mind*. New York: Basic Books.

Benhabib, Seyla. 1988. "The Generalized and the Concrete Other: the Kohlberg-Gilligan Controversy and Feminist Theory." In *Feminism as Critique on the Politics of Gender*, eds. Seyla Benhabib and Drucilla Cornell. Minneapolis, MN: University of Minnesota Press, 77–95.

1989. "Liberal Dialogue Versus a Critical Theory of Discursive Legitimation." In *Liberalism and the Moral Life*. Cambridge, MA: Harvard University Press.

1991. "Models of Public Space: Hannah Arendt, the Liberal Tradition, and Jürgen Habermas." In *Habermas and the Public Sphere*, ed. Craig Calhoun. Cambridge, MA: MIT Press, 73–98.

1992. *Situating the Self: Gender, Community and Postmodernism in Contemporary Ethics*. New York: Routledge.

1995. "Feminism and Postmodernism: an Uneasy Alliance." In *Feminist Contentions: a Philosophical Exchange*, Seyla Benhabib, Judith Butler, Nancy Fraser, and Drucilla Cornell. Introduction by Linda Nicholson. New York: Routledge. 17–34.

1996a. "Introduction: the Democratic Moment and the Problem of Difference." In *Democracy and Difference: Changing Boundaries of the Political*, ed. Seyla Benhabib. Princeton, NJ: Princeton University Press, 3–17.

1996b. "Toward a Deliberative Model of Democratic Legitimacy." In *Democracy and Difference: Changing Boundaries of the Political*, ed. Seyla Benhabib. Princeton, NJ: Princeton University Press, 67–94.

Benhabib, Seyla, Judith Butler, Nancy Fraser, and Drucilla Cornell. 1995. *Feminist Contentions: a Philosophical Exchange*. Introduction by Linda Nicholson. New York: Routledge.

Bessette, Joseph M. 1980. "Deliberative Democracy: the Majority Principle in Republican Government." In *How Democratic Is the Constitution?*, eds. Robert A. Goldwin and William A. Schambra. Washington: The American Enterprise Institute for Public Policy Research, 102–16.

1994. *The Mild Voice of Reason: Deliberative Democracy and American National Government*. Chicago, IL: University of Chicago Press.

Beyond the War Foundation. 1991. "Framework for a Public Peace Process: Toward a Peaceful Israeli–Palestinian Relationship." Paper co-authored by participants, moderator and cosponsors of the conference entitled, "Building a Common Future." Stanford, CA: Stanford Center on Conflict and Negotiation.

Bhatt, Ela. 1989. "Toward Empowerment." *World Development*, 17, 7: 1059–65.

Bickford, Susan. 1996. *The Dissonance of Democracy: Listening, Conflict, and Citizenship*. Ithaca, NY: Cornell University Press.

Blanchet, Thérèse. 1984. *Meanings and Rituals of Birth in Rural Bangladesh*. Dhaka: University Press Limited.

1991. "Maternal Health In Rural Bangladesh: An Anthropological Study of Maternal Nutrition and Birth Practices in Nasirnagar, Bangladesh." Dhaka (October).

Bohman, James. 1996. *Public Deliberation: Pluralism, Complexity, and Democracy* Cambridge, MA: MIT Press.

Bohman, James and William Rehg. 1997. Introduction. In *Deliberative Democracy: Essays on Reason and Politics*, eds. James Bohman and William Rehg. Cambridge, MA: MIT Press, ix–xxx.

Bordo, Susan. 1990. "Feminism, Postmodernism, and Gender-Scepticism." In *Feminism/Postmodernism*, ed. Linda J. Nicholson. New York: Routledge, Chapman & Hall, 133–56.

Bowen, John. 1996. "The Myth of Global Ethnic Conflict," *Journal of Democracy* 7, 4: 3–14.

Bruce, Judith. 1989. "Homes Divided." *World Development* 17, 7 (July): 979–91.

Bumiller, Elisabeth. 1990. *May You Be the Mother of a Hundred Sons: a Journey Among the Women of India*. New York: Fawcett Columbine.

Bunch, Charlotte. 1990. "Women's Rights as Human Rights: Toward a Re-Vision of Human Rights." *Human Rights Quarterly* 12, 4 (November): 486–98.

1995. "Transforming Human Rights from a Feminist Perspective." In *Women's Rights, Human Rights: International Feminist Perspectives*, eds. Julie Peters and Andrea Wolper. New York: Routledge, 11–17.

Bunch, Charlotte and Susana Fried. 1996. "Beijing '95: Moving Women's Human Rights from Margin to Center." *Signs: Journal of Women in Culture and Society* 22, 1: 200–4.

Bunch, Charlotte and Niamh Reilly. 1994. *Demanding Accountability: the Global Campaign and Vienna Tribunal for Women's Human Rights*. Rutgers, NJ: Center for Women's Global Leadership.

Burrows, Noreen. 1986. "International Law and Human Rights: the Case of Women's Rights." In *Human Rights: from Rhetoric to Reality*, eds. Tom Campbell, David Goldberg, Sheila McLean, and Tom Mullen. New York: Basil Blackwell, 80–98.

Busia, Abena P. A. 1996. "On Cultures of Communication: Reflections from Beijing." *Signs: Journal of Women in Culture and Society* 22, 1: 204–10.

Butler, Judith. [1992] 1995. "Contingent Foundations: Feminism and the Question of 'Postmodernism.'" In *Feminist Contentions: a Philosophical Exchange*, Seyla Benhabib, Judith Butler, Nancy Fraser, and Drucilla Cornell. Introduction by Linda Nicholson. New York: Routledge, 35–57.

Caplan, Patricia. 1985. *Class and Gender in India: Women and Their Organizations in a South Asian City*. London: Tavistock.

Charles, David. 1988. "Perfectionism in Aristotle's Political Theory: Reply to Martha Nussbaum." *Oxford Studies in Ancient Philosophy*, Suppl. Vol., 185–206.

Charlesworth, Hilary. 1994. "What Are 'Women's International Human Rights'?" In *Human Rights of Women: National and International Perspectives*, ed. Rebecca J. Cook. Philadelphia, PA: University of Pennsylvania Press, 58–84.

Chen, Martha. 1983. *A Quiet Revolution*. Cambridge, MA: Schenkman.

——— 1995. "A Matter of Survival: Women's Right to Employment in India and Bangladesh." In *Women, Culture, and Development: a Study of Human Capabilities*, eds. Martha C. Nussbaum and Jonathan Glover. Oxford: Clarendon Press, 37–57.

Chow, Esther Ngan-Ling. 1996. "Making Waves, Moving Mountains: Reflections on Beijing '95 and Beyond." *Signs: Journal of Women in Culture and Society* 22, 1: 185–92.

Chow, Esther Ngan-Ling, Doris Wilkinson, and Maxine Baca Zinn, eds. 1996. *Race, Class, and Gender: Common Bonds, Different Voices*. Thousand Oaks, CA: Sage Press.

Chowdhry, Geeta. 1995. "Engendering Development? Women in Development (WID) in International Development Regimes." In *Feminism/Postmodernism/Development*, eds. Marianne H. Marchand and Jane L. Parpart. London: Routledge, 26–41.

Christiano, Thomas. 1993. "Social Choice and Democracy." In *The Idea of Democracy*, eds. David Copp, Jean Hampton, and John E. Roemer. Cambridge: Cambridge University Press, 173–95.

——— 1996. *The Rule of the Many: Fundamental Issues in Democratic Theory*. Boulder, CO: Westview Press.

——— 1997. "The Significance of Public Deliberation." In *Deliberative Democracy: Essays on Reason and Politics*, eds. James Bohman and William Rehg. Cambridge, MA: MIT Press, 243–77.

Cohen, G. A. 1993. "Equality of What? on Welfare, Goods, and Capabilities." In *The Quality of Life*, eds. Martha C. Nussbaum and Amartya Sen. Oxford: Clarendon Press, 9–29.

Cohen, Joshua. 1989a. "Deliberation and Democratic Legitimacy." In *The Good Polity*, eds. Alan Hamlin and Philip Pettit. Oxford: Blackwell, 17–34.

——— 1989b. "The Economic Basis of Deliberative Democracy." *Social Philosophy and Policy* 6, 2 (Spring): 25–50.

——— 1993. "Moral pluralism and political consensus." In *The Idea of Democracy*, eds. David Copp, Jean Hampton, and John E. Roemer. Cambridge: Cambridge University Press, 270–91.

——— 1996. "Procedure and Substance in Deliberative Democracy." In *Democracy and Difference: Changing Boundaries of the Political*, ed. Seyla Benhabib. Princeton, NJ: Princeton University Press, 95–119.

——— 1998. "Democracy and Liberty." In *Deliberative Democracy*, ed. Jon Elster. Cambridge: Cambridge University Press, 185–231.

Cohen, Joshua and Joel Rogers. 1992. "Secondary Associations and Democratic Governance." *Politics and Society* 20, 4 (December): 393–472.

Collins, Patricia Hill. [1990] 1991. *Black Feminist Thought: Knowledge, Con-*

sciousness, and the Politics of Empowerment. Boston: Routledge, Chapman and Hall.

Connecticut Post. 1993. "Rights of Women Are Too Often Ignored," June 16.

Connolly, William E. 1991. *Identity\Difference: Democratic Negotiations of Political Paradox.* Ithaca, NY: Cornell University Press.

CEDAW (Convention on the Elimination of All Forms of Discrimination Against Women.) 1979. G.A. Res. 34/180, U.N. Doc. A/Res/34/180. Adopted December 18, 1979.

Cornell, Drucilla. 1995a. "What is Ethical Feminism?" In *Feminist Contentions: a Philosophical Exchange,* Seyla Benhabib, Judith Butler, Nancy Fraser, and Drucilla Cornell. Introduction by Linda Nicholson. New York: Routledge. 75–106.

    1995b. "Rethinking the Time of Feminism." In *Feminist Contentions: a Philosophical Exchange,* Seyla Benhabib, Judith Butler, Nancy Fraser, and Drucilla Cornell. Introduction by Linda Nicholson. New York: Routledge. 145–56.

Crenshaw, Kimberle. 1989. "Demarginalizing the Intersection of Race and Sex: a Black Feminist Critique of Antidiscrimination Doctrine, Feminist Theory and Antiracist Politics." *The University of Chicago Legal Forum:* 139–67.

Crocker, David. 1992. "Functioning and Capability: The Foundations of Sen's and Nussbaum's Development Ethic." *Political Theory* 20, 4 (November): 584–612.

    1995. "Functioning and Capability: the Foundations of Sen's and Nussbaum's Development Ethic." In *Women, Culture, and Development: a Study of Human Capabilities,* eds. Martha C. Nussbaum and Jonathan Glover. Oxford: Clarendon Press, 153–98.

Currie, Dawn. 1994. "Where Women are Leaders: the SEWA Movement in India." Book review. *Journal of Contemporary Asia* 24, 4: 541–545.

Currie, Dawn and Hamida Kazi. 1987. "Academic Feminism and the Process of De-radicalization: Re-examining the Issues." *Feminist Review* 25: 77–98.

Cutrufelli, Maria Rosa. 1983. *Women of Africa: Roots of Oppression.* London: Zed Press.

Dahl, Robert. 1957. "The Concept of Power." *Behavioral Science* 2: 201–15.

    1958. "A Critique of the Ruling Elite Model." *American Political Science Review* 52: 463–9.

    1961. *Who Governs? Democracy and Power in an American City.* New Haven, CT: Yale University Press.

    1989. *Democracy and Its Critics.* New Haven, CT: Yale University Press.

    1997. "On Deliberative Democracy: Citizen Panels and Medicare Reform." *Dissent* (Summer): 54–8.

Dallas Morning News. Editorial. "Human Rights: Violence against Women Must Be Condemned." June 19.

Daly, Brenon. 1993. "Rights Meeting Looks at Plight of Women Refugees." *San Francisco Examiner,* June 19.

Davies, Miranda, ed. 1983. *Third World, Second Sex: Women's Struggles and National Liberation* Vol. I. London: Zed Press.

    ed. 1987. *Third World, Second Sex: Women's Struggles and National Liberation* Vol. II. London: Zed Press.

Davis, Angela. 1984. *Women, Culture, and Politics*. New York: Random House.

D'Costa, Dorothy Bina. 1997. Interviews related to South Asian culture and language.

Dean, Jodi, 1996. *Solidarity of Strangers: Feminism after Identity Politics*. New York: New York University Press.

ed. 1997. *Feminism and the New Democracy: Resiting the Political*. Thousand Oaks, CA: Sage.

Dewey, John. 1920. *Reconstruction in Philosophy*. New York: Henry Holt & Co.

1938. *Logic: the Theory of Inquiry*. New York: Henry Holt & Co.

1939. *Freedom and Culture*. New York: G. P. Putnam's Sons.

[1927] 1954. *The Public and Its Problems*. Chicago, IL: Swallow Press.

[1897] 1972. "Ethical Principle Underlying Education." In *John Dewey: the Early Works, 1895–1898*, Vol. V, ed. Jo Ann Boydston. Carbondale and Edwardsville, IL: Southern Illinois University Press, 54–83.

[1916a] 1980. *Democracy and Education*. In *John Dewey: the Middle Works, 1899–1924*, Vol. IX, ed. Jo Ann Boydston. Carbondale and Edwardsville, IL: Southern Illinois University Press.

[1916b] 1980. "The Need of an Industrial Education in an Industrial Democracy." In *John Dewey: the Middle Works, 1899–1924*, Vol. X, ed. Jo Ann Boydston. Carbondale and Edwardsville, IL: Southern Illinois University Press, 137–43.

[1919] 1982. "Philosophy and Democracy." In *John Dewey: The Middle Works, 1899–1924*, Vol. XI, ed. Jo Ann Boydston. Carbondale and Edwardsville, IL: Southern Illinois University Press, 41–53.

[1922] 1983. *Human Nature and Conduct: an Introduction to Social Psychology*. In *John Dewey: the Middle Works, 1899–1924*, Vol. XIV, ed. Jo Ann Boydston. Carbondale and Edwardsville, IL: Southern Illinois University Press.

[1931] 1985. "The Need for a New Party." In *John Dewey: the Later Works, 1925–1953*, Vol. VI, ed. Jo Ann Boydston. Carbondale and Edwardsville, IL: Southern Illinois University Press, 156–81.

[1941] 1988. "Introduction to *American Journal of Economics and Sociology*." In *John Dewey: the Later Works, 1925–1953*, Vol. XIV, ed. Jo Ann Boydston. Carbondale and Edwardsville, IL: Southern Illinois University Press, 362–3.

[1942] 1989. "Religion and Morality in a Free Society." In *John Dewey: the Later Works, 1925–1953*, Vol. XV, ed. Jo Ann Boydston. Carbondale and Edwardsville, IL: Southern Illinois University Press, 170–83.

[1943a] 1989. "Anti-Naturalism in Extremis." In *John Dewey: the Later Works, 1925–1953*, Vol. XV, ed. Jo Ann Boydston. Carbondale and Edwardsville, IL: Southern Illinois University Press, 46–62.

[1943b] 1989. "Valuation Judgments and Immediate Quality." In *John Dewey: the Later Works, 1925–1953*, Vol. XV, ed. Jo Ann Boydston. Carbondale and Edwardsville, IL: Southern Illinois University Press, 63–72.

[1944] 1989. "Challenge to Liberal Thought." In *John Dewey: the Later Works, 1925–1953*, Vol. XV, ed. Jo Ann Boydston. Carbondale and Edwardsville, IL: Southern Illinois University Press, 261–75.

[1945a] 1989. "Democratic versus Coercive International Organization: the Realism of Jane Addams." In *John Dewey: the Later Works, 1925–1953*, Vol.

XV, ed. Jo Ann Boydston. Carbondale and Edwardsville, IL: Southern Illinois University Press, 192–8.

[1945b] 1989. "Dualism and the Split Atom: Science and Morals in the Atomic Age." In *John Dewey: the Later Works, 1925–1953*, Vol. XV, ed. Jo Ann Boydston. Carbondale and Edwardsville, IL: Southern Illinois University Press, 199–203.

[1946a] 1989. "Introduction to *Problems of Men*." In *John Dewey: the Later Works, 1925–1953*, Vol. XV, ed. Jo Ann Boydston. Carbondale and Edwardsville, IL: Southern Illinois University Press, 154–69.

[1946b] 1989. "The Crisis in Human History: the Danger of the Retreat to Individualism." In *John Dewey: the Later Works, 1925–1953*, Vol. XV, ed. Jo Ann Boydston. Carbondale and Edwardsville, IL: Southern Illinois University Press, 210–23.

[1948a] 1989. "How to Anchor Liberalism." In *John Dewey: the Later Works, 1925–1953*, Vol. XV, ed. Jo Ann Boydston. Carbondale and Edwardsville, IL: Southern Illinois University Press, 248–50.

[1948b] 1989. "American Youth, Beware of Wallace Bearing Gifts." In *John Dewey: the Later Works, 1925–1953*, Vol. XV, ed. Jo Ann Boydston. Carbondale and Edwardsville, IL: Southern Illinois University Press, 242–7.

[n.d.] 1989. "World Anarchy and World Order." In *John Dewey: the Later Works, 1925–1953*, Vol. XV, ed. Jo Ann Boydston. Carbondale and Edwardsville, IL: Southern Illinois University Press, 204–9.

[1932] 1990. "The Making of Citizens: a Comparative Study of Methods of Civic Training, by Charles Edward Merriam: University of Chicago Press, 1931." In *John Dewey: the Later Works, 1925–1953*, Vol. XVII, ed. Jo Ann Boydston. Carbondale and Edwardsville: Southern Illinois University Press, 112–14.

[1947] 1990. "Comments on 'Religion at Harvard.'" In *John Dewey: the Later Works, 1925–1953*, Vol. XVII, ed. Jo Ann Boydston. Carbondale and Edwardsville, IL: Southern Illinois University Press, 135.

Drèze, Jean and Amartya Sen. 1989. *Hunger and Public Action*. Oxford: Clarendon Press.

Dryzek, John S. 1990. *Discursive Democracy: Politics, Policy, and Political Science*. Cambridge: Cambridge University Press.

1996. "Political Inclusion and the Dynamics of Democratization." *American Political Science Review* 90, 3: 475–87.

Dworkin, Ronald. 1978. *Taking Rights Seriously*. Cambridge, MA: Harvard University Press.

1981. "What Is Equality?" *Philosophy and Public Affairs* 10, 3: 185–246; 10, 4: 283–345.

1983. "In Defense of Equality." *Social Philosophy and Policy* 1, 1: 24–40.

1985. *A Matter of Principle*. Cambridge, MA: Harvard University Press.

1986. *Law's Empire*. Cambridge, MA: Harvard University Press.

Elkin, Stephen L. 1987. *City and Regime in the American Republic*. Chicago, IL: University of Chicago Press.

Elster, Jon. [1986] 1997. "The Market and the Forum." In *Deliberative Democracy: Essays on Reason and Politics*, eds. James Bohman and William Rehg. Cambridge, MA: MIT Press, 3–33.

1998a. Introduction. In *Deliberative Democracy*, ed. Jon Elster. Cambridge: Cambridge University Press, 1–18.

1998b. "Deliberation and Constitution Making." In *Deliberative Democracy*, ed. Jon Elster. Cambridge: Cambridge University Press, 97–122.

Enloe, Cynthia. 1989. *Bananas, Beaches, and Bases: Making Feminist Sense of International Relations*. London: Pandora.

1993. *The Morning After: Sexual Politics at the End of the Cold War*. Berkeley, CA: University of California Press.

Erikson, Robert. 1993. "Descriptions of Inequality: the Swedish Approach to Welfare Research." In *The Quality of Life*, eds. Martha C. Nussbaum and Amartya Sen. Oxford: Clarendon Press, 67–83.

Estlund, David. 1993. "Who's Afraid of Deliberative Democracy? On the Strategic/Deliberative Dichotomy in Recent Constitutional Jurisprudence." *Texas Law Review* 71 (June): 1437–77.

1997. "Beyond Fairness and Deliberation: the Epistemic Dimension of Democratic Authority." In *Deliberative Democracy: Essays on Reason and Politics*, eds. James Bohman and William Rehg. Cambridge, MA: MIT Press, 173–204.

Evans, Joyce. 1993. "Women Ask for End to the Violence." *Milwaukee Sentinel*, June 21.

Ferree, Myra Marx and Patricia Yancey Martin, eds. 1995. *Feminist Organizations: Harvest of the New Women's Movement*. Philadelphia, PA: Temple University Press.

Fishkin, James S. 1991. *Democracy and Deliberation: New Directions for Democratic Reform*. New Haven, CT: Yale University Press.

1992. *The Dialogue of Justice: Toward a Self-Reflective Society*. New Haven, CT: Yale University Press.

1995. *The Voice of the People: Public Opinion and Democracy*. New Haven, CT: Yale University Press.

1996. "The Televised Deliberative Poll: an Experiment in Democracy." *The Annals of the American Academy of Political and Social Science* 546 (July): 132–40.

Flax, Jane. 1990. "Postmodernism and Gender Relations in Feminist Theory." In *Feminism/Postmodernism*, ed. Linda J. Nicholson. New York: Routledge, Chapman & Hall, 39–62.

1995. "Race/Gender and the Ethics of Difference: a Reply to Okin's 'Gender Inequality and Cultural Differences.'" *Political Theory* 23, 3: 500–10.

Fraser, Nancy. [1989] 1991. "What's Critical about Critical Theory? The Case of Habermas and Gender." In *Feminist Interpretations and Political Theory*, eds. Mary Lyndon Shanley and Carole Pateman. University Park, PA: Pennsylvania State University Press, 253–76.

1992. "Rethinking the Public Sphere: a Contribution to the Critique of Actually Existing Democracy." In *Habermas and the Public Sphere*, ed. Craig Calhoun. Cambridge, MA: MIT Press, 109–42.

1995. "Politics, Culture and the Public Sphere: Toward a Postmodern Conception." In *Social Postmodernism: Beyond Identity Politics*, eds. Linda Nicholson and Steven Seidman. Cambridge: Cambridge University Press, 287–312.

Fraser, Nancy and Linda Nicholson. 1990. "Social Criticism without Philosophy: an Encounter between Feminism and Postmodernism." In *Feminism/Postmodernism*, ed. Linda J. Nicholson. New York: Routledge, Chapman & Hall, 19–38.

Freedman, Estelle. 1990. "Theoretical Perspectives on Sexual Difference: an Overview." In *Theoretical Perspectives on Sexual Difference*, ed. Deborah L. Rhode. New Haven, CT: Yale University Press, 257–61.

French, Joan. 1987. "Organizing Women through Drama in Rural Jamaica." In *Third World, Second Sex: Women's Struggles and National Liberation* Vol. II, ed. Miranda Davies. London: Zed Press, 147–54.

1992. "A place for feminism in the Third World." *PanoScope* (July): 28.

Friedman, Elisabeth J. 1995. "Women's Human Rights: The Emergence of a Movement." In *Women's Rights, Human Rights: International Feminist Perspectives*, eds. Julia Peters and Andrea Wolper. New York: Routledge, 18–35.

Friedman, Elisabeth J., Kathryn Hochstetler, and Ann Marie Clark. 1998. "Defining Communities: Latin Americans at UN Conferences on the Environment, Human Rights, and Women." *American Political Science Association*, September 3–6.

Fuss, Diane. 1989. *Essentially Speaking: Feminism, Nature, and Difference*. New York: Routledge.

Galston, William A. 1989. "Community, Democracy, Philosophy: the Political Thought of Michael Walzer." *Political Theory* 17, 1 (February): 119–30.

Gambetta, Diego. 1998. "'Claro!': an Essay on Discursive Machismo." In *Deliberative Democracy*, ed. Jon Elster. Cambridge: Cambridge University Press, 19–43.

Gannon, Kathy. 1996. "Rebels Use Fear, Punishment to Impose Strict Islamic Law." *Associated Press*, September 30, 1996.

Gardner, Katy. 1991. *Songs at the River's Edge: Stories from a Bangladeshi Village*. London: Virago.

Geuss, Raymond. 1981. *The Idea of a Critical Theory: Habermas and the Frankfurt School*. Cambridge: Cambridge University Press.

Giddens, Anthony. 1977. *Studies in Social and Political Theory*. London: Hutchinson.

1979. *Central Problems in Social Theory: Action, Structure and Contradiction in Social Analysis*. Berkeley, CA: University of California Press.

Gillespie, Marcia Ann. 1995. "About the Verdict..." *Ms.* 6, 3: 1.

Gilligan, Carol. [1982] 1993. *In a Different Voice: Psychological Theory and Women's Development*. Cambridge, MA: Harvard University Press.

Global Co-operation for a Better World. 1990. "The Global Vision Statement." Collected and collated from people from 129 countries by Global Co-operation for a Better World coordinated worldwide by the Brahma Kumaris World Spiritual University.

Gluck, Sherna Berger. 1998. "Whose Feminism, Whose History? Reflections on Excavating the History of (the) US Women's Movement(s)." *Community Activism and Feminist Politics: Organizing Across Race, Class, and Gender*, ed. Nancy Naples. New York: Routledge, 31–56.

Goetz, Anne Marie, 1991. "Feminism and the Claim to Know: Contradictions in Feminist Approaches to Women in Development." *Gender and International Relations*, eds. Rebecca Grant and Kathleen Newland. Bloomington, IN: Indiana University Press, 133–57.

1992. "Gender and Administration." *IDS Bulletin* 23, 4 (October): 6–17.

1995a. "Who Takes the Credit? Gender, Power, and Control Over Loan Use in Rural Credit programs in Bangladesh." *World Development* 24, 1: 45–63.

1995b. "Institutionalizing Women's Interests and Gender-Sensitive Accountability in Development." *IDS Bulletin* 26, 3 (July): 1–10.

ed. 1997. *Getting Institutions Right for Women in Development*. London: Zed Books.

Goetz, Anne Marie and Rina Sen Gupta. 1995. "Who Takes the Credit? Gender, Power, and Control Over Loan Use in Rural Credit Programs in Bangladesh." *World Development* 24, 1: 45–63.

Goodman, Ellen. 1993. "Tribunal a Success Amid Horror Stories, 'Women's Rights Are Human Rights, Too.'" *Boston Globe*, June 18.

Gould, Carol C. 1993. "Feminism and Democratic Community Revisited." In *Democratic Community: NOMOS XXXV*, eds. John W. Chapman and Ian Shapiro. New York: New York University Press, 396–413.

Grant, Jaime M. 1996. "Building Community-Based Coalitions from Academe: the Union Institute and the Kitchen Table: Women of Color Press Transition Coalition." *Signs: Journal of Women in Culture and Society* 21, 4 (Summer): 1024–33.

Green, Rayna. 1982. "Diary of a Native American Feminist." *MS* 11 (July/August): 170–2, 211–13.

Greenhalgh, Susan. 1991. "Women in the Informal Enterprise: Empowerment or Exploitation?" Population Council Research Division. Working Paper No. 33.

Gunnell, John G. 1997. "Why There Cannot Be a Theory of Politics." *Polity* 29, 4: 519–37.

Gunning, Isabell. 1991–92. "Arrogant Perception, World-Traveling and Multicultural Feminism: the Case of Female Genital Surgeries." *Columbia Human Rights Law Review* 23: 189–248.

Gutmann, Amy. 1990. "Moral Conflict and Political Consensus." *Ethics* 101 (October): 64–88. Reprinted in *Liberalism and the Good*, eds. R. Bruce Douglass, Gerald Mara, and Henry Richardson. New York: Routledge: 125–47.

1993a. "The Challenge of Multiculturalism in Political Ethics." *Philosophy and Public Affairs* 22, 3 (Summer): 171–206.

1993b. "The Disharmony of Democracy." In *Democratic Community: NOMOS XXXV*, eds. John W. Chapman and Ian Shapiro. New York: New York University Press, 126–60.

1994a. "Preface" and "Introduction." In *Multiculturalism: Examining the Politics of Recognition*, ed. Amy Gutmann. Princeton, NJ: Princeton University Press, ix–xii and 3–24.

ed. 1994b. *Multiculturalism: Examining the Politics of Recognition*. Princeton, NJ: Princeton University Press.

1995. "Civic Education and Social Diversity." *Ethics* 105 (April): 557–79.

Gutmann, Amy and Dennis Thompson. 1996. *Democracy and Disagreement*. Cambridge, MA: Belknap Press of Harvard University Press.

Gwaltney, John Langston. 1980. *Drylongso: a Self-Portrait of Black America*. New York: Vintage.

Habermas, Jürgen. 1984. *Theory of Communicative Action*. Vol. I: *Reason and the Rationalization of Society*, trans. Thomas McCarthy. Boston, MA: Beacon Press.

1987. *Theory of Communicative Action*. Vol. II: *Lifeworld and System: a Critique of Functionalist Reason*, trans. Thomas McCarthy. Boston, MA: Beacon Press.

1989a. *The New Conservatism: Cultural Criticism and the Historians' Debate*, ed. and trans. Shierry Weber Nicholsen. Cambridge, MA: MIT Press.

1989b. *The Structural Transformation of the Public Sphere*, trans. Thomas Burger with Frederick Lawrence. Cambridge, MA: MIT Press.

1990. *Moral Consciousness and Communicative Action*, trans. Christian Lenhardt and Shierry Weber Nicholsen. Cambridge, MA: MIT Press.

1992. *Postmetaphysical Thinking: Philosophical Essays*, trans. William Mark Hohengarten. Cambridge, MA: MIT Press.

1994. "Struggles for Recognition in the Democratic Constitutional State," trans. Shierry Weber Nicholsen. In *Multiculturalism: Examining the Politics of Recognition*, ed. Amy Gutmann. Princeton, NJ: Princeton University Press, 107–48.

1996. *Between Facts and Norms: Contributions to a Discourse Theory of Law and Democracy*, trans. William Rehq. Cambridge, MA: MIT Press.

Hampshire, Stuart. 1989. *Innocence and Experience*. Cambridge, MA: Harvard University Press.

Hansberry, Lorraine. 1969. *To Be Young, Gifted and Black*. New York: Signet.

Haraway, Donna. 1988. "Situated Knowledges: the Science Question in Feminism and the Privilege of Partial Perspective." *Feminist Studies* 14, 3 (Fall): 575–90.

Harris, Angela. 1990. "Race and Essentialism in Feminist Legal Theory." *Stanford Law Review* 42, 58 (February): 581–616.

1994. "Commentary." In Kwame Anthony Appiah, *Identity Against Culture: Understandings of Multiculturalism*. Berkeley, CA: Regents of the University of California, 43–9.

Hashemi, Syed, Sidney Ruth Schuler, and Ann P. Riley. 1996. "Rural Credit Programs and Women's Empowerment in Bangladesh." *World Development* 24, 4: 635–53.

Hassan, Riffat. 1991. "The Issue of Woman–Man Equality in the Islamic Tradition." In *Women's and Men's Liberation: Testimonies of Spirit*, ed. Leonard Grob, Riffat Hassan, and Haim Gordon. New York: Greenwood Press, 65–82.

Heyes, Cressida J. 1997. "Anti-Essentialism in Practice: Carol Gilligan and Feminist Philosophy." *Hypatia* 12, 3 (Summer): 142–63.

Heywood, Leslie and Jennifer Drake, eds. 1997. *Third Wave Agenda: Being Feminist, Doing Feminism*. Minneapolis, MN: University of Minnesota Press.

al-Hibri, Azizah. 1982. "A Study of Islamic Herstory: or How Did We Ever Get Into This Mess?" *Women's Studies International Forum* 5, 2: 207–19.

Hirschman, Albert. 1970. *Exit, Voice and Loyalty: Responses to Decline in Firms, Organizations, and States*. Cambridge, MA: Harvard University Press.

1994. "Social Conflicts as Pillars of Democratic Market Society." *Political Theory* 22, 2 (May): 203–18.

Hirschmann, Nancy. 1989. "Freedom, Recognition and Obligation: A Feminist Approach to Political Theory." *American Political Science Review* 83, 4 (December): 1227–44.

1996a. "Toward a Feminist Theory of Freedom." *Political Theory* 24, 1: 46–67.

1996b. "Domestic Violence and the Theoretical Discourse of Freedom." *Frontiers* 16, 1: 126–51.

1998. "Western Feminism, Eastern Veiling, and the Question of Free Agency." *Constellations* 5, 3: 345–68.

Hirshman, Mitu. 1995. "Women and Development: a critique." In *Feminism/Postmodernism/Development*, eds. Marianne H. Marchand and Jane L. Parpart. London: Routledge, 42–55.

Hirst, Paul. 1992. "Comments on 'Secondary Associations and Democratic Governance.'" *Politics and Society* 20, 4 (December): 473–80.

Hoagland, Sarah Lucia. 1988. *Lesbian Ethics: Toward New Value*. Palo Alto, CA: Institute of Lesbian Studies.

Holmes, Stephen. 1988. "Gag rules or the politics of omission." In *Constitutionalism and Democracy: Studies in Rationality and Social Change*, eds. Jon Elster and Rune Slagstad. Cambridge: Cambridge University Press, 19–58.

hooks, bell. 1984. *Feminist Theory: from Margin to Center*. Boston, MA: South End Press.

1990. *Yearning: Race, Gender, and Cultural Politics*. Boston, MA: South End Press.

Hosken, Fran. 1981. "Female Genital Mutilation and Human Rights." *Feminist Issues* 1, 3 (Summer): 3–23.

Human Development Report. 1996. New York: Oxford University Press.

Huspek, Michael and Kathleen E. Kendall. 1991. "On Withholding Political Voice: an Analysis of the Political Vocabulary of a 'Non-political' Speech Community." *The Quarterly Journal of Speech* 77, 1 (February): 1–19.

International Covenant on Civil and Political Rights. 1966. G.A. Res. 2200(XXI), 21 UN GAOR, Supp. (No. 16) at 52, UN Doc. A/6316. Adopted December 16, 1966.

Jahan, Roushan. 1995. "Men in Seclusion, Women in Public: Rokeya's Dream and Women's Struggles in Bangladesh." In *The Challenge of Local Feminisms: Women's Movements in Global Perspective*, ed. Amrita Basu. Boulder, CO: Westview Press, 87–109.

Jayawardena, Kumari. 1986. *Feminism and Nationalism in Third World*. London: Zed Books Ltd.

Jeffery, Patricia. 1997. "Agency, Activism, and Agendas." In *Appropriating Gender: Women's Activism and Politicized Religion in South Asia*, eds. Patricia Jeffery and Amrita Basu. New York: Routledge, 221–43.

Jhabvala, Renana and Namrata Bali. n.d. *My Life, My Work: a Sociological Study of SEWA's Urban Members*. Ahmedabad, India: Self Employed Women's Association.

Jung, Courtney and Ian Shapiro. [1995] 1996. "South Africa's Negotiated Transition: Democracy, Opposition, and the New Constitutional Order." In *Democracy's Place*. Ithaca, NY: Cornell University Press, 175–219.

Kahin, George McTurnan. 1956. *The Asian-African Conference, Bandung, Indonesia, April 1955.* Ithaca, NY: Cornell University Press.

Kapadia, Karin. 1995. "Where Angels Fear to Tread?: 'Third World Women' and 'Development.'" *The Journal of Peasant Studies* 22, 2 (January): 356–68.

Kardam, Nüket. 1991. *Bringing Women In: Women's Issues in International Development Programs.* Boulder, CO: Lynne Rienner Publishers.

Katz, Lee Michael. 1993. "UN Tribunal Puts Focus on Women, Abuse." *USA Today,* June 15.

Kay, Michael. 1996. "Utility consumers converge for Fishkin-like forum." *Austin American-Statesman.* Austin, TX: June 5, 1996: B1, B5.

Keck, Margaret and Kathryn Sikkink. 1998. *Activists Beyond Borders: Advocacy Networks in International Politics.* Ithaca, NY: Cornell University Press.

Kelley, Stanley, Jr. 1992. Book Review. *American Political Science Review* 86, 4: 1043.

Keynes, John Maynard. [1923] 1971. *A Tract on Monetary Reform.* In *The Collected Writings of John Maynard Keynes,* Vol. IV. London: Macmillan St Martin's Press for the Royal Economic Society.

Knight, Jack and James Johnson. 1994. "Aggregation and Deliberation: on the Possibility of Democratic Legitimacy." *Political Theory* 22, 2 (May): 277–96.

1997. "What Sort of Political Equality Does Democratic Deliberation Require?" In *Deliberative Democracy: Essays on Reason and Politics,* eds. James Bohman and William Rehg. Cambridge, MA: MIT Press, 279–319.

Krüger, Lorenz. 1993. "Commentary on Putnam." In *The Quality of Life,* eds. Martha C. Nussbaum and Amartya Sen. Oxford: Clarendon Press, 158–64.

Kymlicka, Will. 1989. *Liberalism, Community, and Culture.* Oxford: Clarendon Press.

Lal, R. B. and S. C. Seal. 1994. *General Rural Health Survey: Singur Health Centre 1994.* Calcutta: All-India Institute of Hygiene and Public Health.

Lâm, Maivân Clech. 1994. "Feeling Foreign in Feminism." *Signs: Journal of Women in Culture and Society* 19, 4 (Summer): 865–92.

Leonard, Stephen T. 1990. *Critical Theory in Political Practice.* Princeton, NJ: Princeton University Press.

Lewis, Anthony. 1996. "Anatomy of Disaster." *New York Times,* January 5.

Littleton, Christine. 1987. "Reconstructing Sexual Equality." *Southern California Law Review* 75: 1279–337.

Lugones, María. 1990. "Playfulness, 'World' Travelling, and Loving Perception." In *Making Face, Making Soul/Haciendo Caras: Creative and Critical Perspectives by Women of Color,* ed. Gloria Anzaldúa. San Francisco, CA: Aunt Lute Foundation Books, 390–402.

Lukes, Steven. 1974. *Power: a Radical View.* London: Macmillan.

Luskin, Robert, James S. Fishkin, Norman Bradburn, Morris Fiorina, Stanley Kelley, Warren E. Miller, and W. Russell Neuman. 1996. "Roundtable on Deliberative Polls in the United States and the United Kingdom." *American Political Science Association Meeting,* September 1.

Mainwaring, Scott, Guillermo O'Donnell, and J. Samuel Valenzuela, eds. 1992.

Issues in Democratic Consolidation: the New South American Democracies in Comparative Perspective. Notre Dame, IN: University of Notre Dame Press.

Manin, Bernard. 1987. "On Legitimacy and Political Deliberation," trans. Elly Stein and Jane Mansbridge. *Political Theory* 15, 3 (August): 338–68.

Mansbridge, Jane. 1988. "Motivating Deliberation in Congress." In *E Pluribus Unum: Constitutional Principles and the Institutions of Government*, ed. Sarah Baumyartner Thurow. Lanham, MD: University Press of America, 59–86.

1992. "A Deliberative Theory of Interest Representation." In *The Politics of Interests: Interest Groups Transformed*, ed. Mark P. Petracca. Boulder, CO: Westview Press, 32–57.

1993. "Feminism and Democratic Community." In *Democratic Community: NOMOS XXXV*, eds. John W. Chapman and Ian Shapiro. New York: New York University Press, 339–95.

1996. "Using Power/Fighting Power: The Polity." In *Democracy and Difference: Changing Boundaries of the Political*, ed. Seyla Benhabib. Princeton, NJ: Princeton University Press, 46–66.

al-Marayati, Laila. 1998. Interview by Melinda Penkava. *Talk of the Nation.* National Public Radio, August 24, 1998.

March, James G. and Johan P. Olsen. 1995. *Democratic Governance.* New York: Free Press.

Marchand, Marianne H. 1995. "Latin American Women Speak on Development: Are We Listening Yet?" In *Feminism/Postmodernism/Development*, eds. Marianne H. Marchard and Jane L. Parport. London: Routledge, 56–72.

Marchand, Marianne and Jane L. Parpart. 1995a. "Exploding the Canon: an Introduction/Conclusion" In *Feminism/Postmodernism/Development*, eds. Marianne H. Marchand and Jane L. Parpart. London: Routledge, 1–22.

eds. 1995b. *Feminism/Postmodernism/Development.* London: Routledge.

Marx, Karl. [1843] 1967. "Letter to A. Ruge, September 1843." In *Writings of the Young Marx on Philosophy and Society*, eds. and trans. Loyd D. Easton and Kurt H. Guddat. New York: Doubleday Anchor, 211–15.

Mathews, David. 1994. *Politics for People: Finding a Responsible Public Voice.* Urbana, IL: University of Illinois Press.

Matilal, Bimal Krishna. 1989. "Ethical Relativism and Confrontation of Cultures." In *Relativism: Interpretation and Confrontation*, ed. Michael Krausz. Notre Dame, IN: University of Notre Dame Press, 339–62.

Matynia, Elzbieta. 1995. "Finding a Voice: Women in Postcommunist Central Europe." In *The Challenge of Local Feminisms: Women's Movements in Global Perspective*, ed. Amrita Basu. Boulder, CO: Westview Press, 374–404.

Mayer, Ann Elizabeth. 1995. "Rhetorical Strategies and Official Policies on Women's Rights: the Merits and Drawbacks of the New World Hypocrisy." In *Faith and Freedom: Women's Human Rights in the Muslim World.* Mahnaz Afkhami, ed. Syracuse, NY: Syracuse University Press, 104–32.

Mernissi, Fatima. 1991. *The Veil and the Male Elite: A Feminist Interpretation of Women's Rights in Islam.* Reading, MA: Addison-Wesley.

1992. *Islam and Democracy: Fear of the Modern World*, trans. Mary Jo Lakeland. Reading, MA: Addison-Wesley.

1995. "Arab Women's Rights and the Muslim State in the Twenty-first Century: Reflections on Islam as Religion and State." In *Faith and Freedom:*

Women's Human Rights in the Muslim World, ed. Mahnaz Afkhami. Syracuse, NY: Syracuse University Press, 33–50.

Merriam, Charles Edward. 1931. *The Making of Citizens: a Comparative Study of Methods of Civic Training*. Chicago, IL: University of Chicago Press.

Michelman, Frank I. 1986. "Traces of Self-government." *Harvard Law Review* 100, 1: 4–77.

1997. "How Can the People Ever Make the Laws? A Critique of Deliberative Democracy." In *Deliberative Democracy: Essays on Reason and Politics*, eds. James Bohman and William Rehg. Cambridge, MA: MIT Press, 145–71.

Mill, John Stuart. 1963. *Essays on Politics and Culture by John Stuart Mill*, ed. Gertrude Himmelfarb. New York: Anchor Books.

[1869] 1970. *The Subjection of Women*. In *Essays on Sex Equality*, ed. Alice S. Rossi. Chicago, IL: University of Chicago Press, 123–242.

[1859] 1974. *On Liberty*, ed. Gertrude Himmelfarb. New York: Penguin Books.

Miller, David. 1992. "Deliberative Democracy and Social Choice." *Political Studies* Special Issue 40: 54–67.

Miller, Francesca. 1991. *Latin American Women and the Search for Social Justice*. Hanover: University Press of New England.

Minh-ha, Trinh T. 1987. "Difference: 'A Special Third World Women Issue.'" *Feminist Review* 25: 5–22.

Ministry of Foreign Affairs Republic of Indonesia. 1955. *Asia-Africa Speaks from Bandung*. Transcripts of speeches. Djakarta: Ministry of Foreign Affairs Republic of Indonesia.

Mohanty, Chandra Talpade. 1991a. "Introduction." In *Third World Women and the Politics of Feminism*, eds. Chandra Talpade Mohanty, Ann Russo, and Lourdes Torres. Bloomington, IN: University of Indiana Press, 1–47.

[1984] 1991b. "Under Western Eyes: Feminist Scholarship and Colonial Discourses." In *Third World Women and the Politics of Feminism*, eds. Chandra Talpade Mohanty, Ann Russo, and Lourdes Torres. Bloomington, IN: University of Indiana Press, 51–80.

1995. "Feminist Encounters: Locating the Politics of Experience." In *Social Postmodernism: Beyond Identity Politics*, eds. Linda Nicholson and Steven Seidman. Cambridge: Cambridge University Press, 68–86.

Mohanty, Chandra Talpade, Ann Russo, and Lourdes Torres, eds. 1991. *Third World Women and the Politics of Feminism*. Bloomington, IN: University of Indiana Press.

Moraga, Cherrie. 1993. "From a Long Line of Vendidas: Chicanas and Feminism." In *Feminist Frameworks*, eds. Alison M. Jaggar and Paula S. Rothenberg. New York: McGraw-Hill, 203–12.

Morgan, Robin. 1984. *Sisterhood is Global: the International Women's Movement Anthology*. New York: Anchor Press/Doubleday.

1996a. "The NGO Forum: Good News and Bad." In *Beijing and Beyond: Toward the Twenty-first Century of Women*. *Women's Studies Quarterly* 24, 1–2: 46–53.

1996b. "The UN Conference: out of the Holy Brackets and into the Policy Mainstream." In *Beijing and Beyond: Toward the Twenty-first Century of Women*. *Women's Studies Quarterly* 24, 1–2: 77–83.

Morris, Debra and Ian Shapiro. 1993. "Editor's Introduction." In *John Dewey:*

the Political Writings, eds. Morris, Debra and Ian Shapiro. Indianapolis, IN: Hackett Publishing Company, Inc., ix–xix.

Moseley, Ray. 1993. "Women Recount Stories of Violence, Exploitation." *Chicago Tribune*, June 17.

Moser, Caroline O. N. 1989. "Gender Planning in the Third World: Meeting Practical and Strategic Gender Needs." *World Development* 17, 11: 1799–825.

Mostov, Julie. 1992. *Power, Process, and Popular Sovereignty*. Philadelphia, PA: Temple University Press.

Mouffe, Chantal. 1991. "Democratic Citizenship and the Political Community." In *Community at Loose Ends*, ed. Miami Theory Collective. Minneapolis, MN: University of Minnesota Press.

(1992) 1995. "Feminism, Citizenship, and Radical Democratic Politics." In *Social Postmodernism: Beyond Identity Politics*, eds. Linda Nicholson and Steven Seidman. Cambridge: Cambridge University Press, 315–31.

Mozert v. Hawkins City Board of Education, 827 F.2nd 1058 (6th Cir. 1987), *cert. denied*, 484 U.S. 1066. 1988.

Nagel, Thomas. 1987. "Moral Conflict and Political Legitimacy." *Philosophy and Public Affairs* 16 (Summer): 215–40.

An-Na'im, Abdullahi Ahmed. 1994. "State Responsibility Under International Human Rights Law to Change Religious and Customary Laws." In *Human Rights of Women: National and International Perspectives*, ed. Rebecca J. Cook. Philadelphia, PA: University of Pennsylvania Press, 167–88.

Naples, Nancy, ed. 1998a. *Community Activism and Feminist Politics: Organizing Across Race, Class, and Gender*. New York: Routledge.

1998b. "Women's Community Activism and Feminist Activist Research." *Community Activism and Feminist Politics: Organizing Across Race, Class, and Gender*, ed. Nancy Naples. New York: Routledge, 1–27.

1998c. "Women's Community Activism." *Community Activism and Feminist Politics: Organizing Across Race, Class, and Gender*, ed. Nancy Naples. New York: Routledge, 327–49.

Narayan, Uma. 1997. *Dislocating Cultures: Identities, Traditions, and Third World Feminism*. New York: Routledge.

National Issues Convention. 1996. "National Issues Convention Deliberative Poll Reveals Significant Change in Delegates' Views on Key Issues." Press Release, National Issues Convention, January 25.

Nicholson, Linda, ed. 1990. *Feminism/Postmodernism*. New York: Routledge.

Nicholson, Linda and Steven Seidman, eds. 1995. *Social Postmodernism: Beyond Identity Politics*. Cambridge: Cambridge University Press.

Nino, Carlos Santiago. 1996. *The Constitution of Deliberative Democracy*. New Haven, CT: Yale University Press.

Nussbaum, Martha C. 1986a. *The Fragility of Goodness: Luck and Ethics in Greek Tragedy and Philosophy*. Cambridge: Cambridge University Press.

1986b. "Therapeutic arguments: Epicuras and Aristotle." In *The Norms of Nature: Studies in Hellenistic Ethics*, eds. Malcolm Schofield and Gisela Striker. Cambridge: Cambridge University Press, 31–74.

1988a. "Nature, Function, and Capability: Aristotle on Political Distribution." *Oxford Studies in Ancient Philosophy*, Suppl. Vol., 145–84.

1988b. "Non-relative Virtues: an Aristotelian Approach." *Midwest Studies in Philosophy* 13: 32–53.

1988c. "Reply to David Charles." *Oxford Studies in Ancient Philosophy*, Suppl. Vol., 206–14.

1990. "Aristotelian Social Democracy." In *Liberalism and the Good*, eds. R. Bruce Douglass, Gerald Mara, and Henry Richardson. New York: Routledge, 203–52.

1992. "Human Functioning and Social Justice: in Defense of Aristotelian Essentialism." *Political Theory* 20, 2 (May): 202–46.

1993a. "Non-relative Virtues: an Aristotelian Approach." In *The Quality of Life*, eds. Martha C. Nussbaum and Amartya Sen. Oxford: Clarendon Press, 242–69.

1993b. "Commentary on Onora O'Neill: Justice, Gender, and International Boundaries." In *The Quality of Life*, eds. Martha C. Nussbaum and Amartya Sen. Oxford: Clarendon Press, 324–35.

1995a. "Introduction." In *Women, Culture, and Development: a Study of Human Capabilities*, eds. Martha C. Nussbaum and Jonathan Glover. Oxford: Clarendon Press, 1–34.

1995b. "Human Capabilities, Female Human Beings." In *Women, Culture, and Development: a Study of Human Capabilities*, eds. Martha C. Nussbaum and Jonathan Glover. Oxford: Clarendon Press, 61–104.

1995c. "Aristotle on Human Nature and the Foundations of Ethics." In *World, Mind, and Ethics: Essays on the Ethical Philosophy of Bernard Williams*, eds. J. E. J. Altham and Ross Harrison. Cambridge: Cambridge University Press, 86–131.

1995d. "Emotions and Women's Capabilities." In *Women, Culture, and Development: a Study of Human Capabilities*, eds. Martha C. Nussbaum and Jonathan Glover. Oxford: Clarendon Press, 360–95.

1995e. "'Lawyer for Humanity:' Theory and Practice in Ancient Political Thought." In *Theory and Practice: NOMOS XXXVII*, eds. Ian Shapiro and Judith Wagner DeCew. New York: New York University Press, 181–215.

Nussbaum, Martha C. and Jonathan Glover, eds. 1995. *Women, Culture, and Development: a Study of Human Capabilities*. Oxford: Clarendon Press.

Nussbaum, Martha C. and Amartya Sen. 1989. "Internal Criticism and Indian Rationalist Traditions." In *Relativism: Interpretation and Confrontation*, ed. Michael Krausz. Notre Dame: University of Notre Dame Press, 229–325.

Nussbaum, Martha C. and Amartya Sen, eds. 1993. *The Quality of Life*. Oxford: Clarendon Press.

O'Donnell, Guillermo and Philippe C. Schmitter. 1986. *Transitions from Authoritarian Rule: Tentative Conclusions about Uncertain Democracies*. Baltimore, MD: Johns Hopkins University Press.

Ofei-Aboagye, Rosemary Ofeibea. 1994. "Altering the Strands of the Fabric: a Preliminary Look at Domestic Violence in Ghana." *Signs: Journal of Women in Culture and Society* 19, 4 (Summer): 924–38.

Okin, Susan Moller. 1979. *Women in Western Political Thought*. Princeton, NJ: Princeton University Press.

1989. *Gender, Justice and the Family*. Basic Books: New York.

1994. "Gender Inequality and Cultural Difference." *Political Theory* 22, 1 (February): 5–24.

1995a. "Response to Flax." *Political Theory* 23, 3 (August): 511–16.

1995b. "Inequalities between the Sexes in Different Cultural Contexts." In *Women, Culture, and Development: a Study of Human Capabilities*, eds. Martha C. Nussbaum and Jonathan Glover. Oxford: Clarendon Press, 274–97.

1997. "Culture, Religion, and Female Identity Formation: Responding to a Human Rights Challenge." Unpublished manuscript, April.

1998. "Feminism, Women's Human Rights, and Cultural Differences." *Hypatia* 13, 2 (Spring): 32–52.

Oloka-Onyango, J. and Sylvia Tamale. 1995. "'The Personal is Political,' or Why Women's Rights are Indeed Human Rights: an African Perspective on International Feminism." *Human Rights Quarterly* 17, 4: 691–731.

O'Neill, Onora. 1993. "Justice, Gender, and International Boundaries." In *The Quality of Life*, eds. Martha C. Nussbaum and Amartya Sen. Oxford: Clarendon Press, 303–23.

Ong, Aihwa. 1988. "Colonialism and Modernity: Feminist Re-presentations of Women in Non-Western Societies," *Inscriptions* 3/4: 79–93.

Pala, Achola O. 1977. "Definitions of Women and Development: an African Perspective." *Signs: Journal of Women in Culture and Society* 3, 1 (Autumn): 9–13.

Papanek, Hanna. 1997. "Development Planning for Women." *Signs: Journal of Women in Culture and Society* 3, 1 (Autumn): 14–21.

Parekh, Bhikhu. 1992. "The Cultural Particularity of Liberal Democracy." *Political Studies* Special Issue 40: 160–75.

Parikh, Indria J. and Pulin K. Garg. 1989. *Indian Women: an Inner Dialogue.* New Delhi: Sage Publications.

Park, Lisa Sun-Hee. 1998. "Navigating the Anti-Immigrant Wave." In *Community Activism and Feminist Politics: Organizing Across Race, Class, and Gender*, ed. Nancy Naples. New York: Routledge, 175–95.

Parpart, Jane L. 1993. "Who is the 'Other'? a Postmodern Feminist Critique or Women and Development Theory and Practice." *Development and Change* 24, 3 (July): 439–64.

1995. "Deconstructing the Development 'Expert.'" In *Feminism/Postmodernism/Development*, eds. Marianne H. Marchand and Jane L. Parpart. London: Routledge, 221–43.

Pateman, Carole. 1970. *Participation and Democratic Theory.* Cambridge: Cambridge University Press.

1988. *The Sexual Contract.* Stanford, CA: Stanford University Press.

Phillips, Anne. 1991. *Engendering Democracy.* University Park, PA: Pennsylvania State University Press.

[1992a] 1993a. "Democracy and Difference: some Problems for Feminist Theory." In *Democracy and Difference*. University Park, PA: Pennsylvania State University Press, 90–102.

[1992b] 1993b. "Must Feminists Give Up on Liberal Democracy?" In *Democracy and Difference*. University Park, PA: Pennsylvania State University Press, 103–22.

Posadskaya, Anastasia. 1995. "Democracy Without Women Is No Democracy." In *The Challenge of Local Feminisms: Women's Movements in Global Perspective*, ed. Amrita Basu. Boulder, CO: Westview Press, 351–73.

Prinz, Roland. 1993. "Women Tell of Worldwide Abuse at UN Tribunal." *Associated Press*, June 16.

Przeworski, Adam. 1998. "Deliberation and Ideological Domination." In *Deliberative Democracy*, ed. Jon Elster. Cambridge: Cambridge University Press, 140–60.

Putnam, Hilary. 1993. "Objectivity and the Science–Ethics Distinction." In *The Quality of Life*, eds. Martha C. Nussbaum and Amartya Sen. Oxford: Clarendon Press, 143–57.

Putnam, Robert D. 1993. *Making Democracy Work: Civic Traditions in Modern Italy*. Princeton, NJ: Princeton University Press.

Radin, Margaret Jane. 1990. "The Pragmatist and the Feminist." *Southern California Law Review* 63, 6: 1699–726.

Rasekh, Zohra, Heidi M. Bauer, M. Michele Manos, and Vincent Iacopino. 1998. "Women's Health and Human Rights in Afghanistan." *The Journal of the American Medical Association* 280, 5: 449–55.

Rasmussen, David M. 1990. *Reading Habermas*. Cambridge, MA: Basil Blackwell.

Rasmussen, Douglas B. 1990. "Liberalism and Natural End Ethics." *American Philosophical Quarterly* 27, 2 (April): 153–61.

Rathgeber, Eva M. 1995. "Gender and Development in Action." In *Feminism/Postmodernism/Development*, eds. Marianne H. Marchand and Jane L. Parpart. London: Routledge, 204–20.

Rawls, John. 1971. *A Theory of Justice*. Cambridge, MA: Belknap Press of Harvard University Press.

——— 1982. "Social Utility and Primary Goods." In *Utilitarianism and Beyond*, eds. Amartya Sen and Bernard Williams. Cambridge: Cambridge University Press, 159–86.

——— 1985. "Justice as Fairness: Political not Metaphysical." *Philosophy and Public Affairs* 14 (Summer): 223–51.

——— 1987. "The Idea of an Overlapping Consensus." *Oxford Journal of Legal Studies* 7: 1–25.

——— 1988. "The Priority of Right and Ideas of the Good." In *Philosophy and Public Affairs* 17, 4: 251–76.

——— 1993. *Political Liberalism*. New York: Columbia University Press.

——— 1997. "The Ideal of Public Reason Revisited." *The University of Chicago Law Review* 64, 3: 765–807.

Raz, Joseph. 1991. "Morality as Interpretation." *Ethics* 101 (January): 392–405.

Razavi, Shahra and Carol Miller. 1995a. *From WID to GAD: Conceptual Shifts in the Women and Development Discourse*. Geneva: United Nations Research Institute for Social Development, February.

——— 1995b. *Gender Mainstreaming: a Study of Efforts by the UNDP, the World Bank, and the ILO to Institutionalize Gender Issues*. Geneva: United Nations Research Institute for Social Development, August.

Reifenberg, Anne. 1993. "It's the Year of Women at UN Rights Congress." *Dallas Morning News*, June 14.

Riding, Alan. 1993. "Women Seize Focus at Rights Forum." *New York Times*, June 16.

Rockefeller, Steven. [1992] 1994. "Comment" on Charles Taylor's "The Politics of Recognition." In *Multiculturalism: Examining the Politics of Recognition*, ed. Amy Gutmann. Princeton, NJ: Princeton University Press, 87–98.

Rogoff, Barbara. 1990. *Apprenticeship in Thinking: Cognitive Development in Social Context*. Oxford: Oxford University Press.

Rollins, Judith. 1985. *Between Women: Domestics and Their Employers*. Philadelphia, PA: Temple University Press.

Rorty, Richard. 1982. *Consequences of Pragmatism (Essays: 1972–1980)*. Minneapolis, MN: University of Minnesota Press.

Rosaldo, Michelle Zimbalist and Louise Lamphere, editors. 1974. *Women, Culture and Society*. Stanford, CA: Stanford University Press.

Rose, Kalima. 1992. *Where Women are Leaders: The SEWA Movement in India*. London: Zed Books.

Ross, Lee and Andrew Ward. 1996. "Naive Realism: Implications for Social Conflict and Misunderstanding." In *Values and Knowledge*, eds. Terrance Brown, Edward S. Reed, and Elliot Turiel. Mahwah, NJ: Lawrence Erlbaum, 103–35.

Rouse, Shahnaz. 1998. "The Outsider(s) Within: Sovereignty and Citizenship in Pakistan." In *Appropriating Gender: Women's Activism and Politicized Religion in South Asia*, eds. Patricia Jeffry and Amrita Basu. New York: Routledge, 53–70.

Rousseau, Jean-Jacques. [1762] 1968. *The Social Contract*. Maurice Cranston. New York: Penguin.

el Saadawi, Nawal. 1982. "Woman and Islam." *Women's Studies International Forum* 5, 2: 193–206.

Safire, William. 1993. *Safire's New Political Dictionary*. New York: Random House.

Salole, Gerry. 1991. "Participatory Development: The Taxation of the Beneficiary?" *Journal of Social Development in Africa* 6, 2: 5–16.

Sanders, Lynn M. 1997. "Against Deliberation." *Political Theory* 25, 3: 347–76.

Sangari, Kumkum and Sudesh Vaid, eds. (1989) 1990. *Recasting Women: Essays in Indian Colonial History*. New Brunswick, NJ: Rutgers University Press.

Saunders, Harold H. 1993. "Responding to Future Ethnic Conflicts: The Lessons of Yugoslavia." Conference Report for Spoleto, Italy (May 22–24, 1993) and Airlie House, Warrenton, VA (July 18–20, 1993).

Scanlon, Thomas. 1975. "Preference and Urgency." *The Journal of Philosophy* 72, 19: 659–61.

    1982. "Contractualism and Utilitarianism." In *Utilitarianism and Beyond*, eds. Amartya Sen and Bernard Williams. Cambridge: Cambridge University Press, 103–28.

Schumpeter, Joseph A. [1943] 1947. *Capitalism, Socialism and Democracy*. New York: Harper.

Scott, James C. 1985. *Weapons of the Weak*. New Haven, CT: Yale University Press.

    1990. *Domination and the Arts of Resistance: Hidden Transcripts*. New Haven, CT: Yale University Press.

Seabright, Paul. 1993. "Pluralism and the Standard of Living." In *The Quality of Life*, eds. Martha C. Nussbaum and Amartya Sen. Oxford: Clarendon Press, 393–409.

Seitz, Virginia Rinaldo. 1995. *Women, Development, and Communities for Empowerment in Appalachia.* Albany, NY: State University of New York Press.

Selliah, S. 1989. *The Self-Employed Women's Association, Ahmedabad, India.* Geneva: International Labour Office.

Selsky, Andrew. 1996. "Taliban Promises to Ease Restrictions on Women." *Associated Press.* November 1, 1996.

Sen, Amartya. 1984. *Resources, Values and Development.* Cambridge, MA: Harvard University Press.

1985. *Commodities and Capabilities.* Amsterdam: Elsevier Science Publishers.

1990a. "More than 100 Million Women Are Missing." *New York Review of Books* 37 (December 20): 61–6.

1990b. "Justice: Means versus Freedoms." *Philosophy and Public Affairs* 19, 2 (Spring): 111–21.

1990c. "Gender and Cooperative Conflicts." In *Persistent Inequalities: Women and World Development*, ed. Irene Tinker. New York: Oxford University Press, 123–49.

1993. "Capability and Well-Being." In *The Quality of Life*, eds. Martha C. Nussbaum and Amartya Sen. Oxford: Clarendon Press, 30–53.

1995. "Is the Idea of Purely Internal Consistency of Choice Bizarre?" In *World, Mind, and Ethics: Essays on the Ethical Philosophy of Bernard Williams*, eds. J. E. J. Altham and Ross Harrison. Cambridge: Cambridge University Press, 19–31.

Sen, Gita and Caren Grown. 1987. *Development, Crisis, and Alternative Visions: Third World Women's Perspectives.* New York: Monthly Review Press.

Shaheed, Farida. 1994. "Controlled or Autonomous: Identity and the Experience of the Network, Women Living under Muslim Laws." *Signs: Journal of Women in Culture and Society* 19, 4 (Summer): 997–1019.

1995. "Networking for Change: the Role of Women's Groups in Initiating Dialogue on Women's Issues." In *Faith and Freedom: Women's Human Rights in the Muslim World.* Syracuse, NY: Syracuse University Press, 78–103.

Shange, Ntozake. 1975. *For Colored Girls Who Have Considered Suicide/When the Rainbow Is Enuf.* New York: Macmillan.

Shapiro, Ian. 1988. "A Comment on John Harsanyi's 'Democracy, Equality, and Popular Consent.'" In *Power, Inequality, and Democratic Politics: Essays in Honor of Robert Dahl*, eds. Ian Shapiro and Grant Peeher. Boulder, CO: Westview Press, 284–90.

1989a. "Gross Concepts in Political Argument." *Political Theory* 17, 1 (February): 51–76.

1989b. "Three Fallacies Concerning Majorities, Minorities, and Democratic Politics." In *NOMOS XXXII: Majorities and Minorities, Political and Philosophical Perspectives*, eds. John Chapman and Alan Wertheimer. New York: New York University Press, 79–125.

1990. *Political Criticism.* Berkeley, CA: University of California Press.

1994. "Three Ways to Be a Democrat." *Political Theory* 22, 1 (February): 124–51.

1996a. "Elements of Democratic Justice." *Political Theory* 24, 4 (November): 579–619.

1996b. *Democracy's Place.* Ithaca, NY: Cornell University Press.

Shue, Henry. 1980. *Basic Rights: Subsistentce, Affluence, and US Foreign Policy.* Princeton, NJ: Princeton University Press.

Sirianni, Carmen. 1993. "Learning Pluralism: Democracy and Diversity in Feminist Organizations." In *Democratic Community: NOMOS XXXV,* eds. John W. Chapman and Ian Shapiro. New York: New York University Press, 283–312.

Smiley, Marion. 1993. "Feminist Theory and the Question of Identity." *Women and Politics* 13, 2: 91–122.

Smith, Jane and Yvonne Y. Haddad. 1982. "Eve: Islamic Image of Woman." *Women's Studies International Forum* 5, 2: 135–44.

Soares, Vera, Ana Alice Alcantra Costa, Cristina Maria Buarque, Denise Dourado Dora, and Wania Sant'Anna. 1995. Brazilian Feminism and Women's Movements: a Two-Way Street." In *The Challenge of Local Feminisms: Women's Movements in Global Perspective,* ed. Amrita Basu. Boulder, CO: Westview Press, 302–23.

Sorensen, Georg. 1993. *Democracy and Democratization: Processes and Prospects in a Changing World.* Boulder, CO: Westview Press.

Spalter-Roth, Roberta and Ronnee Schreiber. 1995. "Outsider Issues and Insider Tactics: Strategic Tensions in the Women's Policy Network during the 1980s." In *Feminist Organizations: Harvest of the New Women's Movement,* eds. Myra Marx Ferree and Patricia Yancey Martin. Philadelphia, PA: Temple University Press, 105–27.

Sparks, Holloway. 1997. "Dissident Citizenship: Democratic Theory, Political Courage, and Activist Women." *Hypatia* 12, 4: 74–110.

Spelman, Elizabeth. 1983. "Aristotle and the Politicization of the Soul." In *Discovering Reality: Feminist Perspectives on Epistemology, Metaphysics, Methodology, and Philosophy of Science,* eds. Sandra Harding and Merrill B. Hintikka. Boston, MA: D. Reidel, 17–30.

1988. *Inessential Woman: Problems of Exclusion in Feminist Thought.* Boston: Beacon.

Spodek, Howard. 1994. "The Self-employed Women's Association (SEWA) in India: Feminist, Gandhian Power in Development." *Economic Development and Cultural Change* 43, 1: 193–202.

Spragens, Thomas A., Jr. 1990. *Reason and Democracy.* Durham, NC: Duke University Press.

Stamp, Patricia. 1991. "Presentation Elaboration." In *The Future for Women in Development: Voices from the South,* eds. Nancy O'Rourke. Ottawa: The North–South Institute/L'Institut Nord–Sud, 64–5.

Stephen, Lynn. 1997. *Women and Social Movements in Latin American.* Austin, TX: University of Texas Press.

Stokes, Susan. 1998. "Pathologies of Deliberation." In *Deliberative Democracy,* ed. Jon Elster. Cambridge: Cambridge University Press, 123–39.

Sunstein, Cass R. 1988. "Beyond the Republican Revival." *Yale Law Journal* 97: 1539–90.

1993. *The Partial Constitution*. Cambridge, MA: Harvard University Press.

1995. "On Legal Theory and Practice." In *Theory and Practice: NOMOS XXXVII*, eds. Ian Shapiro and Judith Wagner DeCew. New York: New York University Press, 267–87.

Tate, Claudia, ed. 1983. *Black Women Writers at Work*. New York: Continuum.

Taylor, Charles. 1985. *Philosophy and the Human Sciences: Philosophical Papers 2*. Cambridge: Cambridge University Press.

1993. "Explanation and Practical Reason." In *The Quality of Life*, eds. Martha C. Nussbaum and Amartya Sen. Oxford: Clarendon Press, 208–41.

[1992] 1994. "The Politics of Recognition." In *Multiculturalism: Examining the Politics of Recognition*, ed. Amy Gutmann. Princeton, NJ: Princeton University Press, 25–74.

Taylor, Verta. 1989. "Social Movement Continuity: the Women's Movement in Abeyance." *American Sociological Review* 54, 5 (October): 761–75.

Timm, Father R. W. and Philip Gain. 1992. *Bangladesh: State of Human Rights, 1991*. A Report by Bangladesh Manobadhikar Samonnoy Parishad (Coordinating Council for Human Rights in Bangladesh – CCHRB). Dhaka: Nishat Printers.

Tinker, Irene. 1990. "A Context for the Field and for the Book." In *Persistent Inequalities: Women and World Development*, ed. Irene Tinker. New York: Oxford University Press, 3–13.

Tomasi, John. 1995. "Kymlicka, Liberalism, and Respect for Cultural Minorities." *Ethics* 105 (April): 580–603.

Tucker, Cynthia. 1993. "Humanity Begins at Home: a Woman's Right to Freedom from Abuse." *Atlanta Constitution*, June 19.

Tully, James. 1995. *Strange Multiplicity: Constitutionalism in an Age of Diversity*. Cambridge: Cambridge University Press.

Udayagiri, Mridula. 1995. "Challenging Modernization: Gender and Development, Postmodern Feminism and Activism." *Feminism/Postmodernism/Development*, eds. Marianne H. Marchand and Jane L. Parpart. London: Routledge, 159–77.

United Nations Convention on the Rights of the Child. 1989. Annex GA Res. 44/25 Doc. A/Res/4425. Adopted November 20, 1989.

United Nations Development Program. 1993. *Human Development Report*. New York: Oxford University Press.

1996. *Human Development Report*. New York: Oxford University Press.

United States v. *Virginia* 116 S.Ct. 2264. 1996.

Universal Declaration of Human Rights. 1948. G.A. Res. 217A(III), U.N. Doc. A/810, adopted December 10, 1948.

Valdés, Margarita M. 1993. "Julia Anna: Women and the Quality of Life: Two Norms or One." In *The Quality of Life*, eds. Martha C. Nussbaum and Amartya Sen. Oxford: Clarendon Press, 297–302.

Viswanath, Vanita. 1991. *NGOs and Women's Development in Rural South India: A Comparative Analysis*. Boulder, CO: Westview Press.

Walczewska, Slawka, ed. 1992. *Kobiety Maja Glos [Women Have the Floor]*. Kraków: Covivum.

Wali, Sima. 1995. "Muslim Refugee, Returnee, and Displaced Women:

Challenges and Dilemmas." In *Faith and Freedom: Women's Human Rights in the Muslim World*, ed. Mahnaz Afkhami. Syracuse, NY: Syracuse University Press, 175–83.

1997. "A Fundamentalist Regime Cracks Down on Women: an Interview by Gayle Kirshenbaum." *Ms.* 7, 6: 12–18.

Walzer, Michael. 1977. *Just and Unjust Wars*. New York: Basic Books.

1980. *Radical Principles: Reflections of an Unreconstructed Democrat*. New York: Basic Books.

1981. "Philosophy and Democracy." *Political Theory* 9, 3 (August): 379–99.

1983. *Spheres of Justice*. New York: Basic Books.

1984. "Liberalism and the Art of Separation." *Political Theory* 12, 3 (August): 315–30.

1987. *Interpretation and Social Criticism*. Cambridge, MA: Harvard University Press.

1988. *The Company of Critics: Social Criticism and Political Commitment in the Twenty First Century*. New York: Basic Books.

1990a. "The Communitarian Critique of Liberalism." *Political Theory* 18,1 (February): 6–23.

1990b. "What Does it Mean to be an American?" *Social Research* 57 (Fall): 591–614.

1991. "The Idea of Civil Society." *Dissent* (Spring): 293–304.

1993. "Objectivity and Social Meaning." In *The Quality of Life*, eds. Martha C. Nussbaum and Amartya Sen. Oxford: Clarendon Press, 165–77.

1994a. *Thick and Thin: Moral Argument at Home and Abroad*. Notre Dame, IN: University of Notre Dame Press.

1994b. "Comment on Charles Taylor's 'The Politics of Recongition'." In *Multiculturalism: Examining the Politics of Recognition*, ed. Amy Gutmann. Princeton, NJ: Princeton University Press, 99–103.

1995. "The Politics of Rescue." *Social Research* 62, 1 (Spring): 53–66.

Wang, Zheng. 1996. "A Historic Turning Point for the Women's Movement in China." *Signs: Journal of Women in Culture and Society* 22, 1: 192–99.

Warren, Mark. 1996a. "Deliberative Democracy and Authority." *American Political Science Review* 90, 1 (March): 46–60.

1996b. "What should we expect from more democracy?: Radically Democratic Responses to Politics." *Political Theory* 24, 2 (May): 241–70.

Waters, Elizabeth and Anastasia Posadskaya. 1995. In *The Challenge of Local Feminisms: Women's Movements in Global Perspective*, ed. Amrita Basu. Boulder, CO: Westview Press, 351–73.

Weber, Max. (1919) 1989. "Science as a Vocation." In *Max Weber's Science as a Vocation*, eds. Peter Lassman, Irving Velody, and Herminio Martins. London: Unwin Hyman, 3–31.

Webster's Third International Dictionary. 1993. Springfield, MA: Merriam-Webster.

Weedon, Chris. 1997. *Feminist Practice and Poststructuralist Theory*. Oxford: Blackwell.

Weithman, Paul J. 1995. "Contractualist Liberalism and Deliberative Democracy." *Philosophy and Public Affairs* 24, 4 (Fall): 314–43.

West, Cornell. 1989. *The American Evasion of Philosophy: a Genealogy of Pragmatism*. Madison, WI: University of Wisconsin.

White, Sarah C. 1992. *Arguing with a Crocodile: Gender and Class in Bangladesh*. University Press Limited: Dhaka.

Williams, Bernard. 1995. "Replies." In *World, Mind, and Ethics: Essays on the Ethical Philosophy of Bernard Williams*, eds. J. E. J. Altham and Ross Harrison. Cambridge: Cambridge University Press, 185–224.

Williams, Patricia J. 1991. *The Alchemy of Race and Rights*. Cambridge, MA: Harvard University Press.

Wilson, Ara. 1996. "Lesbian Visibility and Sexual Rights at Beijing." *Signs: Journal of Women in Culture and Society* 22, 1: 214–18.

Wisconsin v. *Yoder* 406 US 205. 1972.

Wolf, Susan. 1995. "Commentary on Martha Nussbaum: Human Capabilities, Female Human Beings." In *Women, Culture, and Development: a Study of Human Capabilities*, eds. Martha C. Nussbaum and Jonathan Glover. Oxford: Clarendon Press, 105–15.

Worsley, Peter. 1984. *The Three Worlds: Culture and World Development*. London: Weidenfeld and Nicolson.

Wright, Richard. 1956. *The Color Curtain: a Report on the Bandung Conference*. Cleveland, OH: World Publishing Company.

Wright, Robin. 1993. "Women Take Reins: World Sees More Leaders, More Calls for Justice." *Los Angeles Times*, June 30.

Young, Iris Marion. 1990a. *Justice and the Politics of Difference*. Princeton, NJ: Princeton University Press.

1990b. "The Ideal of Community and the Politics of Difference." In *Feminism/Postmodernism*, ed. Linda J. Nicholson. New York: Routledge, 300–23.

1994. "Gender as Seriality: Thinking about Women as a Social Collective." *Signs: Journal of Women in Culture and Society* 19, 3: 713–38.

1996. "Communication and the Other: Beyond Deliberative Democracy." In *Democracy and Difference: Changing Boundaries of the Political*, ed. Seyla Benhabib. Princeton, NJ: Princeton University Press, 120–35.

1997a. *Intersecting Voices: Dilemmas of Gender, Political Philosophy and Policy*. Princeton, NJ: Princeton University Press.

1997b. "Difference as a Resource for Democratic Communication." In *Deliberative Democracy: Essays on Reason and Politics*, eds. James Bohman and William Rehg. Cambridge, MA: MIT Press, 383–406.

Zein Ed-Dīn, Nazīrah. [1928] 1982. "Removing the Veil and Veiling." *Women's Studies International Forum* 5, 2: 221–6.

Index